Please renew/return this item by the last date shown.

So that your telephone call is charged at local rate,
please call the numbers as set out below:

	From Area codes 01923 or 0208:	From the rest of Herts:
Renewals:	01923 471373	01438 737373
Enquiries:	01923 471333	01438 737333
Minicom:	01923 471599	01438 737599

L 32b

- 6 MAY 2000

L 33

D1345042

Ruskin and Venice

for Filippo and Damon

Ruskin and Venice

Jeanne Clegg

JUNCTION BOOKS   LONDON

© 1981 Jeanne Clegg

First published in Great Britain by

Junction Books Ltd
33 Ivor Place
London NW1

ISBN 0 86245 ~~001 X~~
019 5

The jacket illustration shows Ruskin in 1856 and a view from the bell-
tower of San Giorgio Maggiore, photograph by C. Naya (Ditta Oswaldo
Böhm, Venice), c 1860. The photograph shows the old bell-tower of
St Mark's with stalls around the base, Dr Rima's floating swimming-
baths in St Mark's Basin, gas lamps along the lower arcade of the Ducal
Palace, and the arcade, it seems, whitewashed on the inside as described
by Ruskin writing to his father on 11 September 1845. The five arches
at the east end of the arcade remained walled up until the 1880s;
Ruskin complains about them being used as a urinal in a letter to
his father of 5 October 1851 (*Letters from Venice*, pp. 31-2).

Printed by Nene Litho, Earls Barton, Northants.
Bound by Weatherby Woolnough, Wellingborough, Northants.

Contents

Preface and Acknowledgements

When Ruskin was 44 his father began to hope that he would soon have had enough of continental journeys, 'for he was a young Traveller & we have all been abroad a great part of every year'.[1] But long experience of travelling was no reason why Ruskin should give it up in middle age; for he did not go abroad in search of novelty. Mountains in Switzerland, towns and cities in France and northern Italy had become as familiar to him as south London, Oxford or the Lake District. And they had probably taught him as much, even though he had relatively little to do with the inhabitants of these foreign parts. For Ruskin associated conscious learning with things seen rather than with things read or heard, with places rather than with men or institutions. In each place he found, perhaps, only what he had been looking for; but he had a gift for finding exactly that.

Ruskin visited Venice eleven times. He went first at sixteen in 1835, for the last time in 1888, aged sixty-seven. Journeys to Venice, then, span the whole of Ruskin's working life, for he did not recover from the madness that began in 1889, though he lived another eleven years. Often Ruskin stayed in Venice only a week or two. On three occasions he remained there for several months. Each visit, whether long or short, brought variations in Ruskin's experience and descriptions of the city. Sometimes the differences are important, at others less so; hence the extremely uneven divisions of this book.

There are three main sections. The first deals with the two family tours of 1835 and 1841, and Ruskin's vision of Venice as the most romantic of city-landscapes. Under this heading come the history of the evolution of that view, inherited from his childhood reading, and an account of his attempts to reproduce it in literary endeavours of 1835-36. These early productions, a Byronic poem, a novel and a play, were left unfinished. Further experience of Venice as landscape, acquired in 1841, would prove useful as Ruskin turned to criticism. In his first important book, *Modern Painters* I (1843), Turner is the only true painter of the Venetian dream.

The second group of journeys comprises Ruskin's first as an independent critic in 1845, the last Italian family holiday of 1846 and

1

the two long winter residences of 1849-50 and 1851-52 which produced *The Stones of Venice*. Simpler poetic images of Venice were rejected as Ruskin grew in knowledge of the city's painters, particularly Tintoretto, and its Byzantine and Gothic buildings. Appreciation of the past went together with revulsion from the present. Venice now takes on two aspects, one ideal and ancient, the other modern and ruinous. It was this more complicated city that produced the second half of *Modern Painters* II (1846), brought revisions to *Modern Painters* I (3rd edition 1846), influenced parts of *The Seven Lamps of Architecture* (1849) and generated the three volumes of *Stones* (1851-53). This last book, however, is less consistent and confident than criticism has recognized. Ruskin's accomplishment as an author at this stage conceals religious and political uncertainties which were only to be resolved during the subsequent seventeen-year absence from Venice. In old age Ruskin was reluctant to re-issue *Stones*, condemning it both for Protestant bigotry and for bringing nineteenth-century England creditably out of the comparison with the Italian city.

After 1860 the relationship is different. In *Modern Painters* V the two nations are compared not for what they represent at present, but for their achievement at their times of greatest power and prosperity. Venice in her prime, Giorgione's Venice, is used to dramatize the triumph of the 'English death', capitalism, in Turner's London. The last series of journeys to Venice consists of some brief trips from Verona in 1869, the group tours of 1870 and 1872, a long, lonely stay from September 1876 to May 1877 and the final visit of 1888. 1869 and 1870 brought new work on Tintoretto, the subject of the most controversial of Ruskin's first year's lectures as Slade Professor of Art at Oxford. Study of Carpaccio in 1870 and 1872 provided material for *Fors Clavigera*, the monthly pamphlet begun in 1871. Through *Fors* Ruskin founded a utopian society, the Guild of St George, named for one of the saints whose lives Carpaccio had told. Another, St Ursula, Ruskin associated with Rose La Touche, whom he loved. Association became identification after Rose's death in 1875. The winter spent in Venice in 1876-77 brought Ruskin delirious visions of both personal and public significance. In *Fors* the ancient city is offered to industrial England as a model of political, commercial and social relations and practice. *St Mark's Rest* (1877-84) and the Academy *Guide* (1877) instruct the English traveller in reverence for a Venice shrine of saints and heroes and denounce the attitudes of modern tourist handbooks. As Ruskin knew, his mental control was now precarious. Venice, provoking both excitement and anger, was dangerous. During the last decade of his writing life he directed others, among them young Venetian disciples, in making records of the remnants of ideal Venice for the Guild Museum near Sheffield. He paid a last visit, in 1888, but had to be brought home early.

Little of this is evident from *Praeterita*. Ruskin meant his auto-biography to explain 'How I learned the things I taught' (XXXV, 368n.).* But he does not include Venice among the 'centres of my life's thought' (XXXV, 156). Ruskin lists only three, Rouen, Geneva and Pisa, adding quickly 'All that I did at Venice was bye-work' (XXXV, 156). Geneva, which here stands for the Alps, had perhaps been as important to him as Venice. But nothing he wrote out of his knowledge of Rouen or Pisa competes with this Venetian 'bye-work'. In *Praeterita*, written in his last years, Ruskin persists in seeing himself as having been coerced, or seduced, into this monumental distraction, calling Venice 'a vain temptation' (XXXV, 296).

At one point he almost admits Verona to the circle of his tutress cities, but again excludes Venice (XXXV, 371). This time, however, Ruskin explains why. If it had not been for the events of 1845,

> I should ... have written, *The Stones of Chamouni*, instead of *The Stones of Venice*; and the *Laws of Fésole*, in the full code of them, before beginning to teach in Oxford: and I should have brought out in full distinctness and use what faculty I had of drawing the human face and form with true expression of their higher beauty.
>
> But Tintoret swept me away at once into the 'mare maggiore' of the schools of painting which crowned the power and perished in the fall of Venice; so forcing me into the study of the history of Venice herself; and through that into what else I have traced or told of the laws of national strength and virtue. I am happy in having done this so that the truth of it must stand; but it was not my own proper work ... (XXXV, 372).

Here Ruskin alludes to a saying attributed to Tintoretto: 'Lo studio della pittura è faticoso, e sempre si fa il mare maggiore' (the study of painting is a hard labour, and the sea grows ever wider). He was fond of quoting this (see IV, 26-7 and XVI, 318), though sometimes, as here, wishing it were not such an accurate description of his own experience. If, in reminiscence, Ruskin belittles the role of Venice in his life's work, it was because he could all too easily have seen the place as having taken over too much of his life. He could blame Venice and her painters not just for the time denied to geology and drawing, but also for the whole effort to trace 'the laws of national strength and virtue' and to apply those laws in practice. Ruskin could see the ridiculous side to both what he had done and to what he might have done. That he might have written 'The Stones of Chamouni' or finished *The Laws of Fésole*

*For this and other abbreviations used in the text and Notes see List of Abbreviations.

is not impossible. Other versions of his 'proper work' are clearly mischievous. Speaking again of the 1845 journey in the 1883 Epilogue to *Modern Painters* II, Ruskin wrote:

And very solemnly I wish that I had gone straight home that summer, and never seen Venice, or Tintoret! Perhaps I might have been the Catholic Archbishop of York, by this time — who knows! building my cathedral there, in emulation of the Cardinal's at Westminster — instead of a tiny Sheffield museum (IV, 352-3).

'Seen her, that is to say, with men's eyes', Ruskin adds in a note. Of his childhood visits to Venice he retained the happiest memories (XXXV, 294-5). In 1845 Ruskin had repudiated his child's ways of seeing and feeling. In old age he made attempts to recover childhood, putting in question the adult work that had led him to the impossible condition of trying to undo European catastrophe from a cottage art gallery near Sheffield. For Verona, as for Pisa, Geneva, Rouen, he had felt a more constant affection. For that reason those cities have a consistency and static quality in Ruskin's writings which Venice, more complex, more problematic and more diverse in what she had to offer of good or bad, never has.

In each case one must look to what Ruskin wrote at that time, to what he made of Venice in his books, to the more immediate thoughts expressed in letters and diaries. Few authors have received the attention of editors as good as Cook and Wedderburn so soon after their deaths. More recent scholars have done much to compensate for their selectivity, their reticence on subjects that some of Ruskin's relatives and friends, though not Ruskin himself, thought should not be made public. But much remains unpublished, including much that can help with an understanding of Ruskin's relations with Venice. Not all the poems of the early years appear in the second volume of the Library Edition, and one that escaped is the only thing Ruskin wrote on the spot on his first visit to Venice. As editor of Ruskin's letters, Van Akin Burd is unequalled. His edition of the family correspondence makes accessible much of the background to the early continental holidays. Among the wealth of manuscript and transcript material in the Ruskin Galleries at Bembridge, Isle of Wight, are travel diaries kept by Ruskin's father and cousin; these provide slight but reliable framework to the family tours. Thanks to Harold Shapiro the letters of the 1845 journey are now easily available, but for most visits the published record is less complete. The Bodleian transcripts of letters and diaries made by Alexander Wedderburn when he was working on the Library Edition are essential material for any aspect of Ruskin's life, but are particularly useful for the poorly documented visit of 1849-50. From the Bembridge collection of John James Ruskin's letters to his son we can deduce something of the missing half of the correspondence of that winter. They also illuminate the Ruskin letters of 1851-52 edited by J.L. Bradley. Mary Lutyens's editions of Effie Ruskin's correspondence are, of course, invaluable sources of information for the *Stones* period. No such convenient concentration of material exists for the last journeys, except for that of 1872, of which James S. Dearden has given clear and detailed account. Rawdon Brown the English scholar resident in Venice for most of his life, was crucial in keeping Ruskin in contact with the city during his later years. Only a small selection of their correspondence has been published; letters in the Bodleian, British Library and in Venice are therefore important sources for the 1860s and 1870s. For the winter of 1876-77 the largely unpublished letters to Joan Severn are most helpful, for it is here that Ruskin's Venetian work is least easily detachable from his personal life. Finally there is the matter of contacts and disciples Ruskin made in Venice in the latter part of his life. Except for two letters to Ruskin in the John Rylands University Library of Manchester little written record of them survives in this country. Here Cook and Wedderburn were not able, and understandably did not aim to achieve complete documentation. They do not seem to have contacted Giacomo Boni at the time of preparing the Library Edition, and it was not until Eva Tea began Boni's biography that further evidence of their relationship, in the form of rather Italianate transcriptions, came to England. For Ruskin's letters to Alvise Zorzi they seem to have drawn on what Zorzi himself published, and so missed Ruskin's last and most urgent letter to him. This they might not have published in any case. When the firm of George Allen, Ruskin's pupil, assistant and later publisher, contacted Angelo Alessandri, they asked only for the letters bearing on art criticism. Alessandri therefore sent less than half of the letters he had received, and of course none of the drafts of his own letters to Ruskin. The rest were not, in fact, of a kind to reveal anything intimate, but the editors did miss an opportunity to complete the record of a master-pupil relationship. Although one can always hope that further traces of Ruskin may come to light in Italy, the fragmentary nature of much of what does survive suggests that the rest is meagre. This does not make it less exciting to find in Venice, odd letters in the Marciana (some pasted into Rawdon Brown's copy of *Fors Clavigera*), two more in the Armenian convent, an inscription in the set of books Ruskin gave to the Academy, his pupils' registration forms in the Academy school archives, a photograph of another in a trunk in Assisi, half a letter in Bassano, isolated drawings in Roman churches and neglected museums, Ruskin's father's signature in the register of a Florentine library. Certainly it does not make the search any less troublesome to the unfortunate owners and keepers.

My first thanks, however, must go to James S. Dearden, Curator of the Ruskin Galleries, for his patience in answering innumerable questions, guidance through abundance of material at Bembridge and his suggestions as to where else one might look. For permission to use these manuscripts I thank The Ruskin Galleries, Bembridge School, Isle of Wight. For permission to publish previously unpublished writings of Ruskin and John James Ruskin I am grateful to George Allen & Unwin Ltd as the Literary Trustees of John Ruskin. I am indebted to the Oxford University Press for permission to quote from *The Diaries of John Ruskin* edited by Joan Evans and J.H. Whitehouse and Harold Shapiro's edition *Ruskin in Italy: Letters to his Parents 1845*, to John Murray (Publishers) Ltd for allowing quotation from Mary Lutyen's *Effie in Venice* and to the Yale University Press for permission to give extracts from J.L. Bradley's *Ruskin's Letters from Venice 1851-52*. I thank Count Alvise Zorzi for the use of letters from Ruskin to his grandfather, the Trustees of the Pierpont Morgan Library for those from Boni to Ruskin and the Syndics of the Fitzwilliam Museum, Cambridge for letters from Ruskin's father to the Burne-Jones family. For their courtesy in looking out and making available letters, drawings and photographs pertinent to Ruskin's relations with Venetians I am grateful to Mrs Andrea Carruthers, Keeper of the St George's Guild Collection at Reading University, Mr Lawrence Bilton, Curator of the Coniston Museum, Miss Janet Gnosspelius of Liverpool, Mrs M. Guselian of Coniston, signorina Mathilde Morani of Assisi, dottoressa Rosanna Saccardo of the Biblioteca Civica of Mestre, the Fathers of the Armenian Convent of San Lazzaro and professoressa Elena Bassi, Director of the Venetian Academy. To the staffs of civic registries, state archives, museums and libraries in Venice, Verona, Milan, Assisi, Florence and Rome I have gone, often with ingenuous enquiries, and always received helpful answers. I would like to thank particularly the staffs of the Biblioteca Nazionale Marciana, the Biblioteca Civica Correr and the Archivio Fotografico of the Correr.

I have used illustration in this book to show aspects of nineteenth-century Venice to which Ruskin was sensitive but not necessarily sympathetic; hence the presence of contemporary photographs rather than Ruskin's own drawings.[2] For the drawings record features of the city Ruskin admired and wished to preserve, not those which distressed or angered him. For permission to reproduce these illustrations I am grateful to the Museo Civica Correr, the Ditta Oswaldo Böhm of Venice, the Courtauld Institute of the University of London and the Ruskin Galleries, Bembridge.

Until very recently the history of Venice since the fall of the Republic has been much neglected and to make any acquaintance with the city in the nineteenth century one must turn to local and contemporary material. I am much indebted to the British Academy for the Wolfson

Fellowship which has enabled me to spend nine months in Venice collecting material for the completion of this book. I am also grateful to the University of Calabria for the leave of absence which allowed me to take this opportunity.

My study of Ruskin's experience of and work in Venice began, however, as research for a doctorate at Oxford, and I owe special thanks to my supervisor, Miss Rachel Trickett, Principal of St Hugh's, for her support, criticism and advice over many years. To Dr Robin Biswas of Leicester University I have an even older debt of teaching, no less important because informal. I would also like to thank Dr Frank Taylor of Manchester, Professor Dante Della Terza of Harvard, professor Giampiero Franco of Ca' Foscari and Professor Van Akin Burd of New York for their encouragement and advice. For their generosity in giving information and help of many kinds in connection with Ruskin I am grateful to Mrs Dinah Birch of Oxford, Mr Robert Hewison and Dr Catherine Williams of London. There is one Ruskin scholar, however, to whom this book owes more than to any other single person; without Tim Hilton it would simply never have got written.

I must also thank those who, without sharing a special interest in Ruskin, have helped in many different ways. Three people I can only thank in memory: signora Maria Pennati Alessandri, who welcomed me kindly when I arrived on her doorstep naively asking 'if she had any letters from Ruskin'; professor Angiolo Tursi, whose collection of material relating to foreigners in Italy will not be the same without his guidance and conversation; and Franco Giusberti, to whom I am grateful more than I can say. I would also like to thank Franco's family and my own, who are in a sense represented in the dedication to my nephews. Finally, I owe a great deal to many friends both in Italy and England; but would like to thank especially Bianca Tarozzi, Maria Grossmann and Barbara Gunnell.

List of Abbreviated References

Capital Roman numerals refer to the volume number of *The Works of John Ruskin*, 39 vols., eds. E.T. Cook and Alexander Wedderburn (Library Edition, 1903-12)

Bem.	The Ruskin Galleries, Bembridge, Isle of Wight
Bodl.	The Bodleian Library, Oxford
B.L.	The British Library
Diaries	*The Diaries of John Ruskin*, 3 vols., eds. Joan Evans and J.H. Whitehouse (Oxford, 1956-59)
Family Letters	*The Ruskin Family Letters (1801-1843)*, 2 vols., ed. Van Akin Burd (1973)
Effie in Venice	*Effie in Venice: Unpublished Letters of Mrs John Ruskin Written from Venice between 1849-52*, ed. Mary Lutyens (1965)
Letters from Venice	*Ruskin's Letters from Venice 1851-52*, Yale Studies in English, No. 129, ed. John Lewis Bradley (New Haven, Conn., 1955)
Marciana	Biblioteca Nazionale Marciana, Venice
Ruskin in Italy	*Ruskin in Italy: Letters to His Parents 1845*, ed. Harold I. Shapiro (1972)
Trevelyan Letters	*Reflections of a Friendship: John Ruskin's Letters to Pauline Trevelyan 1848-1866*, ed. Virginia Surtees (1979)

With the exception of the above, a full reference is given to each work on first citation in the notes of each section, but otherwise in shortened form.
Place of publication is London unless otherwise stated.

I   Venice the Romantic

I.1   The English View of Venice before Ruskin

In the late Middle Ages and Renaissance the English tended to admire, and often at the same time hate Italians. During the seventeenth and eighteenth centuries contempt, and sometimes pity, came to replace both admiration and hatred. By the early nineteenth century Italians had become figures in a landscape ransacked for imaginative inspiration, sometimes enhancing, sometimes disturbing romantic atmosphere. Andrew Canepa attributes the transformation in the stereotype to the 'complete reversal in the relative economic and cultural positions of England and Italy'.[1] Of all Italian cities, Venice was perhaps the one which best epitomized the wealth, intellect and power of 1300, and the poverty, pathos, degradation and romance of 1800.

For mediaeval travellers on their way from western Europe to Palestine and the eastern Mediterranean, Venice was the port of embarkation. There out-going English pilgrims and crusaders met in-coming luxury merchandise. In the city they saw the fruits of a prosperity that had been growing ever since about 1000. Their praise of the city begins a tradition of 'glorification of Venice'.[2] One especially enthusiastic Irish friar described coming, in 1323,

> to the famous and renowned city of the Venetians, which, although it is completely set in the sea, yet by the name of its beauty and the merit of its elegance it could be set between the star Arcturus and the shining Pleiades . . . In honour of [St Mark] . . . is a most sumptuous church, built incomparably of marble and other valuable stones, and excellently adorned and worked with bible stories in mosaic. Opposite it is that public square which all things considered has no equal anywhere. To this church is joined almost continuously that famous palace of the Duke of Venice, in which are fed at all times live lions for the glory of the state and the magnificence of its citizens. And opposite this palace near the harbor are two round marble columns, large and high, on the top of one of which, for their magnificence, is the figure of a lion shining in gold like the moon or the sun; and at the west door of the church are two bronze horses likewise always shining.[3]

The description gives a sense of many beautiful things packed into a small space. The writer is impressed, but appreciates that he is meant to be. He marvels at the horses 'always' shining and the lions 'at all times' fed, and knows that it is 'for the glory of the state and the magnificence of its citizens'. Another pilgrim of 1422 was less articulate and more prosaic in his recognition of Venetian power and prosperity:

> Venis stondes alle in the See,
> And Ylez about hir gret plente:
> And Lordez thei ben of diversez placez,
> To telle her Lordschip I have no space:
> But I dar hit so discry,
> Hit is a riche Toun of spicery:
> And of alle other marchandise also,
> And right well vitelet ther to.[4]

Others paid more attention to religious than to commercial matters, but relics and ceremonies too were signs of prosperity and sophistication. 'Rich', suggesting both expense and elaborate workmanship, is the key word in this part of an account of the Corpus Christi Day procession of 1506:

> lytell children of bothe kyndes, gloryously and rychely dressed, berynge in their hands in riche cuppes or other vessayles some pleasaunt floures or other well smellynge or rich stuffe, dressed as aungelles to adorn the sayde processyon.[5]

In the course of the sixteenth century the association between Venice and wealth became fixed in the English language. A set of catch phrases indicating the distinctive attributes of Italian cities came into use as 'Englishmen's interest in foreign countries and their awareness of the differences between them increased enormously'.[6] While Genoa was known as 'the proudest', and Milan 'the greatest', Venice was 'the richest'. For a growing trading nation like England the age-old mercantile greatness of Venice was an achievement to be frankly admired.[7] Whereas now 'the main constituent of the Modern Renaissance concept is Florence; . . . then Italy was seen in terms of Venice'.[8] St Mark's was admired for the costliness of its marbles, and not until the nineteenth century for anything else.[9] The aspect and situation of the city excited little emotional response. Ruskin was disappointed to find that his beloved Sidney 'goes to Venice, and seems unconscious that it is in the sea at all . . .' (XXXV, 294). He thought this illustrated the uniqueness of his joy in the beauty of the city, 'the English mind, high or common, being utterly without trace of the feeling' (XXXV, 294). In fact, like those of any century, sixteenth-century travellers pursued their purposes single-mindedly: 'Diplomatist, merchant and student came back with what he had gone to fetch and no more.'[10] What the Elizabethan Englishmen went to fetch from Italy was above all an education and what George Parks calls 'political intellect'.[11] Florence produced the theoretical literature, the government of Venice offered a living example that could be analysed and discussed. The distinction is reflected in *Othello*, where the Venetian Iago presents himself as a soldier, and deprecates the book-learnt theory of the Florentine Cassio. In an age when a taste for concreteness in political debate was growing, 'The Venetian achievement and the attitudes surrounding it corresponded to the emerging needs of the European nations.'[12] Venice had no equal in renown for stable government, efficient public administration, a balanced, sophisticated constitution and genius in international relations. Courtiers like Sidney went there to learn diplomatic skills, establish contacts, gather information about world affairs and study government at a time when such information was not available in published form in England.[13] But it is clear from Jacobean drama that by the turn of the century interest in Venice had permeated all levels of English society, and was no longer confined to those able to go there. A bumbling counterpart to Sidney turns up in *Volpone*, where Jonson makes Sir Politic-Would-Be go to Venice to learn policy. Of plays by Shakespeare and his contemporaries E.H. Sugden lists fourteen set or partially set in the city, and numerous others containing references to Venetian fashions, terms of address, gondolas, manufactures, the trade in luxury goods, the Turkish wars.[14] There must have been a fund of popular knowledge and curiosity about Venice which playwrights could exploit. Venetian life provided exotic paraphernalia, her administrative principles raised interesting intellectual and moral questions. In *The Merchant of Venice* Shakespeare drew on her fame for strict application of justice, religious tolerance and close regulation of commercial and financial dealings, and her need to protect that fame.

The dramatic possibilities of Venice were only heightened by the ambivalence of her reputation. The civic virtues and learning of Italians in general were thought to be accompanied by licentiousness, subtlety, jealousy, treacherousness, atheism and a talent for murder. Of all Italian cities 'Venice, with Florence as the city of Machiavel, stood in the front rank for this sinister repute.'[15] Ascham's attack on the Italianate Englishman in 1570 was based on his 'experience' of one city, Venice:

> I was once in Italy myself; but I thank God my abode there was but nine days; and yet I saw in that little time, in one city, more liberty to sin, than ever I heard tell of in our noble city of London in nine year.[16]

Around the turn of the century Venetian courtezans were notorious enough for a London brothel to call itself simply 'Venice'.[17] Respectability was no protection against suspicion of licentiousness; a pure demeanour was only achieved by expertise in subtlety. Iago deploys this combination of standard vices to defame Desdemona in Othello's eyes, claiming a native's inside knowledge of the ways of the city:

> In Venice they do let God see the pranks
> They dare not show their husbands; their best conscience
> Is not to leave undone, but keep unknown.[18]

He transfers to Desdemona his own character as a 'super-subtle Venetian' concealing illicit desires.[19] Thus Venice was considered equally suitable as a home for scheming villains like Shylock and Volpone as for the honest, noble-minded Antonio and Bassano. But the vices of Jacobean scoundrels imply intelligence, daring and energy, however perverted; they are consistent with, indeed call for, respect.[20] Even Ascham's scandalized reaction is in a way complimentary: 'The almost obsessive preoccupation of foreigners with the licentiousness of Venice . . . [was] a kind of negative tribute to the more general freedom of Venetian society.'[21]

The seventeenth century was to see a complete change in the English view of Venice. First came the institutionalization of the Venetian myth, then the recognition of her decline as an international power. By the middle of the century a number of the works of the great Venetian historians and constitutional theorists had been translated into English.[22] Whatever their ideology, whatever their allegiances, most English political writers could find some inspiration in that complicated network of councils and offices.[23] Curiosity was intense in a period in which England was having to decide on her own future form of government, and was looking at different models with a view to imitating them.[24] The most public acknowledgement of this occurred in 1644, when the Venetian ambassador was asked by a group of members of parliament to explain the structure and working of the Venetian constitution. In the meantime the material basis of greatness had been eaten away. The seventeenth century was one of economic depression for Italy as a whole as the luxury trades gave way to commerce on a larger scale. English, French and Dutch ships not only used the new Cape route but gradually took over Mediterranean trade as well, and because of privateering and poor relations with the Turks, Venetian merchants would sail under the English flag in preference to their own.[25]

James Howell's *Survay of the Signorie of Venice*[26] is of special interest because known to Ruskin. The book is a high point in the glorification of Venice, yet is sensitive to her diminished strength. It also reflects the delicacy of the English political debate. The view that the Venetian constitution was a mixed system, an elaborate structure of checks and balances, was now giving way to the view that it was an aristocracy.[27] In 1660 Milton, combating the Restoration to the last, denounced 'the fond conceit of something like a duke of Venice'.[28] In 1651 Howell was already suspected of monarchist sympathies. He therefore presented his book as a call to aid Venice, 'the Key and Bulwark of *Europe*' in her struggle against the Turk, 'that monstrous Giant'.[29] This gave pretext for extolling Venetian virtues: a strong and enduring form of government, independence of the Pope, wholesome laws, affinity with England as a maritime nation and one which had never been invaded, her inclination to peace, the patriotism and steadiness of her people, her extensive empire. Howell finds nothing sinister in the rewards offered to informers, nor in the severity with which offenders are punished, nor in the secrecy surrounding the workings of government. Answering the two traditional charges against Venice, subtlety and licentiousness, he pleads that international alliance against her has forced her 'to peece her *Lion's* with a *Foxe's* tayl', but has to admit that she has 'a large conscience . . . under the navill'.[30]

Only here does Howell abandon the personification of Venice as a fair virgin which runs through the whole *Survay*. It was an image which seems to have appealed to John James Ruskin when he came across the book in August 1851. On the 29th of that month he wrote to his son, who was on his way to Venice to finish *Stones*, summarizing passages.[31] As an opponent of Catholic Emancipation and of democratic notions, John James particularly liked Howell's account of the expulsion of the Jesuits, told by the Senate to 'go — take nothing with you — and never return'. He also called attention to one of the reasons given for the Republic's having endured so long: 'not so much that the prince did command well as that the *people* did *obey* well'. The *Survay* was 'a sort of old perhaps coarse foolish in some sort Book', but Ruskin is advised to look at it before closing his second volume of Venetian history.

If he did so, Ruskin would have been pleased by Howell's picture of the government of Venice, but might have thought his praise of her aspect lukewarm:

> Her situation is so rare . . . and her Structures so magnificent and neat, that this *Virgin* Cittie useth to ravish at first sight all Strangers that come to visit Her, specially if they com from the Sea, and not passd through others of the dainty Townes of *Italie*.[32]

Romantic travellers would be ravished by the first sight of Venice, no matter how well travelled they were or however they approached. Howell is typical of his time in placing less emphasis on the city's beauty than on her comforts. A contrast with London may be implied in his pleasure that the streets of Venice are 'so neatly and eevenly pavd, that in the dead of Winter one may walk up and down in a pair of Sattin Pantables and Crimson Silk Stockins and not be dirtied'.[33] And although trade has fallen off of late,

> ther is no outward appearance of poverty, or any kind of decay in this soft effeminat City, but she is still fresh and florishing, abounding with all kinds of comerce, and flowing with all bravery and delight, all which may be had at cheap rates . . .[34]

In future many English travellers would comment on the cheapness of Venice, itself a sign of her comparative economic decline. Venice is now on the defensive, militarily, economically and also geographically, for Howell thought the sea 'doth not love her so *deeply* as he did'.[35] Burnet and Addison were also to discuss the danger of the city being left high and dry; later visitors, among them Shelley, Byron and Ruskin, predict the more romantic catastrophe of submersion.

Eighteen years after Howell's *Survay*, in 1669, came another celebration of the Venetian constitution, laws, secrecy in affairs of state, independence and genius for government. But while Jean Gailhard's *Present State of the Republick of Venice*[36] was extravagant in its praise of the system in principle, it is critical of aspects of state practice. Gailhard cannot excuse secret assassination, and cites wrongful executions as examples of over zealous judicial severity. Such cases were to be much discussed during the later eighteenth century as concern and sympathy shifted on to the individual and away from the state in whose name and at whose hands the victim suffered.[37] Even Gailhard was not sure that the rulers of Venice really had the public interest at heart. He describes the nobility as greedy, dishonest, unjust, arrogant, jealous, hypocritical, 'much self-ended' and generally 'odious'.[38] What was perhaps worse, because ridiculous rather than sinister, he had noticed nobles begging. Of the 'fornication, adultery, incest, sodomy etc.' so common in Venice Gailhard claims he will not speak,[39] though in fact he offers some interesting explanations. He sees government permissiveness in moral matters as deliberate compensation for political repression.[40] On a psychological level he blames the strictness of husbands and fathers; this makes wives and daughters over react and over indulge. Compared to Howell, Gailhard pays more attention to social and cultural life. He notices the churches, and the palaces, which he calls 'Gothick'. His appreciation of the festivals, amusements and healthy air of the lagoon looks forward to the day when the city would become a tourist resort.

During the last quarter of the seventeenth century awareness of decline and criticism of Venice increased. The French were quicker to pounce on the symptoms than the English.[41] The strength of anti-Catholic feeling in England could help sustain a special interest in Venice, for 'Of all states in *Italy* this of *Venice* hangs loose from the Pope most of all.'[42] Gilbert Burnet, who visited Venice in 1685, was attracted by the work of Venetian historians, especially by Paolo Sarpi's hostile account of the Counter-Reformation.[43] At the same time Burnet was alert to signs of decline. In comparison to the mainland, where he saw great misery and a falling population, he claimed for Venice 'an incredible Wealth, and a vast plenty of all things in this place'.[44] Yet his grumbles about the food and living conditions indicate that the plenty was not so vast. Burnet complained that the wine was watered and the meat boiled before being roasted, no doubt to counteract toughness. Other experiences were unfamiliar without being exotic or pleasant. The bread was unleavened and cooked in an oven 'too much heated, so that the crum is as dough, when the crust is as hard as stone'.[45] Venetians 'have nothing convenient' in their houses, there being 'no apartments, no Closets or Back-stairs'; the beds are made of iron to prevent infestation by vermin, the chairs hard and upright.[46] Like Gailhard, Burnet approves of the institutions of government, although it seems that they are already in need of defence. The unlimited power of the Inquisition of State, 'so much censured by strangers', is, on the contrary, 'the greatest glory, and the chief security of this Republick'.[47] But Burnet sees a grave threat to that security in the rapid deterioration in the moral and religious characters of the rulers of Venice. They are coarsely atheist and they are cowardly; the Turkish wars are being fought by mercenaries[48] while the *broglio* is 'full of graceful young Senators and Nobles ... [who] stay at home managing their intrigues ... and dissolving their spirits among their Courtisans'.[49] The atheism, intrigues and courtesans are not new, but the cowardice and effeteness are. So too is Burnet's special condemnation of Venetian women with whom 'the first step without any preamble or preparative is downright beastliness'. Since they are also ignorant and idle, he pronounces them 'the insipidest creatures imaginable'. Nuns and clergy are also accused of 'ignorance and vice'.[50] Consistently Burnet interprets licentiousness not as an expression of hyper-active sexuality but as a form of laziness, a shirking of responsibility to state or society. Similarly he associates plotting and scheming not with over-reaching ambition and perverted intelligence but with political ignorance and shortsightedness.

Burnet stands at the beginning of a long tradition which attributes the decline of Venice to the moral and cultural degeneration of her citizens, a tradition which was eventually to produce *The Stones of Venice*. And it is interesting that Burnet has, in common with Ruskin but not with his predecessors, a strong interest in Venetian architecture, although his tastes are naturally neo-classical. He praises painting and Palladian churches, and is unimpressed by St Mark's except for the mosaics; though it had obviously cost a great deal, it is 'dark and low'.[51] Burnet also notices the Venetian disregard for the Ducal Palace that was to disgust many future visitors, Ruskin included:

> The nobleness of the staircases, the riches of the Halls, and the beauty of the whole building, are much prejudiced by the beastliness of those that walk along, and that leave their marks behind them, as if this were a common house of Office, then so noble a Palace.[52]

By the time Addison visited Venice at the turn of the century she was hardly to be taken seriously as a European power. Addison still thought she might recover her old magnificence but the only aspect of present Venetian strength he found worthy of remark was her ability to defend herself by pulling up the stakes marking the deeper channels in the lagoon.[53] Of the whole array of methods used by government to maintain stability Addison is critical, although he thinks the ends wise.[54] But the political interest of Venice has really now been exhausted, to be poorly compensated for by that of her entertainments. Addison was enchanted by the opera, the theatre, by acrobatic displays and by the gondoliers singing Tasso.[55] And as a resort Venice is made the more attractive by the low cost of magnificence, for gondolas, Addison remarks, are so much cheaper than keeping horses and carriage.[56]

Addison's *Remarks* were to be quoted by many of those who followed him around Italy.[57] He was to have an even greater influence in Italy itself. Several Venetian imitations of the *Spectator* appeared during the eighteenth century. Goldoni, meanwhile, was drawing on the plots of Samuel Richardson's novels. For Venetians of this period, like other Italians, looked to England for inspiration, correctives to a decadence they saw in their own culture.[58] The English probably agreed with this self-evaluation. Some of the Venetian arts were now being brought home, but they were hardly of the most serious kind. There was the opera, and 'Venetian windows' (meaning Palladian ones). The Venetian contribution to Strawberry Hill was a design for a ceiling from Sansovino's Library.[59]

In 1749 Walpole wrote to Mann describing a 'jubilee masquerade in the Venetian manner' held at Ranelagh. There were booths like those at the time in Piazza San Marco, with masked shopkeepers selling Dresden china, tea, wine, orange tree bowers, gaming tables, and on the canal 'a sort of gondola, adorned with flags and streamers, and filled with music rowing about'.[60] Walpole, who had recently done his tour, added that there was 'nothing Venetian in it', but such shows must have prepared future visitors to experience the city as an amusement park. Since they usually arrived just in time for Carnival or the Ascension Day ceremony and left soon afterwards, their expectations were probably fulfilled. The great religious-cum-patriotic ceremony of the marriage with the sea soon became a subject to make jokes about. In 1741 Thomas Gray wrote from Florence to his friend West that he was going 'next to Venice by the 11th of May, there to see the old Doge wed the Adriatic Whore'.[61] William Beckford in 1782 did not think it worth describing: 'You have heard enough, and if ever you looked into a show-box, seen full sufficient of this gaudy spectacle, without my enlarging on the topic.'[62]

For those English travellers in search of freer social mores Venice was an ideal refuge. In 1739 Lady Mary Wortley Montagu arranged to meet her lover there. Though he failed to arrive, she remained a year and returned for another year in 1756. She appreciated the 'universal liberty', and told Lady Pomfret that

> it is so much the established fashion for everybody to live their own way, that nothing is more ridiculous than censuring the actions of another. This would be terrible in London, where we have little other diversion.[63]

Ruskin was to notice her lack of interest in 'buildings, or beauty or history' and to be made 'bitterly melancholy' by her thoughtless enjoyment of this 'centre of pleasure'.[64]

Some certainly seem to have gone merely as consumers, like James Boswell in 1765, his 'fancy ... stirred by the brilliant stories I had heard of Venetian courtesans'.[65] Such brilliant stories provided obvious material for Pope in his attack on the Italianate Englishman. The young grand tourist of the *Dunciad* goes first to Rome, which is deplorable enough, but Venice is worse:

> Tyber, now no longer Roman, rolls,
> Vain of Italian Arts, Italian Souls:
> To happy Convents, bosom'd deep in vines,
> Where slumber Abbots, purple as their wines:
> To Isles of fragrance, lilly-silver'd vales,
> Diffusing languor in the panting gales:
> To lands of singing, or of dancing slaves,
> Love-whisp'ring woods, and lute-resounding waves.
> But chief her shrine where naked Venus keeps,
> And Cupids ride the Lyon of the Deeps;
> Where, eas'd of Fleets, the Adriatic main
> Wafts the smooth Eunuch and enamour'd swain.[66]

Neatly, Pope links dissoluteness with naval, and hence economic and political impotence. There is no energy, no fertility in this sexuality, only languor and abandon. Beckford, characteristically, took this notion to its extreme, even though he was not in a position to be moralistic about Venetians:

> Their nerves unstrung by disease and the consequence of early debaucheries, allow no natural flow of lively spirits, and at best but a few moments of false and feverish activity. The approaches of rest, forced back by an immoderate use of coffee, render them weak and listless to like any active amusement, and the facility of being wafted from place to place in a gondola, adds not a little to their indolence. In short, I can scarcely regard their Eastern neighbours in a more lazy light; and am apt to imagine, that instead of slumbering less than other people, they pass their lives in one perpetual doze.[67]

The deglamourization of sexual freedom bears out Canepa's idea that the Englishman's stereotype of the Italian character depended on the relative strength of the two countries. Ascham had been horrified by Venetian depravity and its effect on young Englishmen; Pope is contemptuous. Vice is no longer exciting, dangerous, even wicked. Beckford associates Venetians and their Eastern neighbours in indolence and incapacity, for both had declined as international powers, while England had made enormous advances.

Beckford sees Venetians as indolent, but was not so himself. Other mid-eighteenth-century travellers seem to have been as bored by Venice as Venetians were said to be by life. Boswell told Rousseau that 'For the first week I was charmed by the novelty and beauty of so singular a city, but I soon wearied of travelling continually by water, shut up in those lugubrious gondolas.'[68] Edward Gibbon, who also went in 1765, got over the novelty even more quickly: 'The spectacle of Venice afforded some hours of astonishment and some days of disgust.'[69] He disliked the buildings, and society was closed to foreigners, as he explained to Dorothea Gibbon:

> Of all the towns in Italy, I am the least satisfied with Venice; Objects which are only singular without being pleasing, produce a momentary surprize which soon gives way to satiety and disgust. Old an[d] in general ill built houses, ruined pictures, and stinking ditches dignified with the pompous denomination of Canals; a fine bridge spoilt by two Rows of houses upon it, and a large square decorated with the worst Architecture I ever yet saw, and wonderfull only in a place where there is more land than water: such are the colours I should employ in my portrait of Venice; a portrait certainly true in general, tho' perhaps you should attribute the very great darkness of the shades to my being out of humour with the place. Here are no English, and all communication with the natives . . . is strictly forbid.[70]

Gibbon was wrong about there being 'no English'. It was a vintage year for bad-tempered visitors from England. There was Boswell, and 1765 also saw the arrival of Samuel Sharp, whose *Letters from Italy* were to provoke the sentimentalist counter-attack. With rare pauses for approval, Sharp's account of Venice is one long grumble. His comment that 'Venice, with a few alterations, might appear much more magnificent than it now is'[71] may be the most prosaic ever made about the city. Gibbon had noticed 'ruined pictures', and some dilapidation may also have been evident in the buildings by now. But the remark is typical of Sharp's passion for the modern and smart. He thought Venetian windows 'exceedingly paltry' because made of small panes of glass, while the shutters were 'not painted like ours in *England*', and the 'heavy clumsy tiles' on the roofs 'very much offend the eye'.[72] The canals too he found offensive and gondolas 'dismal'; their gloominess had become a cliché, for says Sharp, 'every body, at first sight, compares the roof you fit in to a hearse'.[73] He insults Venetian dialect by calling it 'a corrupt Italian'.[74] Sharp gives an absurd portrait of a scene in a courtroom (in complete contrast to *The Merchant of Venice*), and adopts a tough policy towards the 'swarms of beggars' in the city, a phenomenon he puts down to the Catholic habit of giving alms.[75] The only objects of curiosity are the function of the *cicisbeo* and the goings-on in the *casine*, matters which tantalized everybody during this period.[76]

Sharp's particularly inflexible brand of prejudice made him a perfect target for satire. Barely a year after the publication of *Letters from Italy*, Lawrence Sterne depicted him in *A Sentimental Journey* as Mundungus, plodding round Europe always 'straight on, looking neither to his right hand or his left, lest Love or Pity should seduce him out of his road'.[77] Sterne's susceptible hero never, of course, extricates himself from France, but his successors were eager to be seduced by modern Italy. The 'hostile tradition' was not extinguished;[78] Ruskin himself would sometimes vent irritation in mindless abuse. But usually his anger expresses serious concern with the state of modern Europe. In this Ruskin's judgements are more interesting than, but nonetheless indebted to, the late eighteenth-century change in attitudes to things foreign and things Italian. English responses to Venice were quite transformed because of this change.[79] Two members of Dr Johnson's circle were instrumental. Both Giuseppe Baretti and Hester Piozzi, formerly Thrale, had obvious reasons for being pro-Italian, and in both cases their allegiances were middle class. Baretti, the Piedmontese critic and lexicographer, spent in all nearly thirty years of his life in England and was a keen anglophile,[80] but could not let Sharp's *Letters* go without prompt rebuttal. His *Account of the Manners and Customs of Italy* made no attempt to rehabilitate the Venetian aristocracy, whom

Baretti thought presumptuous, ignorant, out of date and deceitful, but it did focus sympathetic attention on 'ordinary' Italians.[81] Though himself a moralist rather than a sentimentalist, Baretti's picture of the emerging Italian bourgeoisie and of the populace as an honest, cheerful, warm-hearted, tolerant, forgiving and hospitable, though somewhat simple-minded people, did contribute to the cause of enthusiasm.

It was not until twenty years later, however, that sympathy turned into rapture. In 1784 Mrs Thrale married an Italian singing master, Piozzi, much to the scorn of her family and friends, including Baretti, whose sympathies did not in practice extend down as far as that.[82] The ecstasies of delight reached in her *Observations and Reflections*, which Ruskin knew,[83] betray both her infatuation and her anxiety to defend the nationality of her husband. Venice was a high point in the long honeymoon. She writes of the 'more than magical sweetness of Venetian manners, dialect and address',[84] and interprets government tolerance of intrigues and wanton levity as indulgence on the part of paternalistic rulers who 'love to see her gay and cheerful'.[85] Politically innocent, Mrs Piozzi is almost indifferent to Venetian institutions,[86] but most curious about domestic manners and attitudes. The people are good natured in acknowledging foreign excellence, conversation is natural and not cultivated 'as an art' as in England; Venetian women, unlike English wives, are not terrified of their husbands' anger over accidents to the dinner.[87] Mrs Piozzi writes of 'our dear Venetians' as if they were children, to be praised, and occasionally reproved:

> St. Mark's Place is covered all over in a morning with chicken-coops, which stink one to death; as nobody I believe thinks of changing their baskets: and all about the Ducal palace is made so very offensive by the resort of human creatures for every purpose most unworthy of so charming a place, that all enjoyment of its beauties is rendered difficult to a person of any delicacy; and poisoned so provokingly, that I do never cease to wonder that so little police and proper regulation are established in a city so particularly lovely, to render her sweet and wholesome.[88]

Among buildings, the Ducal Palace was the one most admired. It was 'so beautiful, it were worth while almost to cross the Alps to see that, and return home again'.[89] But Mrs Piozzi was more susceptible to atmosphere and association than to formal effects. She liked moonlight, and thought the undulating floor of St Mark's was meant to 'represent the waves of the sea, and perpetuate marine ideas, which prevail in every thing at Venice'.[90] Attentive to the workings of her own mind, she described herself as if she were the passive victim of an overwhelming, romantic, magical force:

St. Mark's Place, after all I had read and all I had heard of it, exceeded expecta-
tion; such a cluster of excellence, such a constellation of artificial beauties, my
mind had never ventured to excite the idea of within herself . . . It was half an
hour before I could think of looking for the bronze horses . . . The general effect
produced by such architecture, painting, such pillars; illuminated as I saw them
last night by the moon at full, rising out of the sea, produced an effect like
enchantment . . . How does this lovely Piazza di San Marco render a newly-
arrived spectator breathless with delight! . . . though the whole appears
uncrowded, as in the works of nature, not of art . . . This wonderful city realises
the most romantic ideas ever formed of it, and defies imagination to escape her
various powers of enslaving it.[91]

In this, however, Mrs Piozzi was not the first. A few years before
William Beckford had been on perhaps the most romantic grand tour of
all time. He took with him the landscape painter J.R. Cozens, whose
'fragile and illusive' sketches were later to become familiar to Turner.[92]
Beckford had an originality rare in a traveller of any period, and he
knew it. His narrative of the journey, first published privately in 1783,
had a title suitably different from the usual 'Observations', 'Remarks',
'Accounts', and 'Letters': *Dreams, Waking Thoughts and Incidents*. The
diary, and the experience, is contrived, but not less remarkable for that.
Beckford spent most of his time in Venice alone, or affected to do so.
He was not pleased when people forced their company upon him, and
preferred to learn not through talk or reading,[93] but through looking
and elaborating what he saw in his imagination. Beckford moved from
place to place without seeming to know how he did so.[94] He spent one
afternoon under a tree listening to the stories told by the winds, and
another lying in the sea off the Lido: 'My ears were filled with murmur-
ing undecided sounds; my limbs, stretched languidly on the surge, rose
or sunk just as it swelled or subsided.'[95] Like Ruskin, Beckford went to
watch the sunset across the lagoon,[96] and like the imaginary traveller in
The Stones of Venice (IX, 414-15), he approached Venice for the first
time at sunset:

an azure expanse of sea opened to our view, the domes and towers of Venice
rising from its bosom . . . Still gliding forwards, the sun casting his last gleams
across the waves, and reddening the distant towers, we every moment distin-
guished some new church or palace in the city, suffused with the evening rays,
and reflected with all their glow of colouring from the surface of the waters.
The air was still; the sky cloudless; a faint wind just breathing upon the deep
. . . the distant woods of Fusina were lost in the haze of the horizon. We were
now drawing very near the city, and a confused hum began to interrupt the
evening stillness . . .[97]

Beckford was to have no rival in sensitivity to Venetian light and colour until Turner and Ruskin:

A pale greenish light ran along the shores of the distant continent, whose mountains seemed to catch the motion of my boat, and to fly with equal celerity. I had not much time to contemplate the beautiful effects on the waters — the emerald and purple hues which gleamed along their surface.[98]

The 'effects' are emotionally and dramatically suggestive as well as beautiful. As Beckford enters Venice tapers glimmer through awnings, and every gondola has a lantern so that each boat is 'followed by tracks of light, which gleamed and played upon the waters'.[99] Music too reverberates. He sees a barge serenading under a window, gondoliers take up the air, and 'long after I was asleep, the melody seemed to vibrate in my ear'.[100] Beckford observed, but he also liked what 'seemed', cultivated fantasies. Some of these have vaguely to do with Venetian history, which he is original in finding poetic. He thinks of Barbarossa, expects to bump into a Byzantine emperor, dwells on the absence of 'splendid fleets' with nostalgia rather than with scorn, as Pope had done.[101] He went deliberately to shudder under the Bridge of Sighs and, afterwards 'drew chasms and subterranean hollows, the domain of fear and torture, with chains, racks, wheels and dreadful engines in the style of Piranesi'.[102] The Venetian government had been disapproved of before; Beckford made it a source of Gothic horror. As Ruskin noticed, however, his favourite sources of inspiration were classical and neo-classical. Beckford liked the Palladian churches, San Giorgio Maggiore and San Giacomo Redentore, which he compared to Greek temples. In the Ducal Palace he pays his respects to the classical divinities and is caught by the police 'stalking proudly about like an actor in an ancient Grecian tragedy'.[103] At such times the effort of being different shows, as when Beckford goes to Torcello and writes of the cathedral font that he 'longed to have it filled with bats' blood, and to have it sent by way of a present to the sabbath'.[104] Yet Beckford was, as Roderick Marshall says, the first English writer to show 'nature blending with art, love with folly, splendour with decay', a series of paradoxes that was to make Venice a source of imaginative inspiration for the next fifty years or more.[105]

This was not directly due to *Dreams*, which was suppressed and did not reappear until 1834.[106] More immediately influential was John Moore's enormously popular *View of Society and Manners in Italy*.[107] To visual qualities Moore was not particularly sensitive; his imagination fed on the past. He liked 'singular events', and 'the history of no nation presents a greater variety of singular events than that of Venice'.[108] Conspiracies, crimes of state, the stories of the great doges provided him with 'une matière historique éminement propre à l'élaboration poétique . . .'[109] In spite of his title, Moore preferred to do his elaboration without society. In a crowd he felt his ideas 'broken, bruised, and dislocated'.[110] Nevertheless he found St Mark's Square stimulated a chain of association strong enough to withstand interference from contemporary Venetians for some time. You see churches, he says, and think of superstition, Rome, Constantinople; then, 'While you are forcing your way, sword in hand, with the heroic Henry Dandelo, into the capital of Asia, Adam and Eve stop your progress'; you think of Paradise, the Palace recalls the strength of the constitution, the lions' mouths horrify you, and then the sea brings to mind 'a country of *real* freedom'.[111] The country of real freedom did not provide the same scope for mental wanderings: in London, Moore asks, 'what idea can present itself to the imagination, beyond that of snug neatness and conveniency of substantial brick houses?'[112] Ruskin too disliked the neat and substantial buildings of modern England. But he was eventually to turn against the liberal 'Byronic' version of Venetian political history for which Moore was first responsible (X, 8). Moore used his reading of the early history of Venice as an illustration of greatness constructed on democratic principles: 'The independence of Venice was not built on usurpation, nor cemented with blood; it was founded on the first law of human nature; and the undoubted rights of man.'[113] He assembled the evidence to show what happens when oligarchy takes over: 'to the well-being . . . of the State . . . all respect for individuals, all private considerations whatever, and every compunctious feeling of the heart, is sacrificed.'[114]

Previous observers had, on balance, felt the 'well-being of the state' worth the sacrifice of the private individual. Even Mrs Piozzi thought Venetian reserve with foreigners a small price to pay for long-term stability.[115] Moore was probably the first to apply Benthamite principles to the institutions that had once held the admiration of Europe:

> It is believed to be owing to the attention of these courts [the State Inquisition], that the Venetian republic has lasted longer than any other; but, in my opinion, the chief object of a government should be, to render the people happy; and if it fails in that, the longer it lasts, so much the worse.[116]

In any case, Moore thought, tyranny was no protection against threats from outside. If such an attack came, 'it is much to be feared, that the spies, gondoleers, lions mouths, and State Inquisitors, would hardly prevent its success'.[117]

Sixteen years later Venice fell to Napoleon. Unresisted, the French put an end to eleven centuries of independence and a constitution whose only claim to respect in most men's eyes had become its capacity for survival. 1797 moved Wordsworth in his poem 'On the Extinction of the Venetian Republic' to forgive Venice her disgrace in her 'extinction', and recall what she had meant to Howell's generation as 'safeguard of the west', 'eldest Child of Liberty', 'maiden City, bright and free'. Others were less generous. Ignominiously handed over to the Austrians at Campoformio, Venice became accessible to English travellers again between 1798 and 1805. Joseph Forsyth reported mockingly on how readily Venetians had adopted French democratic ways: 'Men of all ranks associated very promiscuously under the arcades; they are free from the old republican distinctions, and they rattle on every subject but their own transformations.'[118] Retaken by the French after Austerlitz, the city was to undergo more radical changes, both in administration and appearance, between 1806 and 1814. When the end of the Napoleonic wars left Venice once more in Austrian hands, her humiliation seemed complete. Impoverished aristocrats sold off palaces, withdrew to the country, or accepted small pensions from the occupying regime. Unlike Milanese nobles they were not to give a lead in national revival. Few foresaw that thirty-five years later the professional classes were to give that lead in one of the most successful revolutions of 1848. In the meantime the demise of Venice, in part already accomplished (by the annihilation of democracy in 1297, by the fall of 1797, by the Austrian occupation of 1814), in part yet to come (as she sank beneath the waves), was taken for granted.

English reactions to the dead or moribund state of Venice varied. For many she became the special victim of Hapsburg aggression in Italy, competing with Florence for the 'auréole du martyre'.[119] Lady Sydney Owenson Morgan, the Irish novelist who spent a year in Italy between 1819 and 1820, was disturbed by the effects of heavy taxation, the drop in population, and warned that 'if the leaden sway' of Austrian rule continued, soon 'not a wreck would remain'.[120] She also deplored the fact that

> while the classical annals of Italy, with all their vices and crimes, make a part of the established education of England, the far nobler history of the Italian Republics, 'les siècles des merites ignorés,' remains but little known.[121]

Successive waves of exiles from Italy now began to arrive in England, their arrival coinciding with and nourishing the growing interest in Italian mediaeval and Renaissance culture and history.[122] But if, in Lady Morgan, liberal views went together with a passion for mediaeval history and sympathy for contemporary Italians, this was not always so. Shelley illustrates how revolutionary views and a love of the literature of Italy could be accompanied by extreme contempt for her present inhabitants:

Venice which was once a tyrant, is now the next worse thing, a slave. For in fact it ceased to be free, or worth our regret as a nation from the moment that the oligarchy usurped the rights of the people. Yet I do not imagine that it ever was quite so degraded as it has been since the French, and especially the Austrian yoke. . . . I had no conception of the excess to which avarice, cowardice, superstition, ignorance, passionless lust, & all the inexpressible brutalities which degrade human nature could be carried, until I had lived a few days among the Venetians.[123]

One might be listening to Ascham pronouncing his verdict after nine days residence. It is in any case questionable whether Shelley could be said to have 'lived . . . among the Venetians'. Contemplating a 'plan/ Never to leave sweet Venice' in *Julian and Maddalo*, Shelley imagines riding alone on the Lido, reading and writing 'Unseen, uninterrupted' in the company of casts of statues. Venetian sculpture does not exist any more than Venetian company; the great virtue of Venice seems to be that 'the town is silent'.[124] Shelley can divide Italy cleanly between natural and human, past and present:

There are *two* Italies — one composed of the green earth and transparent sea and the mighty ruins of ancient time, and aërial mountains and the warm and radiant atmosphere which is interfused through all things. The other consists of the Italians of the present day, their works and ways. The one is the most sublime and lovely contemplation that can be conceived by the imagination of man; the other is the most degraded, disgusting and odious.[125]

It is only the first Italy that appears in Shelley's poems. In *Lines Written among the Euganean Hills* Venice is stripped down to a few essentials and set against a rising sun:

Column, tower, and dome, and spire,
Shine like obelisks of fire,
Pointing with inconstant motion
From the altar of dark ocean
To the sapphire-tinted skies.[126]

'Ocean's nursling', born of water, made of fire, and reaching up into the air, will soon return into her mother element leaving no trace, except for where

     palace gate
With green sea-flowers overgrown
Like the rock of ocean's own,
Topples o'er the abandoned sea
As the tides change sullenly . . .[127]

If Shelley's day-to-day experience of Italy was 'not exempt from the laws, and the all too human impulses, which operate whenever it is a question of the travel experience', neither was Byron's. Barrows describes his life in Italy as a 'rudimentary and fairly blasé version of the Grand Tour'. Yet out of conventional experience both Shelley and Byron made 'something new and highly personal that transposed the English traveler's potential response into a new and higher key'.[128] That 'something' had, in Byron's case, various sides to it. One was historical and incorporating a political message. Both of Byron's Venetian tragedies, *Marin Faliero* and *The Two Foscari*, deal with the sacrifice of the individual to an omniscient and omnipresent state. Byron had done some research into Venetian chronicles for himself, and in the Preface to *Marin Faliero* criticized John Moore for inaccuracy as a historian.[129] But Byron's Venice was not a product of knowledge. In the same Preface he wrote 'Everything about Venice is, or was, extraordinary — her aspect is like a dream, and her history is like a romance.'[130] In the fourth canto of *Childe Harold* Byron uses romantic historical personages to 're-people' Venice with 'the heroic and the free,/The beautiful — the brave — the Lords of earth and sea'.[131] Shakespeare and Otway, enjoying new popularity at the time, provide reinforcements, 'Beings of the Mind', Shylock, Othello, Pierre. Byron could use these idealized or fictional Venetians to replace the modern Venetians, whom he described in the 'Ode on Venice' as crabs creeping through slimy streets. The city herself could be made to rise 'As from the stroke of the Enchanter's wand'[132] under various aspects. In the 'Ode' Byron gave a lurid picture of Venice as a sick man in the throes of a horrible last half hour. In *Childe Harold*, as an extinct maritime civilization soon to sink into the sea, she was a reminder of Tyre and a warning to England, as she was to be for Ruskin.[133] She was also a city with which Byron could identify himself. He, like the Venetians under Austrian rule, was an exile among 'empty halls,/Thin streets and foreign aspects'; Byron stood 'A ruin amidst ruins'.[134] Byron made the crumbling palaces, and gondoliers who no longer sing, more than compensate for the loss of the days when Venice 'was a boast, a marvel, and a show'.[135] Venice became 'the epitome of a paradise now lost',[136] her beauty intensified by approaching death, like the sunset,[137] now to become a most important moment in the traveller's Venetian day. Writing to Thomas Moore, Byron summed up both the imaginative and the mundane attractions in a famous description of Venice as

(next to the East) the greenest island of my imagination. It has not disappointed me; though its evident decay would, perhaps, have that effect upon others. But I have been familiar with ruins too long to dislike desolation. Beside, I have fallen in love . . .[138]

In 1819 Moore was to come to Venice himself and have rather an unfortunate experience. Conditions would have been perfect for a Byronic first sight of the city if Byron in person had not accompanied him on the last stage of his journey. There was

> a glorious sunset when we embarked at Fusina in a gondola, and the view of Venice and the distant Alps (some of which had snow on them, reddening with the last light) was magnificent; but my companion's conversation, which, though highly ludicrous and amusing, was anything but romantic, threw my mind and imagination into a mood not at all agreeing with the scene.[139]

Byron was not there to put everybody off their expectations of the approach to Venice. Lady Morgan described how, as one crossed the blank lagoon,

> memory, no longer deadened by external impressions, sends forth from her *'secret cells'* a thousand fanciful recollections; and as the spires and the cupolas of Venice come forth in the lustre of the mid-day sun, and its palaces, half-veiled in the aërial tints of distance, gradually assume their superb proportions, then the dream of many a youthful vigil is realised; and scenes long gloated over in poetic or romantic pages, gradually form and incorporate, and take their local habitation among real existences — objects of delight to the dazzled eye, as once to the bewildered imagination.[140]

The absence of 'external impressions' sets the mind free to feed off its accumulated resources. The 'half-veiled' spires, cupolas and palaces are not so substantial as to dispel the images summoned, which then mingle with the undefined 'real existences'; and so the dream is 'realised'. The annuals, and poems like Samuel Rogers's extremely popular *Italy*[141] show how prevalent this consciously subjective experience of Venice was during the 1820s and early 30s. Thomas Roscoe, who described the first sight of the city as 'some vision of the deep'[142] is typical. Hazlitt found the city 'magical, dazzling, perplexing', felt 'a mixture of awe and incredulity', and could hardly believe his eyes.[143] Perhaps this was the point, not to believe one's eyes at all, but to trust in the memory and the imagination. Lady Morgan proclaims the victory of the inner over the outer powers of perception when she says that Venice, 'even when seen ... still appears rather a phantasm than a fact'.[144] Many seemed to have passed their time in Venice in a state of confused trance. Rogers went 'gliding up her streets as in a dream'.[145] As Leitch Ritchie approached the centre of the city, people passed him 'like figures in a dream'; when he got to sleep he 'dreamed all night of enchanters, and enchanted ladies, and Childe Harold, and the Arabian Nights'.[146] The annuals supplied a range of romantic narrative, with and without Gothic horror.[147] Set against a scenario of islands, gondolas, music, sunsets, moonlight, exotic costumes and madhouses, plots revolved around unfortunate lovers, jealousy, vengeance, spies, the evil eye, torture and mysterious disappearances. In 1841 James Fenimore Cooper used such material to fill a full-length novel, *The Bravo: A Venetian Story*. It was to infuriate Ruskin during the *Stones of Venice* time. As Cooper explained in the Preface, the novel was to show how defective the European concept of liberty was compared to the American ideal; in the former case the state conceded rights to the people, in the latter the people voluntarily surrendered rights to the state. Venice, once herself a model republic, had by now become the epitome of a repressive regime, and the target of modern republicans.

But most purveyors of Venetian historical nonsense probably thought little about the political implications. They enjoyed the dramatic and sentimental possibilities of Venetian anecdote and ceremonial, and were vaguely aware of 'How much has been transacted . . . on this spot of earth.'[148] But the transactions chosen were hardly distinguishable, in content or in the way they were presented, from the invented episodes. The same atmosphere of enchantment prevails as Thomas Roscoe takes his readers, at various times, to the 'hallowed ground' of Titian's palace, to Byron's to see the scene of his love affairs, to the Bridge of Sighs to think of groaning victims, and to the Rialto where 'a thousand grand rememberances and splendid visions await us'.[149] Venetian history was now as unreal as Venetian fiction: as one anonymous writer put it 'It always was a dream, and will continue a dream for ever.'[150]

The aspect of the city, like her past, suffered from the lack of definition. Hazlitt, as one might expect, was exceptional, paying close attention to the load of ornament, the brilliant colour, and the general richness of Byzantine buildings, though (like Ruskin in *The Seven Lamps* and *Stones* I) condemning their lavishness as a sign of moral intemperance.[151] Otherwise ideas about Venetian architecture seem to have changed little since Burnet. Roscoe still praised the 'chaste and classical taste' of Palladio and regurgitated Joseph Forsyth's comments on St Mark's; it was 'a singular mixture', stylistically 'a fortuitous jumble' outside, while inside it was 'dark, heavy, barbarous, nay, poor'.[152] Joseph Woods, another object of Ruskin's scorn, judged the church extremely ugly and the Ducal Palace even uglier.[153] Those with more expansive temperaments were drawn to them, but because they enhanced the general atmosphere of strangeness and unreality. Ritchie called St Mark's 'a palace of faery'.[154] Lady Morgan went so far as to say that its styles blended 'so barbarously, and yet so beautifully',[155] but could only defend the Ducal Palace for its associations, not as an artefact.[156] William Brockedon described the subject of one plate from a drawing by Samuel Prout as 'the Ducal Palace, in all the grandeur of

its massiveness, and all the topsy-turvy of its architectural character, —
a vast incumbent structure upon an apparently very inadequate
support.'[157] But the drawing itself implied beauty, as did many of the
illustrations that helped to sell this literature. There was as yet no
rationale which would allow the attractions of these buildings to be
expressed in words. The picturesque and ruin sentiment, however,
provided arguments for liking their present dilapidated condition.[158]
Henry Crabb Robinson found 'The monuments of its faded glory . . .
deeply affecting.'[159] Lady Morgan thought that with decay the interest
of the city had

> rather increased than lessened; and in a picturesque point of view, it never
> perhaps was more beautiful, or more striking, than at the present moment . . .
> such majesty of ruin, in such affecting combinations of former splendour and
> actual decay, that their material beauty is heightened by deep moral touches.[160]

In the end taste in architecture brings us back to Byron and the
orthodoxy of the time. A writer in the *Forget-Me-Not* for 1826 defined
the peculiar charm of Venice, as opposed to that of Naples or Rome, as
'that of the *romantic*'.[161] Three years later Henry Crabb Robinson
summed up what had happened to the English view of Venice since the
sixteenth century as he 'entered Italy at Venice, the rich, but *I* say, the
romantic'.[162] The artists, novelists, poets and annual writers of the late
1820s and early 30s confirmed this as the appropriate catchword. It
was at about this time that John James and Margaret Ruskin and their
son began what turned out to be a series of continental journeys.

I.2   1835

Continental travel was not something Ruskin's parents took for granted.
Their extraction, upbringing, and early fortunes would not have induced
them to do so.[1] They first went abroad, taking their six-year-old son
with them, in 1825. It was to see the coronation of Charles X and the
field of Waterloo. One imagines it as a journey of thanksgiving for the
preservation of England from revolution, the restoration of the *ancien
régime*. Others were quicker to take advantage of the secondary consequences. Rogers and Turner had been among those who toured Italy
within five years of the peace. They in turn encouraged a more hesitant
generation of travellers.

Fifty years later Ruskin wrote in *Praeterita*:

> on my thirteenth(?) birthday, 8th February, 1832, my father's partner, Mr.
> Henry Telford, gave me Rogers's *Italy*, and determined the main tenor of my
> life.
>
> At that time I had never heard of Turner . . . But I had no sooner cast eyes on
> the Rogers vignettes than I took them for my only masters, and set myself to
> imitate them as far as I possibly could by fine pen shading.
>
> I have told this story so often that I begin to doubt its time. It is curiously
> tiresome that Mr. Telford did not himself write my name in the book, and my
> father, who writes in it, 'The gift of Henry Telford, Esq.,' still more curiously,
> for him, puts no date: if it was a year later, no matter; there is no doubt however
> that early in the spring of 1833 Prout published his *Sketches in Flanders and
> Germany*. . . . We got the book home to Herne Hill before the time of our usual
> annual tour; and as my mother watched my father's pleasure and mine in look-
> ing at the wonderful places, she said, why should not we go and see some of
> them in reality? My father hesitated a little, then with glittering eyes said —
> why not? (XXXV, 79.)

Praeterita emphasizes the enclosed, protective atmosphere of the
Ruskins' home at Herne Hill, and makes the decision seem daring. Yet
the boldness lay only in transferring established habits across the
Channel. For by 1832 the family, which now included Ruskin's
orphaned cousin, Mary Richardson, were well practised in educational

32

and romantic journeys. Nearly every summer since 1824 they had combined John James Ruskin's business trips with a family holiday. They visited country houses to look at paintings, and regions of beautiful, sublime, picturesque and dramatic scenery.[2] Mountains were preferred, John being a precocious geologist as well as a precocious poet. It was natural that the Alps should now be included in the itinerary. They had followed Wordsworth through the Lake District. Now Prout led them through Germany, Saussure through Switzerland, and Rogers and Turner through north-western Italy.

They had intended going south to Rome, but the heat, it seems, drove them back (XXXV, 80). They did not, in 1833, cross the peninsula to Venice. This did not prevent Ruskin from writing about the city. The main literary production of the tour was an 'Account' in which prose anecdote alternates with poetic transport, with spaces left for illustration, all in imitation of Rogers (II, 340-87). At the end of Mary Richardson's more matter-of-fact journal, however, appear some 'Lines by J.R.' which begin:

> The isles of the ocean are set for her seat
> There are waves at her waist, there are rocks at her feet
> Peerless and proud must the diadem be
> That is meet for the brow of the Queen of the sea.[3]

Ruskin was later to insert this six-stanza poem in a longer work,[4] but its complete lack of particularity, as well as its position in his cousin's journal, suggests that it belongs to the earlier tour.

Some commentators have emphasized the importance of Wordsworth for the young Ruskin. They stress a recommendation to observe closely.[5] Certainly this was to be important. But observation had to compete with preconception and association. The influence of Wordsworth was subdued by that of Scott and of Byron, who between them caused Ruskin 'many a day-dream and many a night-dream'.[6] Literary assumptions about Italian landscape appear in Ruskin's compositions from the age of ten. In 1829 he wrote a poem about Etna, the following year one about Vesuvius.[7] His knowledge was not confined to volcanoes. Planning the 1831 tour of Wales Ruskin anticipated 'scenery which equals that round about Tivoli . . .'[8] The confident comparison was not completely based on fantasy, or at least not on his own fantasy. The plates of Rogers's *Italy* and the *Sketches* of 1833 were perhaps the finest representations of 'wonderful places' Ruskin had seen to date, but they were by no means the first. Nor were they the first reproductions of Turner's or of Prout's work he had come across. Prout, Turner, James Duffield Harding, James Holland and David Roberts, the modern painters Ruskin was later to champion, were prominent among the artists who supplied the annuals of the 1820s and 30s. Years later Ruskin had sentimental memories of how 'the simple family circle looked forward with chief complacency to their New Year's gift of the Annual' (XXXIV, 94). The Ruskins almost certainly owned a complete set of *Friendship's Offering* from 1830 to 1846.[9] The engraving from a drawing of Vesuvius in the volume for 1830 may well have been the first he saw of Turner's work. Prout he had seen something of even earlier:

> the really most precious, and continuous in deep effect upon me, of all gifts to my childhood, was from my Croydon aunt, of the *Forget-me-not* of 1827, with a beautiful engraving in it of Prout's 'sepulchral monument at Verona'.[10]

These yearly gifts were not valued exclusively for their illustrations. Ruskin remembered how the stories 'were read some twenty times a year, during the earlier epoch of teens', and was led to

> wonder a little at my having been allowed so long to sit in that drawing-room corner with only my Rogers's *Italy*, my *Forget-me-not*, the *Continental Annual*, and *Friendship's Offering*, for my working library . . . (XXXV, 141).

Such a library did indeed produce yet another imitator of Byron, rather than the rival Ruskin's father had hoped for. For ten years from 1835 Ruskin was to be a regular contributor of 'third-rate literature'.[11] In *Friendship's Offering* he always had a place, and in its editor, W.H. Harrison, he found (apart from his father) his first literary adviser. Through this association Ruskin became acquainted with a man whose Annual contributions he had much admired, the Rev. Dr George Croly (XXXV, 140). It was surprising to the young Ruskin to learn that Croly 'had never been in Italy. I have read so many brilliant sketches of Venice, Naples and Turin in F.O. that I was much surprised by his denial of personal knowledge.'[12]

Ruskin's first notions of Venice were founded partly on descriptions supplied by those who, like himself, had never been there. This was to change. The journey of 1833 had only awakened the Ruskins' appetite for continental travel. On his return to London John James Ruskin bought travel literature and literature associated with foreign places. Byron had always been in the house; now he purchased Moore's seventeen-volume edition of his works, which included the plays and letters.[13] Not content with Telford's gift, he bought one more copy of Rogers's *Italy*. In 1834 Ruskin's father also bought Bulwer Lytton's *The Last Days of Pompeii* and Rose's sentimental *Letters from the North of Italy*. In 1835 he purchased Forsyth's hostile *Remarks*.[14]

By February of 1835 the next journey was in its planning stage.

This time the Ruskins could exercise personal preferences. John was especially definite. Like Mary Richardson, he was practising French and Italian.[15] He wrote verse letters to his father recommending a westerly route:

> What care we for Germany, leave her, oh leave her
> We will dash down to Paris, and jump on Geneva.[16]

Salvador, their courier, had come out to Herne Hill with maps and 'upset all my favourite schemes', for these had involved taking the carriage along Alpine goat-tracks and ignoring all thought of expense or time.[17] Eventually they had reached some agreement and 'serpentined the journey by/All places of much consequence'. It seems that Venice was less important to the Ruskins than Rome. However, the travellers never arrived at their original destination. At the Hospice of the Great St Bernard on 15 July Ruskin began a long verse letter to his school-friend, Willoughby Jones, in which he explained why they were still in the Alps:

> cholera and plague have come and plague it, we have missed all,
> And now indeed we're all in doubt, and none of us can know,
> How long we shall roam about, or whither we shall go
> Our route we've hardly planned as yet, and such suspense is horrid . . .[18]

Disconcerted, the Ruskins turned into the Tyrol, where they made a casual decision:

> When we to Inspruck got you know how small the distance then is,
> We thought that we might venture by Verona down to Venice . . .[19]

It was now late September. Up to this point Ruskin had kept a prose diary. This he used almost wholly for notes on natural phenomena, mainly the weather and geology. Paris was simply 'Still very warm. Cyan. 9'.[20] In the Alps he drew diagrams of rock strata.[21] But his principal means of recording what he saw was description. He writes, often at length, with clarity and excitement, transitions from the analytic to the imaginative being easily accomplished. Near the Hospice of the Great St Bernard, for example, there was a 'small, deep, calm, transparent lake'. Knowing that 'Ice is lighter than water', Ruskin was surprised to see

> snow in some places sloping down beneath the water of this lake. It however was an excellent test of the colour of the water. It had not the bluish, verdigris green of the lac de Chêde, but a rich olive sort of green . . .[22]

He was tirelessly curious about such matters. Later on the same day he noticed some 'pale and delicate pink' colouring in the snow and 'wished to examine it, but damp clouds, tired mules, coming night, and friends in a hurry, are great enemies to philosophical experiments'.[23] One sympathizes with Mr and Mrs Ruskin and Mary waiting in the cold and damp while John examined pink snow.[24] But the incident does illustrate an independence of mind and an enquiring spirit. Both these and his ability to use language with originality and precision completely deserted Ruskin whenever he was faced with human beings and their works. For Rouen he could summon no less banal and repetitive description than 'one of the most beautiful out of all the beautiful cities of La belle France'.[25] And now, as the party made for Venice, Ruskin records coming down from the mountains into the 'thoroughly romantic, Italian, beautiful, picturesque, filthy and abominable village of Bormio'.[26] Two days later, on 25 September, Ruskin filled the last page of this diary volume. There may have been another, now lost. Or Ruskin may have decided that prose was not the medium by which to describe the even more thoroughly romantic cities of Venice and Verona. Certainly he had other means of expressing himself. One was drawing. In *Praeterita* Ruskin recalled how

> on my first sight of the Ducal Palace . . . I had deliberately announced to my father and mother, and — it seemed to me stupidly incredulous, Mary, that I meant to make such a drawing of the Ducal Palace as never had been made before. This I proceeded to perform by collecting some hasty memoranda on the spot, and finishing my design elaborately out of my head at Treviso. The drawing still exists, — for a wonder, out of perspective, which I had now got too conceited to follow the rules of, — and with the diaper pattern of the red and white marbles represented as a bold panelling in relief. No figure disturbs the solemn tranquillity of the Riva, and the gondolas — each in the shape of a Turkish crescent standing on its back on the water — float about without the aid of gondoliers.[27]

He also momentarily revived his 'poetic diary in the style of "Don Juan" artfully combined with that of "Childe Harold"'(XXXV, 152). This he had abandoned half way through the second canto at Chamonix, having 'exhausted on the Jura all the descriptive terms at my disposal' (XXXV, 152). At Venice he found enough 'new' ones to fill two stanzas with such imagery as 'the weedy step and washen door', the low wailing of a 'victim, unrevenged, of secret midnight slaughter', and the ghosts of senators, doges and *bravi* flitting 'Along the moonlit pavement of St. Mark' (II, 440). Venice is 'Like to a lovely thought in dreamy sleep', and 'like a monument, a tomb'. The imagery is so ready to hand that its use hardly involves any imaginative effort. When

Ruskin's generation sense gloom in Venice it tells us far less about the state of mind or emotions of the author than in Byron's case. Ruskin, certainly, was entirely happy during this first visit, quite unaffected by self-doubt. The letter to Willoughby Jones, begun three months before in the Alps, closes with this cheerful picture of a busy romantic routine:

> And now I'm in the halls so high of Ocean's lovely daughter,
> The gondolas are gliding by like arrows in the water
> Here and there they dart about where far around I see
> The palaces arise from out the blue waves of the sea
> Of marble, marble, wondrous white, they fairylike arise,
> The Doge's is upon my right and near the Bridge of Sighs;
> Oh, Venice is a place to make a tortoise quite ecstatic
> I've crossed her lake, her ocean lake, and seen the Adriatic,
> I've tried St. Mark's by midnight moon and on Rialto walked about,
> A place of terror and of gloom which very much is talked about,
> The gondolier has rowed me by the house where Byron took delight
> The Palace too of Foscari is very nearly opposite,
> But 4 days more, and go we forth, and fast we sail away . . .[28]

Ruskin was probably remembering accurately when in *Praeterita* he described this visit as one of 'pure childish passion of pleasure' (XXXV, 295). On 11 October, the night before they were to sail away, he apparently cried all night.[29]

The Ruskins were home by Christmas. In January 1836 Pedro Domecq, the third member of the Ruskin, Telford, Domecq partnership, left his four daughters to stay at Herne Hill for several weeks. Ruskin fell in love with the eldest of them, Adèle Clothilde. Miserable at her departure, Ruskin composed love poems. He also made attempts at more ambitious forms, a tragic drama and a novel, both set in Venice. In 'Marcolini' Ruskin borrowed names, stage properties, sentiments and the beginnings of a revenge plot interwoven with a story of doomed devotion from Rogers, Byron, Shelley and Shakespeare.[30] Venice provides a background of ruined palaces, lions' mouths, spies, torture, drownings and treachery, a 'secret city' (II, 490) where at any moment the 'song' may be

> stopped by the dagger, and a hundred forms
> Of Proteus death look out from holes and corners
> With horrible glance, and gather from the crowd
> Harvest of lives . . . (II, 500).

The atmosphere is so perilous that the desperation expressed by the characters at the prospect of exile does not seem very plausible (II,

480). But Ruskin's problem was in making the transition from atmosphere to plot, for though these exciting events are much talked of, nothing actually happens. He gave up in the fifth scene. He encountered the same difficulty with 'Velasquez the Novice', the first of the 'Chronicles of St. Bernard' discovered by a poetical young traveller in the library of the Hospice. Velasquez is a mysterious young man of handsome and haughty appearance but 'severe thoughtfulness' of disposition who speaks of 'the light of the love of the departed' in a gondola on the way from Mestre to Venice (I, 538, 542). His interlocutor is Ada, who combines stoutly British patriotism with dreamlike southern beauty (I, 538, 540). This harmonizes with the climate and the sensation of 'being borne in a vessel of dreams through a city of beautiful silence' (I, 540). The atmosphere is enlivened but not broken by prosaic comments from a John Bull character,[31] or by the 'populous and cheerful motion' of innumerable gondolas (I, 544-5). These transport dark-haired maidens, stern senators and flower-girls, and are propelled by gracefully dirty gondoliers or police spies pretending to be such. Palaces, indiscriminately 'rich Grecian' or 'rich Moresco' with 'exquisitely formed Gothic windows', manage to combine splendour with 'darkness, desolation and decay' (I, 544, 548, 549). All of which is only remarkable because it shows how thoroughly Ruskin, at seventeen, had absorbed the romantic vision of Venice.

More interesting than his ability to reproduce that vision is his attempt to sustain it against criticism. For in defending Turner's *Juliet and Her Nurse* against the review in *Blackwood's Magazine* of October 1836 Ruskin was also taking the side of the poets in their battle against the Sharps and Forsyths of the sceptical, hostile tradition. Ruskin puts his argument that Turner's view is 'accurate in every particular' in peremptory fashion (III, 637), but in support of Turner's Shakespearean imagination he becomes gushing:

Many-coloured mists are floating above the distant city, but such mists as you might imagine to be aetherial spirits, souls of the mighty dead breathed out of the tombs of Italy into the blue of her bright heaven, and wandering in vague and infinite glory ... with the beauty of uncertain light ... And the spires of the glorious city rise indistinctly bright into those living mists, like pyramids of pale fire from some vast altar ... (III, 638-9).

The point of this and much more is to show that Turner is only putting on canvas what would have been 'the admiration of the world' if expressed by the 'mind of the poet', the poet in this case being Ruskin relying somewhat on the help of Shelley.[32] Turner had no need of such defence, however, and Ruskin's 'Reply' was not published. He would need to catch up with Turner's knowledge of many things,[33] among them Venetian topography and Venetian light, before he could take a firmer critical stand.

I.3　1841

Just after the return from the continent in December 1835 Ruskin
wrote a brief comic script for a 'Conversation Supposed to be Held
between Mr. R., Mrs. R., Miss R., and Master R., on New-Year's Morning,
1836' (II, 446-8). Mr R. grumbles about the English weather, his dull
work at the office, the gloom of the docks, and speaks longingly of
'when we went/Travelling in Italy; Seeing churches, large and fair, —'.
At this point Miss and Master R. join in an enthusiastic chorus about
gems and marbles, palaces and pictures, lake and mountains. Mrs. R.
berates them, especially her husband, for not appreciating the regular,
healthy comforts of home and a prospering business, and after some
reflection he is reconciled to England.[1] For the next four years the
Ruskins were to confine their holidays to the Lakes, Scotland,
Yorkshire, Derbyshire and Cornwall. They were away from home
enough without more extended journeys. John James Ruskin, as
always, had to travel for custom. In January Ruskin took up residence
in Christ Church, his mother and cousin in Oxford High Street. Not all
his academic work interested the young man greatly, but he had much
else to do besides. There was drawing, poetry, natural history, first
writings on architecture and growth in knowledge of modern landscape
artists, especially Turner.[2] By the spring of 1840 Ruskin had been given
four of his paintings, had got to know Godfrey Windus's collection, and
in June of that year met the artist. He would use the Italian tour of
1840-41 to 'get experience in scenery' for himself,[3] and discover that
the 'chief sources of Venetian happiness' were exclusively Turnerian
(III, 255). But the immediate reason for going and for interrupting
Oxford work for so long was another. In April 1840 Ruskin manifested
faint symptoms of consumption, was taken home, and received doctor's
orders to winter in the south. Whether or not his health had been
affected by hearing, belatedly, of Adèle's engagement and then of her
marriage in March, he would continue to grieve over her and himself
during this nine-month journey. 'Venetian happiness' would offer some
consolation. For though Ruskin had invented a special link between
Adèle and that city, it was not a painful association. Venice had been to
him 'a place of dreams . . . a refuge from all other thoughts'.[4]

The main objective was not Venice but several months in the warmth of Rome and Naples. On the way south Ruskin brought his expertise in views to bear on each town. Le Puy was 'quite noble — a little dry', and Valence 'thoroughly Italian, but nothing distingué'.[5] Sometimes his responses were more emotional. At Fréjus he

> thanked God for giving me a few more such hours and scenes, while my sight is still so far perfect. If it gets weaker, I think I shall stay in Italy or Switzerland. What have I to go home for?[6]

Tuscany did not impress him. Lucca was 'an ugly little town', Pisa 'very uninteresting', and though the galleries of Florence were 'impressive enough', the town itself was 'stupid'.[7] In Rome and the Campagna, however, Ruskin found a wealth of picturesque effects. In the ghetto he found material for his 'Proutist' style of drawing (XXXV, 277). In the countryside he picked out Poussin clouds, Hurlstone peasants, Copley Fielding hailstorms and complete Turners constantly.[8] In 'an odd fit of industry' he began reading Sismondi's *Histoire des républiques italiennes au moyen-age*.[9] But four days later he declared 'The history of these rubbishy little republics is as confused as Thucydides . . .'[10] In such moods, he could find no pleasure, even in scenery. Once, while raging at himself on the Pincian for his inability to feel or possess the beauty before him, he noticed two nursemaids with their charges, one baby 'a larger animal' than the first, and then 'a couple of moustachioed beasts'. They were all quite insensitive to the scene '— but still *happy*'.[11] Ruskin was different in both respects. The happiness of others caused him pain, and their misery was not always amenable to the picturesque outlook. At Paestum he

> Sat for a quarter of an hour, alone, on the steps of the temple of Ceres, and tried to work myself into a little serious feeling about it; but it wouldn't do. As long as I kept to the bold, shattered, grassy foundation, with its waving weeds and glancing lizards, it was all very well; but one glance on the ugly, ragged plain and miserable white-washed cottages destroyed the whole effect, and a yellow swineherd . . . completed the interruption . . . The whole affair a great bore.[12]

Ruskin was not at his best in the south. Rome made him 'dread to return'.[13] There he had begun to 'long for Venice and the Alps' in December.[14] As the party travelled north after Easter Ruskin declared himself 'sick of strange places. I shall be glad so to get to Padua and see something to remind me of old times.'[15] He had spent only two weeks in this north-eastern corner of Italy, but he felt it peculiarly his own. Arriving in Venice on 6 May he wrote in his diary:

Thank God I am here! It is the Paradise of cities and there is a moon enough to make half the sanities of earth lunatic, striking its pure flashes of light against the grey water before the window; and I am happier than I have been these five years — so happy — happier than in all probability I ever shall be again in my life, I feel fresh and young when my foot is on these pavements, and the outlines of St. Mark's thrill me as if they had been traced by A[dèle']s hand. This and Chamouni are my two homes of earth; there might have been another, but that has become all pain. Thank God I am here![16]

There is an element of self-dramatization in such an entry as in that of Fréjus, and that of the Pincian incident. Having lost his love, Ruskin has lost his natural home, and must be grateful if he can find a spiritual one in exile. Incapable of the pleasures easily available to the less sensitive, he must make the most of this special delight.

Yet Ruskin was wrong when, in *Praeterita*, he discounted this entry as written in ignorance and a state of emotional imbalance (XXXV, 296). His ten days in Venice were not self-indulgent. They brought some hard work, difficulties and self-criticism. The first problem was those 'pure flashes of light'. Ruskin 'did not enjoy' his first day's drawing as he had expected to because 'I could not draw well for the dazzling light of the water, and got flushed and uncomfortable — so, vanity of vanities!'[17] On the next day he seems to have tried somewhere darker, but was still

Excessively sulky and bored about my drawing to day — could not get on; drew like a child, and did not like the general effects of the narrow canals; disappointed in the ordinary houses.[18]

On the ninth day he thought over the problem and concluded, without much satisfaction, that

On the whole, I should say that the exquisite grace and finish of pieces of ordinary-life architecture about Rome spoiled one for the *common* houses here . . . On the other hand, I think a single passage of the grand canal or the Piazzetta worth all Rome and Naples together; but the whole is not up to my recollection of it . . . I have got all wrong with my drawing . . .[19]

Then, three days later, he seems to begin to realize what the trouble was:

What a delicious afternoon I spent yesterday in St. Mark's — trying to get the local colour of the church. It was such a pleasure to have one's eye kept on those beautiful and strange details . . . and to be able to . . . look round on the vast square and bright evening sky . . . I never took so luxurious a drawing in my life

. . . feeling I was doing something, and that with no picturesque ugliness, but with an object which it is delight to have one's eyes drawn to. Then when I left the square . . . there was a light such as Turner in his maddest moments never came up to . . . I am disappointed in the pictures of the place — they so seldom compose well and their detail is so rich in colour that it is penance to draw in grey, and requires months for days to use anything else. The best bits are hackneyed, which is another bore. There is a curious contrast between those last two entries . . .[20]

It was not a question of 'vanity of vanities', but of choice of subject and materials. The pencil drawing technique that had served the 'ordinary-life architecture' of Rome and Naples was unsuited to the city he now saw. The Venice that gave him happiness had light and colour and monumental outlines, details 'beautiful and strange', but no 'picturesque ugliness', was difficult to 'compose well'. It was Turner's Venice, not Prout's. Soon Ruskin was writing to Edward Clayton, his friend at Oxford: 'After a thorough spell of drawing, I have put up my pencils — rather sulkily, by-the-bye: for this place is quite beyond everybody but Turner . . .'[21] He did not realize that he had found another way. Ruskin could describe what he could not yet draw. As soon as he stopped straining to make scenes compose well he could enjoy them again. In the evening of his first disappointing day he had found St Mark's Square 'worth any thing — everything'. The band was playing, the crowd in exotic costumes moving through twilight, shadows, rising lamplight, moonlight, the last of daylight reminiscent of moonlight.[22] Having sulked all the second morning a row out towards the Lido 'put me a little right again', and then he saw how

A heavy thunder cloud came over the Doge's palace in the twilight, and rapid limitless flashes of silent lightning showed first behind its ridges, as the rockets rose from behind the smoke of St. Angelo; then retired over the Lido, lighting the whole noble group of the Salute with a bluish spectral white, as every flash touched on it with vague, mysterious gracefulness — Turner's own — the edges of the dome dark against the reflected lightning on the ground of sky. I must try if I cannot give the effect some time.[23]

Ruskin had already 'given the effect'.

One would think from Ruskin's diary that he was travelling alone. He writes of what he sees and feels, and hardly ever mentions anyone else or what they are doing. When he does go somewhere with other members of his family, he gives no indication of their presence. Mary Richardson, who noted what she, her aunt, uncle and cousin were doing every morning, afternoon and evening, tells what he omits. On the evening Ruskin had been so impressed by St Mark's Square he had been

accompanied by his father.[24] Mary went with him on his farewell visit
to St Mark's.[25] One day they had all gone together to the Lido.[26]
Ruskin wrote 'I have been to Lido to day.'[27] Much of the time he
was alone. Mary Richardson's most usual note of his doings is 'John to
drawing again.'[28] Meanwhile the others went shopping, to the Arsenal,
found their way along the alleys to the Rialto, went to picture galleries.
They were content to perform the pleasant duties of any traveller. But
Ruskin differed less in what he did and saw than in how he reacted. He
went to the Academy galleries, but made no note of Titian's
Assumption, about which Mary Richardson had been enthusiastic.[29] He
did notice a Veronese, but pronounced it 'intensely ridiculous' because
the clothes were anachronistic.[30] Ruskin took either less or more
interest in things than might have been conventional. Mary Richardson
remarked, in due order, on the mosaics, carvings, sculptures and bronze
horses of St Mark's, the treasures put on view on Mondays and
Fridays.[31] Ruskin tried to 'get the local colour'.[32] He paid closer attention, more selectively. The only sculptures he speaks of are the three
angles of the Ducal Palace: 'I wonder why two of the chief corner
stones of the Doge's Palace should be representations of human weakness?'[33] This was a question that would still interest him thirty years
later (XXIX, 34). During the next two days he gave further details, and
looked at the Solomon corner.[34] He tried to read the inscriptions and
the figures on the capital beneath, announcing 'I shall test Mr Prout by
this when I get home, though I fear he won't bear it.'[35] Ruskin tested
Byron too. He went over the supposedly horrific prisons and torture
chambers of the Ducal Palace, and reported that 'there had been a slight
proportion of . . . gammon about it'.[36] He was ready, too ready
perhaps, to notice discrepancies, changes in himself and in the town:

> a little of my romance is going. The canals are I think shallower, and I am sure
> dirtier, than they were of old; and I have lost the childish delight at the mere
> floating and dashing — the joy of watching the oars and waves . . . The town
> seems perhaps more prosperous than when we were here before, but it is evident
> that the nature of the people is changed; and all that is now doing and erecting
> disagrees with things of old.[37]

Ruskin never, even in his sixties, lost childish delight in rowing and the
boats of Venice. The 'evident' change in the nature of the people is hard to
credit. But the town probably was more prosperous, and the canals may
well have been shallower,[38] and Ruskin's sense of romance was changing
if not going. Mary Richardson, John James and Margaret Ruskin were
content to repeat the patterns of 1835, or make minimal variations on
them. They had come via Fusina instead of Mestre 'for a change'. They
saw the Giudecca, the Salute, the Custom's House and the Ducal Palace,

all of which had its fairy enchanting effect the same as on a first visit. We went to the same hotel ... About one we went out for a little turn in the Piazza St Marco which struck us as much as on a first visit.[39]

On future tours Ruskin too would tend to go to the same hotel, visit the same places. But even when most apparently repetitive, his reactions would always be different in some way, never quite 'the same as on a first visit'.

From Naples in February 1841 Ruskin had written to Edward Clayton, shortly to be ordained:

> The least speaking or reading makes me hoarse ... so how I am to preach I cannot tell ... I have begun a work of some labour which would take me several years to complete; but I cannot read for it, and do not know how many years I may have for it. I don't know if I shall even be able to get my degree; and so I remain in a jog-trot, sufficient-for-the-day style of occupation ...[40]

1842 dispersed many uncertainties, saw the 'work of some labour' truly begun. It was to displace the idea, cherished by Margaret Ruskin, that he should take orders. It was also to prove that he was stronger in health than he thought. In the spring of that year Ruskin took his degree. He also saw, and formed a passion for, Turner's Swiss mountain drawings (XXXV, 309-10). Shortly afterwards the Ruskins left for a summer in Switzerland. There Ruskin was again enraged by hostile reviews of paintings Turner had shown at the Royal Academy. The pamphlet he resolved to write grew into *Modern Painters: Their Superiority in the Art of Landscape Painting to All the Ancient Masters Proved by Examples of the True, the Beautiful, and the Intellectual, from the Works of Modern Artists, Especially from Those of J.M.W. Turner, Esq., R.A.*[41] The book was the first of five volumes of a work that would be completed only in 1860. But *Modern Painters* I was written quickly, at the new family home on Denmark Hill, in the winter of 1842-43.

It was more concerned with English and Swiss than with Italian subjects, with skies and mountains and water than with cities. Yet Venice had a place among landscapes. Before discussing the truths of nature one by one, Ruskin wished to give a summary illustration of how only a painter's love of nature enables him to paint her (III, 255). That it might be 'proved by deliberate investigation of facts, and in no way [be] left dependent upon feeling or imagination', he offers 'a comparison of the kind of truths impressed upon us in the painting of Venice by Canaletti, Prout, Stanfield, and Turner'. At first sight Canaletto seems to create the illusion that 'we are in our beloved Venice again'. We then notice that he is 'lurid and gloomy ... has lost the flashing, dazzling, exulting light, which was one of our chief sources of Venetian happiness'. One house we recognize, but instead of rich arabesques, 'beautiful as a dream', we have 'Five black dots'. Of the next house we remember shattered marble shafts, 'greened by the weeds ... gliding over the illumined edges and delicate fissures ... the wild sea-weeds and crimson lichens drifted and crawled with their thousand colours and fine branches over its decay ...' Canaletto gives fifty-five bricks all the same size, a thick black line for the roof and six ripples for the base: 'And this is what people call "painting nature!" ' He sees

heaps of earth and mortar, with water in between ... But what more there is in Venice than brick and stone — what there is of mystery and death, and memory and beauty — what there is to be learned or lamented, to be loved or wept — we look for to Canaletti in vain.

Prout has the picturesque decay, but as Ruskin had foreseen fails the test of architecture:

we begin to feel that we are in Venice ... But let us look a little closer; we know those capitals very well; their design was most original and perfect, and so delicate ... what have we got for them here? Five straight strokes of a reed pen! No, Mr. Prout, it is not quite Venice yet (III, 256).

Stanfield has the air and good light, feeling for truth of architecture and water, but

there is nothing to hope for or find out, nothing to dream of or discover; we can measure ... This cannot be nature, for it is not infinity. No, Mr. Stanfield, it is scarcely Venice yet.

Turner is supreme:

white, flashing fulness of dazzling light, which the waves drink and the clouds breathe, bounding and burning in intensity of joy ... Do we dream, or does the white forked sail drift nearer, and nearer yet ... It pauses now; but the quivering of its bright reflection troubles the shadows of the sea, those azure, fathomless depths of crystal mystery, on which the swiftness of the poised gondola floats double, its black beak lifted like the crest of a dark ocean bird, its scarlet draperies flashed back from the kindling surface, and its bent oar breaking the radiant water into a dust of gold. Dreamlike and dim, but glorious, the unnumbered palaces lift their shafts out of the hollow sea, — pale ranks of motionless flame — their mighty towers sent up to heaven like tongues of more eager fire, — their grey domes looming vast and dark, like eclipsed worlds ... Yes, Mr. Turner, we are in Venice now (III, 257).

The difference between this Venice and that of the 'Many-coloured mists' and 'aetherial spirits' of 1836 shows Ruskin's growing skill in prose description. The colours are clearer, the dream more powerful. This is probably Ruskin's most eloquent version of Venice the romantic in its pure form. He would try one more poem on a Venetian subject, the 'Madonna dell' Acqua'.[42] But there the imagery of weeds and sunset and ocean birds appears tired and conventional again, and though they continue to reappear in later writings, they are put to a different use. For Ruskin was now to undergo changes. When, three years later, he came to revise *Modern Painters* I for the third edition, he would cut the description of Turner's Venice and substitute a much longer one of a different kind (see III, 169, n.). He would still attack Canaletto, but for his failure to show Venice before she was ruined by decay rather than for his failure to show the beauty of decay itself (III, 213-15). Between 1843 and 1846 Ruskin came to have more respect for 'bricks and mortar'. Of Prout's mannerism he did not change his opinion, but the artist had been offended by this passage, and Ruskin gave instead a more detailed appreciation of the aspects of his work he did admire (III, 217-20). Of Turner Ruskin would say that Venice was the one Italian city in which he encountered no difficulties (III, 244), that one of his Venetian paintings, 'with sunlight and moonlight mixed, was . . . the most perfectly *beautiful* piece of colour of all that I have seen produced by human hands, by any means, or at any period' (III, 250). This emphasizes Turner as a painter, not his conception of Venice, timeless, 'dreamlike and dim'. That city would be displaced into the past, and modern painters of Venice make room for Venetian painters.

II   The Stones of Venice

II.1   1845

A month after returning home in 1841 Ruskin was sent to Leamington to spend some weeks in the care of a doctor trusted by his parents. Bored, he looked over his old diaries, commenting on what he had seen and felt going down through France exactly one year before. He judged himself 'nearly ready for another start already. I feel rather poetical about Naples and Rome, and yearn for Milan again, and my beloved Alps . . .'[1] In fact Ruskin did not go back to Rome, or anywhere south of Rome, for over thirty years. Nor would he ever again 'feel rather poetical' about any part of Italy. After 1843 Ruskin's new purpose as a critic would alter the nature of Italian travel. *Modern Painters* I had been thick with detailed analysis, drawn from long study of natural phenomena, illustrating 'Ideas of Truth' in painting. At twenty-four Ruskin was less well prepared to speak of the representation of 'Ideas of Power', 'Ideas of Beauty' and 'Ideas of Relation', the other categories proposed. He could not then anticipate how long, and how many volumes, it would take to complete this work. Examples, however, could clearly not be drawn only from a handful of despised seventeenth-century painters, and an equally limited number of contemporary artists, only one of whom Ruskin considered great. To write of 'Ideas of Beauty, the subject of *Modern Painters* II, Ruskin needed a greater knowledge of art.

It took him two years to conclude that this meant he must go to Italy. 1843-44 was a time of preparation. Writing his autobiography, forty years later, Ruskin could not recall how his 'picture knowledge' had grown during the early 1840s. He remembered only George Richmond's telling him that as a colourist Veronese was far superior to Rubens: 'No more was needed. From that moment I saw what was meant by Venetian colour' (XXXV, 337). In fact this was only one of many similar exchanges with George Richmond, his brother Tom and Joseph Severn, his friend. When Ruskin had frequented their studio in Rome in 1840 and 1841, his 'Protestantism and Proutism' had made him sceptical of their preference for Italian over Dutch and Flemish art (XXXV, 277). A few months later, however, Ruskin noted in his diary some remarks of Severn's comparing Turner to 'the old Italian school', contrasting him with Rembrandt.[2] In May 1843 he summarized in his diary a conversation with Tom Richmond about Michaelangelo and Raphael, then a remark by a dealer named Woodburn to the effect that collectors always begin by buying the Dutch School and end with the Italian.[3] Letters to George Richmond of this year, 1843, show Ruskin growing in admiration of Fra Angelico. Having seen some Raphaels of Woodburn's he decided that 'REMBRANDT WON'T do.'[4] But Ruskin's hesitation in tackling 'Ideas of Beauty' probably had less to do with questions of schools than with what he anxiously called his 'unnatural horror of the unnatural'.[5] He spoke of this as the time when he 'held off in fear and trembling' from painters of the human figure.[6] By June 1843, however, Ruskin had devised a programme of study including Raphael, 'the early school of Italy', a renewed assault on Italian language and history. He also stated that 'I must necessarily go to Italy', but seems to have made no definite plans.[7] That autumn Ruskin was reading Alexis Francois Rio's *De la poésie chrétienne dans son principe, dans sa matière, et dans ses formes* (1836).[8] This was a highly enthusiastic interpretation of early Italian painting. Rio showed where in art might be found the mediaeval ideal Carlyle exemplified in Abbot Samson's monastery in *Past and Present* (1843). Carlyle's book, with Cobbett's *History of the Protestant Reformation in England and Ireland* (1824-26) and Southey's *Sir Thomas More: or Colloquies on the Progress and Prospects of Society* (1829-31), were to be of help to Ruskin in using the middle ages to criticize nineteenth-century England.[9] It may have been George Richmond who introduced him to these writings, though neither Ruskin nor the Richmond circle were exclusively mediaevalist in their taste. In February 1844 Ruskin went with Severn to the Royal Academy and 'saw a Giorgione which I believe I shall never forget'.[10] In August, returning from a holiday in Switzerland, he had a few days in the Louvre. On the 12th Ruskin wrote to George Richmond asking for guidance about pictures he might miss without his help. At this point Ruskin still wanted 'to go everywhere at any time, and be in twenty places at once' (XXXVI, 39). The first three days in Paris, however, made sure the next journey would be to Italy:

I have had a change wrought in me, and a strong one, by this visit to the Louvre, and know not how far it may go, chiefly in my full understanding of Titian, John Bellini, and Perugino and my being able to abandon everything to them, or rather being *un*able to look at anything else.[11]

Ruskin's new professional purpose made him 'heartless enough' to go abroad, for the first time, without his parents (see XXXV, 312). He kept no diary on the 1845 journey, but wrote daily to his father. The letters are full of self-analysis, statements of intellectual change similar

to that experienced in Paris, but often more painful. On the way down
into Italy Ruskin describes picturesque scenes not unlike those of
1840-41.[12] Something different comes with his first session of hard
work at Lucca, where he was studying as much architecture as painting.

> It is a woeful thing to take an interest in anything that man has done. Such
> sorrow as I have had this morning in examining the marble work on the fronts
> of churches. Eaten away by the salt winds from the sea, splintered by frost
> getting under the mosaics, rent open by the roots of weeds (never < taken >
> cleared away), fallen down from the rusting of the iron bolts that hold them,
> cut open to make room for brick vaultings and modern chapels, plastered over
> in restorations, fired at by the French, nothing but wrecks remaining – & those
> wrecks – *so* beautiful . . . I shall have to go back to M[onte] Rosa, I think, or
> I shall get to hate the human species, [of] our days, worse than any Timon.[13]

For the first time Ruskin sees buildings as artefacts, not as features in a
landscape. Decay, previously attractive to him, is now lamentable. And
with interest in what man has done goes hatred of a present which
neglects, destroys and then restores. Florence provoked even more
violent 'antiquarian feelings', and self-doubt:

> I have been developing stores <of> upon stores, heaps on heaps of things that I
> cannot explore nor learn. I have been discovering at every step new darknesses –
> about me – new incapacities in myself . . . there is the sorrow of seeing a whole
> nation employed in destroying the most precious of its heritages, and sinking
> deeper & deeper every day into apathy, ignorance & sensuality . . . the race of
> Giotto & Orcagna & Dante were a very different people from those of the
> present day . . .[14]

What these 'very different people' were like Ruskin could not yet say.
He was not 'studying a branch of science in which I feel steady progress, but gathering together a mass of evidence from a number of
subjects, & I have to think before every thing that I see of its bearings
in a hundred ways'.[15] It required 'a good deal of courage' to work in
this way. Ruskin could not tell where it might lead him.

It seemed to be taking him away from his old self. One day in June
Ruskin walked up to Fiesole:

> As I was coming down again, I found myself, unexpectedly, standing on the *very*
> spot, at the end of the cypress avenue, where five years ago – I stood, refusing
> to look at the Giottos in the little chapel, and running up to this point to see the
> mountains. What a wonderful change in me since then.[16]

Now he saw nothing of nature, being always 'in dark chapels, dusty streets, marble galleries, or between dead walls'.[17] In August, after three months of art study, Ruskin went to the Alps to track down Turner sites. But he was disappointed in the mountains and uneasy at the thought of the urgent work to be done in the cities.

Ruskin did not abandon the study of nature in 1845, but he did reject the practice of poetry. This was because of another change in himself, one which puzzled him at first: 'I don't know how it is, but I almost always see two sides of a thing at once, now — in matters poetical — & I never get strongly excited without perceiving drawbacks & imperfections . . .'[18] Olive trees reminded him of Oxford shops selling olive oil, a commercial association which interfered with Biblical ones. Ruskin could not then decide 'whether the poetry or prose of life be its humbug . . .' He was in no mood to write the poem about mountains his father had requested. Eventually Ruskin produced 'Mont Blanc Revisited', but was not happy with it. John James agreed that it was 'feeble', suggesting that 'Your poetry at present has got among your prose . . .'[19] By July Ruskin had decided that the change was permanent. Describing his life as 'too comfortable & regular, too luxurious, too hardening', he did not 'see how it is at all possible for such a person to write good poetry'. Ruskin believed that he had 'made great progress . . . since that poetical time', the result being that

> I perceive several singular changes in the way I now view Italy. With much more real interest — I take a far less imaginative or delightful one. I read it as a book to be worked through & enjoyed, but not as a dream to be interpreted. All the romance of it is gone, and nothing that I see ever makes me forget that I am in the 19th century.[20]

His father was sceptical.[21] Ruskin insisted that he had taken 'a different direction of likings'.[22] Formerly he had hated history and political science. Now he was 'always at Sismondi', studying Italian constitutions with 'great interest' and had acquired a 'quiet, truth-loving, fishing, reasoning, moralizing temperament'.

Ruskin wrote little more poetry after 1845 but was not about to become a historian or a political scientist in any usual sense. Very soon in practice, and later in principle, he was to look to the past as a source of imaginative and moral truth, not for literal fact or constitutional theory. In this Ruskin was to follow through instincts expressed by his father, who could

> only half like the dismissal of Imagination — The deepest passion the finest Imagination & the highest Talent emit the greatest proportion of Truth   Your *true* men are your great men — The passionless unimaginative & stupid everyday

men are the walking Falsehoods of the earth — Shakespeare, Dante, Virgil, Milton, Wordsworth — Turner Titian & Tintoretto, are full of Truth . . . I hold History to be half Lies & Fable to be half Truth.[23]

If Ruskin did not, in September 1845, accept this solution to his dilemma, it was probably because he was still thinking of imaginative effort in terms of some not very good poetry. His new experience of Italy was certainly not compatible with pictures offered by childhood reading or his own derivative productions. Ruskin swung between the two, one moment pronouncing 'all Mr. Rogers sentiment . . . entire humbug', the next raging at modern Italians for having 'taken the whole feeling of the country away from me'.[24] He looked for consolation in 'my poor dear, beloved Verona', anticipating that Venice would have too much 'twang of manufacture and trade about it', too much 'reference to art' and be '*too* showy' to be poetical.[25] In this confused state of mind, Ruskin began the last stage of his journey. He intended staying only a short time in Venice, drawing little architecture, merely checking up on already formed impressions of Titian, Veronese and the Bellinis, and for the most part drawing canal scenes with James Duffield Harding, his old art master.[26] In fact he stayed five weeks, found the 'out of door art' more instructive than in any other Italian city and Venetian paintings revelatory, felt the canal drawing a waste of time. Ruskin left Venice feeling 'upset in all my calculations'.[27]

In planning his visit Ruskin reckoned without change in himself or Venice. His expectations were anachronistic and escapist. Ruskin reassured his parents that he would not take the railway, now open as far as Mestre:

Thank heaven it isn't finished across the lagune yet, and I trust once more to have the pleasure of the quiet float to Venice without being transported to Greenwich or Liverpool in unsweetened imagination.[28]

On 10 September he took a gondola from Mestre 'in order to recall to mind as far as I could our first passing to Venice'.[29] It had not occurred to Ruskin that the railway bridge, now two weeks from completion, would alter the famous approach, block off that long-celebrated first sight of the city rising from the sea. He had been in Venice on 10 May 1841, the date the first piles had been driven into the lagoon, but had not taken notice. Now Ruskin could only wish he were without sight or feeling. He pronounced the great Roman-style structure worse than 'the Greenwich railway', the city 'as nearly as possible like Liverpool'. The next day, 11 September, he told his father: 'Of all the fearful changes I ever saw wrought in a given time, that on Venice since I was last here beats. It amounts to destruction . . .'[30] For two weeks Ruskin's letters to his father consisted of accounts of calamities detailing the annihilation of Venice by decay, restoration and modernization.

Ruskin was only in part correct in thinking that the changes had come upon Venice since his last visit. His impression of the palaces on the Grand Canal 'mouldering down as if they were all leaves & autumn had come suddenly' was clearly mistaken.[31] Decay was too far advanced to have been of recent origin. The Ca' Foscari was 'all *but* a total ruin — the rents in its walls are half a foot wide'.[32] Of the courtyard of another palace there remained only

> one shattered brick wall with the vestiges of the insertion of the marble arches, the well in the centre, and a few capitals of the columns beside it, & one noble claw of a supporting lion. Two turkeys were wandering among the weeds, where the garden had been, but not a leaf now remaining except grass & nettle.[33]

This 'violently affected' Ruskin. Previously he had not appreciated capitals and arches, 'the beauty of the fragments'.[34] In 1835 and 1841 he had made Proutesque drawings of whole buildings. Now he did little bits of windows and mouldings, to serve as records. Harding, who kept to picturesque views, said Ruskin's efforts would '"frighten the Daguerreotype into fits"'.[35] It was an apt comment, for his ex-pupil was enthusiastically buying daguerreotypes, and later trained his personal servant, Hobbes, in the use of the camera.

Ruskin never lost a feeling for natural decay, though after 1845 he would stress the expressive power of cracks and stains rather than formal effects. One of his charges against architectural restoration was that it cancelled the signs of the passage of time:

> they are *scraping* St Mark's clean. Off go all the glorious old weather stains, the rich hues of the marble which nature, mighty as she is, has taken ten centuries to bestow — and already the noble corner farthest from the sea, that on which the sixth part of the age of the generations of man was dyed in gold, is reduced to the colour of magnesia . . .[36]

The Austrians had begun restoring on St Mark's in 1818. This was the first time Ruskin had noticed their work. From now on he would consistently condemn, as destructive of art and of historical record, all restoration other than the use of external supports making no pretence of being of earlier date. Those were old-fashioned methods. Nineteenth-century restorers up to the late 1870s were more drastic. Ruskin's Venetian work was carried out during the most intense period of demolition and reconstruction. Now, in 1845, he drew details of the Ca' d'Oro while the work went on around him.[37] Ca' Foscari and the Fondaco dei Turchi were among many to be so treated.

Not all attempts to correct the dilapidated state of Venetian buildings were undertaken with the intention of imitating the original.
Ruskin did not stay at the Hotel Danieli (the old Palazzo Dandolo), on
this visit, perhaps because it was being renovated. Until 1840 the Dal
Niel family had owned only the second floor; now that they had
bought the first as well, they had given the palace a new façade. Ruskin
reported: 'All its rich red marble front is covered with a smooth,
polished, bright white stucco, painted in stripes . . . in imitation of
marble, with a grand blue sign in brilliant relief.'[38]

There were other colourful developments nearby. The lower arcade
of the Ducal Palace had been whitewashed on the inside, attracting the
eye 'in forcible manner to the black & yellow sentry boxes now in
bright relief'. Railings closing these arches used by the guards were also
painted in the Austrian colours, which 'agreeably contrasted' with some
green and white public baths built in the water just off the quay in
front of the Palace.[39] There had been floating baths in the San Marco
Basin every summer since the early 1830s, but the Ruskins may have
been just too late or too early to see them on previous visits. Those he
now remarked on were boldly advertised in three languages. Like
Danieli's 'grand blue sign', this was evidently meant to attract tourists.
Another development reminded Ruskin of a holiday resort nearer
home: 'Just below the bridge of sighs, a bright brick house is building,
square as a Margate lodging house.'[40] Not ten years later, plans were to
be put forward for a much larger structure in the same place. The Riva
degli Schiavoni was to have been extended outwards by 70 metres to
allow the construction of a gigantic complex of hotel, theatre, cafés,
baths and other facilities. Ruskin did not learn of this unrealized
project, nor of ideas to run a boulevard along the Grand Canal, nor the
one to extend the railway to San Giorgio Maggiore and throw a bridge
across the Basin to St Mark's Square.[41] But Ruskin noticed enough, in
1845, to realize the strength of the move to turn Venice into a modern
city. He detested all such change, the 'iron station', the 'omnibus
gondolas', the new iron bridges and the filling in of canals — like the
bridge across the lagoon part of a tendency to shift the emphasis of
commercial and also personal movement from water to land.[42] Another
civic amenity also horrified Ruskin: 'gas lamps! . . . in grand new iron
posts of the last Birmingham fashion . . . Imagine the new style of
serenades — by gas light.'[43] Gas street illumination had been brought to
Venice in 1843. She was ahead of other Italian cities in this respect.
As regards modernization, Ruskin was probably accurate in remarking
that great changes had taken place since his last journey. The early
1840s was a time of rapid economic advance for Venice. But it is also
true that change in the city coincided with change in Ruskin. On
previous visits his perception of cities had been mediated by

contemporary literature or painting. In 1845 Ruskin proves himself, for the first time, as attentive, detailed and independent in observation of urban history as he had formerly been in investigation of natural history. In 1841 'all that is now doing and erecting' had vaguely intruded on his preoccupation with Venice as landscape.[44] In 1845, aware of the past and of human artefact in way that he had not been previously, Ruskin is newly sensitive, even hypersensitive, to the changes taking place:

> There is no single spot, east or west, up or down, where her spirit remains – the modern work has set its plague spot everywhere – the moment you begin to feel, some gaspipe business forces itself on the eye, and you are thrust into the 19th century, until you dream, as Mr Harding did last night, that your very gondola has become a steamer.[45]

From this date Venice would not represent a place out of time, out of this world, an escape from the nineteenth century and England. Indeed Ruskin perceives a special connection between Venice and his own country, special because the modernization of Venice conflicts so dramatically with the inherited vision. For the 'plague spots' he might blame, on alternate days, the Austrians ('these despotic governments'), the Venetians (' "porci battizati" '), or the French ('a cursed nation').[46] Far more frequent are analogies with Greenwich, Margate, Birmingham and Liverpool, analogies which hint at a different historical responsibility.

Ruskin would always suffer waves of regret for Venice the romantic, and sometimes managed to re-create her image. Once, on this visit, he floated down the Grand Canal by moonlight, for Venice 'looks like itself by night, neither decay visible nor repairs'.[47] But, more important, the city offered scope for new uses of the imagination. Prout's drawings no longer stood the test, but the buildings were found to be greater works of art.[48] Venice had been 'hackneyed' by common painters,[49] but uncommon painters had also worked there. Ruskin found 'among the wrecks of Venice, authority for all that Turner has done of her'.[50] Titian, Giorgione and Veronese had literally painted Venice, covering whole palaces with frescoes:

> imagine what Venice must have been with their hues blazing down into the sea & up again. There <is> are a fragment or two of Giorgione left yet on one palace – purple & scarlet, more like a sunset than a painting.[51]

The re-creation of Venice's past demanded more of the imagination than did sympathy with 'Mr Rogers sentiment'. The greatest challenge of all, and least expected, was Tintoretto.

For ten days Ruskin had been so engrossed in outdoor drawing that he had not looked at pictures. On 23 September he wrote to his father of what had happened to him and Harding in the Academy that day:

> I have been quite overwhelmed today by a man whom I had never dreamed of — Tintoret. I always thought him a good & clever & forcible painter, but I had not the smallest notion of his enormous powers. Harding has been as much taken aback as I have, but he says he is 'crumbled up' while I feel encouraged & excited by the good art.[52]

The next day they both went to the Scuola di San Rocco:

> I have had a draught of pictures today enough to drown me. I never was so utterly crushed to the earth before any human intellect as I was today, before Tintoret. Just be so good as to take my list of painters, & put him in the school of Art at the top, top, top of everything, with a great big black line underneath him to stop him off from everybody — and put him in the school of Intellect, next after Michael Angelo. He took it so entirely out of me today that I could do nothing at last but lie on a bench & laugh. Harding said that if he had been a figure painter, he never could have touched a brush again, and that he felt more like a flogged schoolboy than a man — and no wonder. Tintoret don't seem to be able to stretch himself till you give him a canvas forty feet square — & then, he lashes out like a leviathan, and heaven and earth come together.[53]

Of all Ruskin's single experiences of the works of one painter this discovery of Tintoretto in September 1845 was the one he remembered as having revealed his 'function as an interpreter'. He 'had seen that day the Art of Man in its full majesty for the first time; and that there was also a strange and precious gift in myself enabling me to recognize it, and therein ennobling, not crushing me'.[54] At this time Ruskin had especially needed to 'feel encouraged & excited by the good art', to 'lie on a bench & laugh'. He had learnt much and admired much on this journey, but nothing in his studies had given such intellectual exhilaration. Now Ruskin found that his was not the abstract, unimaginative occupation he had thought. He had 'a strange and precious gift', enabling him to follow this painter: 'Away he goes, heaping host on host, multitudes that no man can number — never pausing, never repeating himself — clouds & whirlwinds & fire & infinity of earth & sea, all alike to him. . .'[55]

The categories of artists Ruskin had drawn up in July had to be revised.[56] The Venetians had dominated Class III, 'the School of *Painting* as such', but Ruskin had spoken derogatively of '*art* per se'.[57] Tintoretto, sent to the 'top, top, top' of his school, made him admit 'As for *painting*, I think I didn't know what it meant till today. . .'[58] Another of

Ruskin's schools had been headed, in rambling and uncertain fashion, 'General Perception of Nature human & divine, accompanied by more or less religious feeling. The School of the *Great* Men. The School of Intellect.'[59] In this category were assembled a miscellaneous collection of artists, none of them Venetian. Ruskin had declared the Venetian constitution 'tyrannical government . . . made hereditary', to have impeded 'the development of intellect. Venice leaves us no writers, and in art she leaves us a school entirely devoted to the musical part of it . . . of art as a medium of mind, she <leaves> knows nothing.'[60] Tinrotetto disproved that argument and made intellect in painting definable and recognizable. Ruskin set out 'to calculate the number of feet square he has covered with mind in Venice'.[61]

These paintings confirmed one impression he had already formed. They were evidence of the difference between past and present. In Venice Ruskin heard from his father that Joseph Severn had publicly recommended a return to fresco. He pronounced this 'monstrously absurd . . . you might as well throw a covey of chickens into the Atlantic as our R-A's into fresco'.[62] To Severn he wrote:

> It isn't of any use to try and do anything for such an age as this. We are a different race altogether from men of the old time; we live in drawing rooms instead of deserts; and work by the light of chandeliers instead of volcanoes. I have been perfectly prostrated these two or three days back by my first acquaint-ance with Tintoret; but then I feel as if I had got introduced to a being from a planet a million of miles nearer the sun, not to a mere earthly painter. As for our little bits of R.A.'s, calling themselves painters, it ought to be stopped directly. One might make a mosaic of R.A.'s, perhaps; with a good magnifying glass, big enough for Tintoret to stand with one leg upon . . . if he balanced himself like a gondolier.[63]

Turner would be the only exception to this rule, but this could also be explained by referring to the Venetian painter. Ruskin claimed to have 'at last' discovered who had been Turner's master.[64]

If Ruskin's new confidence now allowed him to lecture Severn, one of those who had first introduced him to Venetian art, it also made Harding's company burdensome. Harding had no wish to spend all his time in galleries. But he left soon after the San Rocco experience, so Ruskin no longer had to 'go & draw boats & cucumbers'.[65] A new artist acquaintance, William Boxall, was a friend of Wordsworth and of George Richmond. From Boxall Ruskin got 'a little good sympathy', for he shared his new interest.[66] It was a time of year when Venice was 'horribly full of English & musquitoes'.[67] Among the visitors was Anna Jameson, also 'writing something about old art'. After some conversa-tion Ruskin told his father that she 'knows as much of art as the cat'.[68] Ruskin, proud of his new knowledge, was pleased with himself, and in the end with Venice. He could still enjoy the usual Venetian diversions — rowing out to the islands to collect shells, eating ices in the Piazza in the evenings.[69] Ruskin felt 'less miserable' having 'seen the extent of the *present* evil & made up my mind to it'.[70] He was 'mighty sorry' when he left, finally, in the middle of October.[71] Work and excitement had kept him active. At Padua Ruskin collapsed with a feverish illness and made his way back to England exhausted.

Nevertheless, *Modern Painters* II was written that winter and appeared in April 1846. This volume belies its title. Far from praising modern painters at the expense of ancient masters, as he had done in *Modern Painters* I, Ruskin does the reverse, though his ancients are not now French and Dutch seventeenth and eighteenth century but Italian Renaissance and pre-Renaissance. Symmetry, a sign of 'high moral discipline', is sought by both Tuscans and Venetians; it is 'one of the principal faults in the landscapes of the present day, that the symmetry of nature is sacrificed to irregular picturesqueness' (IV, 127). The main objects of attack, however, are contemporary figure painters. The Venetians always introduced portraiture into their work; now all individuality is masked under an 'unhappy prettiness and sameness'. Such portraiture as does exist 'must make the people of the nineteenth century the shame of their descendants, and the butt of all time'. Its subjects are shown proudly posturing; for true dignity we must look to

Venice, where we find their victorious doges painted neither in the toil of battle nor the triumph of return: nor set forth with thrones and curtains of state, but kneeling, always crownless, and returning thanks to God for His help; or as priests interceding for the nation in its affliction (IV, 190-3).

Venetian sensuousness Ruskin does criticize, yet it is only the modern world that has made the nude obscene:

for that daring frankness of the old men, which seldom missed of human grandeur, even when it failed of holy feeling, we have substituted a mean, carpeted, gauze-veiled, mincing sensuality of curls and crisping-pins, out of which, I believe, nothing can come but moral enervation and mental paralysis (IV, 196-8).

In discussing the imagination, Ruskin is unwilling to speak of anyone but the three painters cited by his father, Turner, Titian and Tintoretto (IV, 244). He had been unable to offer chapter titles when planning this section before the 1845 journey.[72] Venice had supplied material for a definition. Excitedly and at length, Ruskin describes the works of Tintoretto seen there. The San Rocco experience of 'human intellect' informs his perception of 'Imagination Associative', which produces 'always a governed and perfect whole; evidencing in all its relations the weight, prevalence, and universal dominion of an awful inexplicable Power; a chastising, animating, and disposing Mind' (IV, 248). Ruskin has in mind no 'merely earthly painter' in writing of 'Imagination Penetrative', which

> never stops at . . . outward images of any kind; it ploughs them all aside, and plunges into the very central fiery heart; nothing else will content its spirituality; whatever semblances and various outward shows and phases its subjects may possess go for nothing; it gets within all fence, cuts down to the root, and drinks the very vital sap of that it deals with . . .(IV, 250-1).

Not all, but much of the praise of Venetian painters in *Modern Painters* II is of human qualities, either depicted or expressed through their work. The humble dignity of the doge portraits, the daring frankness of the nudes, the ordering intellect and fierce spirituality of the imaginative genius were to appear again in Ruskin's writings. Gradually he would populate his (till now empty) city of Venice with a race of heroes, whose characteristics are, at least in part, generalized from the personalities of her painters, and especially from Tintoretto. In this *Modern Painters* II looks forward to *The Stones of Venice*, as it does in other respects. In a long note to his introductory chapter (cancelled from the 1883 edition and thereafter), Ruskin gives a select catalogue of European monuments destroyed by neglect or conversion (IV, 31-2). It was partly because he felt the total annihilation of this heritage to be so near that Ruskin was to turn to architecture and postpone for ten years, the writing of further volumes of *Modern Painters*. Moreover this destruction, like the building of the railways and the utilitarian philosophies of 'this working age', are here seen as symptoms of moral decay accompanying peace and prosperity. Against this Ruskin warns in words that anticipate the titles of his two Venetian histories: 'Let us beware that our rest become not the rest of stones . . .' (IV, 29-31).

II.2   1846

Towards the end of the 1845 journey John James Ruskin had been unable to conceal how much he missed his son. In mid-September he told him that he had begun 'wearying . . . to hear of you turning homewards'.[1] Then came the long delay in Venice. His father must have accused him of failing to respect plans for a family holiday the following year, for Ruskin wrote a letter that was both defensive and defiant:

> You seem surprised at my stopping at Venice: — first I did not know you were going there next year. I knew of Annecy & Carrara, but of no where else — secondly, if I had, I should still have staid . . .[2]

He told his father that complete destruction was imminent. This John James Ruskin probably thought exaggerated. At Brig Ruskin found more letters 'full of complaints of my stay at Venice', and again at Lausanne 'a short letter from my Father, full of most unkind expressions of impatience at my stay at Venice'.[3] Ruskin stifled an impulse to write an angry reply, pretended he had never received the letter, and put it all down to 'the ungoverned expression of extreme though selfish affection'. The 1846 tour would demonstrate to his father why he had taken so long. It would compensate for separation, and also make up for Ruskin's previous deficiency in another respect. In 1845 he had written to his mother:

> I think there is such a change come over me lately that there will be no more disagreements between us as to where we shall go or what we shall do, for my childishnesses are, I am (in one respect) sorry to say, nearly gone, & now, wherever I am, in church, palace, street, or garden, there is always much that I can study & enjoy — and although I am just as selfwilled as ever, yet my tastes are so much more yours, & my father's, that I think we shall travel more happily than we did . . .[4]

John James Ruskin crossed through the phrase 'I think we shall travel more happily than we did'.[5] In *Praeterita* Ruskin was to observe his wishes by omitting to speak of the holiday 'disagreements'. In this letter he is probably thinking of the 1840-41 tour, when he had so often refused to fit in with the normal round of activities, especially in the matter of looking at works of art. Ruskin now promised reparations:

> you will find me a little more of the cicerone than I used to be, and perhaps something of a guide where I was formerly only an incumbrance. I am looking forward with infinite delight to the prospect of showing my father all my new loves, making him decipher the sweet writing of Simon Memmi in the Campo Santo, and leading him into the dark corners of the cloisters of St Mark, where my favourite Fra Angelicos look down from the walls like visions . . .[6]

Ruskin had just declared himself willing to go anywhere his parents liked, even to Baden Baden or Scotland. But it is evident that he is not about to submit to his parents' preferences. He will lead now that his tastes have overtaken theirs. John James Ruskin was, in fact, eager to share his son's interests. They set off on 2 April, three weeks before the publication date of *Modern Painters* II. The 1845 route was taken in reverse. They arrived for their fortnight's stay in Venice on 14 May, taking the gondola across the lagoon. John James reported

> singing very good & touching — Mrs R especially affected. Large front corner Room Danielis   John rowed me down the grand Canal Music 60 in Band St Marks Place. Saw Daughter of Emperor of Russia . . .[7]

This evening must have been gratifying. He was 'a slave to Music Militaire',[8] and loved nobility. After that there seems to have been little time for such things. Mr Ruskin was taken round St Mark's, the Ducal Palace, the Academy, the Scuola di San Rocco, the Manfrini and Mocenigo Palaces and at least eleven churches. In his diary he hurriedly listed paintings and made brief notes of what is clearly Ruskin's commentary:

> Academy. Titians assumption Tintorettos Miracle of St Mark Adam & Eve — Death of Abel. J. Bellinis Madonna — many beautiful Bonifazios. — P. Veroneses grand Supper with Pharisee — Dwarf Dog & Titians first & last pictures Geo Richmonds favourite Basaiti Christs agony . . . *Schola di St Rocco* immense Tintorettos — *Crucifixion* from which John took picture annunciation — homely in Ruined shed Slaughter of Innocents no Butchery *Flight* into Egypt — ass beautiful ascension — most sublime — the winged angels & mother . . .[9]

The whole of John James Ruskin's journal covering the stay in Venice in 1846 is filled with notes similar to these, except for a curious passage that appears just before the departure for Padua. It is apparently copied from his diary of five years before, for it is headed 'Note on Venice 10 May 1841':

To the Eye of an Artist Venice must be the Region of Paradise Every form that can charm or attract seems around you. Every Building is dyed in every shade of Colour without one Violent effect — The Waters reflect Houses Palaces bright with a thousand hues but all soft & harmonious The City is beautiful in Silver Light of morning & radiant in Gold as day declines. Every dome & spire & mast seem to give out some inward Lights rather than merely to reflect the Rays of Light shed upon them They seem arrayed in Glory & you feel almost surprized when this Lustre departs with the setting Sun. There is till Sunset a perfect mirror brightness in the distant water — a smooth silky softness on the Canals The water having no depth nor swell, only hives & licks & crouches at the feet of the Palaces that rise from out its bed. The plash of the Water to the stroke of the Gondoliers oar hath a sort of [illegible] in it. The Gondola skims & darts over the Water so smoothly & noiselessly that you seem to glide on air.

One suspects that John James is taking refuge in memories of a less demanding city. The weather must have made instruction in Venetian art all the more exhausting:

We have three days of excessive heat, crowned last night by a storm of thunder, lightning, hail and wind beyond all I ever heard or saw. The City was wrapt in continuous flame for two or three hours and to-day in place of being better — it is hotter — pleasant climate where you can scarcely breathe or move.[10]

It seems that 'Mrs R suffered from heat at Venice', and it got worse as they travelled down through Tuscany.[11] By the time they turned towards home at the end of July she had 'got thin' and her husband was suffering from an attack of dysentery.[12] They had not been so far south in mid-summer before, and were now in their early sixties. Neither John James nor Margaret Ruskin ever came to Italy again.

Their son meanwhile did not feel the heat.[13] He took every opportunity to further his researches, filling his diary with work notes. Some concern an extension of the problem that had troubled Ruskin in 1841, the effects of light and shadow on water, and how colour is reflected.[14] He would quote these diary notes in *Modern Painters* I, which he was revising for its third edition (III, 501). With that in mind he also made further studies of Titian and Tintoretto, concentrating on their treatment of landscape.[15] Architectural work also continued. There are notes on St Mark's and Murano mosaics, sculptural ornament on the church and the palace, the shapes of arches and the need for irregularity in proportion.[16] Here John James Ruskin could not attempt to follow. To W.H. Harrison, who had enquired whether there would be anything new for the annuals, he replied from Venice:

I regret to say there is no chance of this; my son has not written a Line of poetry and he says he cannot produce any by setting himself to it as a work — he does not I am sorry to say regret this . . . He is cultivating Art at present searching for real knowledge but to you and me this knowledge is at present a sealed Book. It will neither take the shape of picture nor poetry. It is gathered in scraps hardly wrought for he is drawing perpetually but no drawing such as in former days you or I might compliment in the usual way by saying it deserved a frame — but fragments of everything from a Cupola to a Cartwheel but in such bits that it is to the common eye a mass of Hieroglyphics — all true — truth itself but Truth in mosaic.[17]

Ruskin was giving his father a practical demonstration of the changes of which he had told him in 1845, changes John James Ruskin had not taken quite seriously.

For himself, Ruskin used the journey to reappraise the experiences of the year before. Writing to George Richmond from Lucerne on the way home Ruskin summarized his impressions and spoke of his intentions:

Italy is quite killing now for anyone who cares about it; the destruction I saw last year gave me a good idea of the extent of it, but none of its *pace*. The rate at which Venice is going is about that of a lump of sugar in hot tea. It is the same everywhere — one roar of 'Down with it — rase it — rase it, even to the ground' from one side of Europe to the other, and such idiocies building everywhere, instead — all nations agreeing to be unnational, apeing each other in ape's tricks . . . I have got some useful bits of detail . . . especially in architecture — though in Italy I lost the greater part of my time because I had to look over the first volume of *Modern Painters*, which I wanted to bring up to something like the standard of knowledge in the other . . . I am not going to write any more for some time, for I have got a kind of stagger this year in Italy; the Romanism there is so awful, and the whole state of the people so wrong, that I think there their art can only have done them mischief — and I want to learn more of the real bearings of it on their history before I venture any more assertions. It is an awkward thing to come from Venice to Florence. After that Venetian Academy, Padua and the Campo Santo don't come nice at all; nobody held his own but Masaccio . . .[18]

Ruskin would have been especially sensitive to the evils of Romanism at this time. He feared that the 'frequent expressions of admiration for Romanist works of art' in *Modern Painters* II might cause him to be bracketed with other graduates of Oxford, Puseyite and worse.[19] Ruskin was all the more nervous about Italian religious art because he could not make up his mind:

whether it had not been better for Italy on the whole that none had existed . . .
I dare not say; it is a subject requiring attentive examination before writing
anything further respecting such art; and unfortunately it is almost impossible to
carry on an investigation of this kind without spending more time abroad than
I can spare . . .[20]

His immediate task, the revision of *Modern Painters* I, could be
completed without venturing assertions on the matter. Italian painters
appear only as the forgotten forbears of the modern school of landscape (III, 170-84). This was difficult to sustain. Neither Titian nor
Tintoretto had cared to describe even the city in which they lived. The
lagoon sunset beloved by Ruskin was visible daily from Titian's house,
but 'never received image from his hand' (III, 171). Ruskin wished to
praise their 'imaginative abstraction' (III, 170), yet cannot with any
consistency propose this as a model:

> the whole field of what they have done is so narrow, and therein is so much of
> what is only relatively right, and in itself false or imperfect, that the young and
> inexperienced painter could run no greater risk than the too early taking them for
> teachers; and to the general spectator their landscape is valuable rather as a means
> of peculiar and solemn emotion, than as ministering to or inspiring the universal
> love of nature. Hence while men of serious mind, especially those whose pursuits
> have brought them into continued relations with the peopled rather than the
> lonely world, will always look to the Venetian painters as having touched those
> simple chords of landscape harmony which are most in unison with earnest and
> melancholy feeling; those whose philosophy is more cheerful and more extended,
> as having been trained and coloured among simple and solitary nature, will seek
> for a wider and more systematic circle of teaching . . . they are not intended for the
> continual food but the occasional soothing of the human heart . . . (III, 172).

Ruskin is clearly forcing his argument here, but it is interesting that
he thought it necessary to do so, to allow for the existence of a philosophy of the 'peopled world' as distinct from a cheerful, Wordsworthian
philosophy inspired by 'simple and solitary nature'. He could not yet
define this urban morality but when he did come to do so, in *The
Stones of Venice*, the seriousness and melancholy here attributed to
Titian and Tintoretto were to be among its essential components.
Though Titian and Tintoretto were 'not . . . to be blamed' for their
neglect of the particular truths of Venice (III, 170), Canaletto was. In
the first edition of *Modern Painters* I Ruskin has compared Canaletto's
Venice of 'bricks and mortar' with a romantic landscape version of the
city as he had experienced it at sixteen and twenty-two (III, 255-6).
Now he compares that artist's work with a picture of a more recently
discovered Venice of the past:

Let the reader, with such scraps of evidence as may still be gleaned from under the stucco and paint of the Italian committees of taste, and from among the drawing-room innovations of English and German residents, restore Venice in his imagination to some resemblance of what she must have been before her fall. Let him, looking from Lido or Fusina, replace, in the forests of towers, those of the hundred and sixty-six churches which the French threw down; let him sheet her walls with purple and scarlet, overlay her minarets with gold, cleanse from their pollution those choked canals which are now the drains of hovels, where they were once vestibules of palaces, and fill them with gilded barges and bannered ships; finally, let him withdraw from this scene, already so brilliant, such sadness and stain as had been set upon it by the declining energies of more than half a century, and he will see Venice as it was seen by Canaletto; whose miserable, virtueless, heartless mechanism, accepted as the representation of such various glory, is, both in its existence and acceptance, among the most striking signs of the lost sensation and deadened intellect of the nation at that time; a numbness and darkness more without hope than that of the Grave itself, holding and wearing yet the sceptre and the crown, like the corpses of the Etruscan kings, ready to sink into ashes at the first unbarring of the door of the sepulchre.[21]

This city of purple and gold and scarlet is no less highly coloured than the former, but the colours now are in the buildings, not in the mists or the reflections in the water. It is a city of artefact more than of scenery; it is inhabited and has a history of a kind. First there were the men who sheeted the walls of Venice with colour and bannered her ships, then those of 'lost sensation and deadened intellect', the generations responsible for Canaletto's existence and acceptance, and now, finally, there are 'the Italian committees of taste', the English and German residents. A rudimentary version of the Fall of Venice has been outlined.

Six months after the third edition of *Modern Painters* I came out a fourth was going to press and Ruskin was referring to the volume as 'my rubbishy book'.[22] He was in poor spirits, suffered from minor ailments, and was in an uncertain frame of mind. Ruskin told his old Oxford tutor Brown that he was still 'entirely open to conviction one way or the other' on the matter of the relations between art and religion, and lacked the 'profound sense of religion' needed to tackle it correctly.[23] He talked of 'reading Divinity and History constantly, as . . . studies not to be separated', but seems not to have done so.[24] In *Praeterita* Ruskin was to say that after 1845

my Denmark Hill life resolved itself into the drudgery of authorship and press correction, with infinite waste of time in saying the same things over and over to the people who came to see our Turners (XXXV, 367).

It was probably in this manner that Ruskin spent the winter of 1847-48, the winter of his engagement to Euphemia Chalmers Gray, known to the Ruskins as Effie.

It is likely that Ruskin and Effie had planned to leave for Switzerland and Venice immediately after their marriage.[25] But by the time their wedding took place on 10 April 1848 an Italian journey was out of the question. There had been street riots in Milan since September 1847.[26] In January 1848 Clinton Dawkins, the British Consul in Venice, reported a sudden change in the atmosphere there too. There were incidents at the Opera. A boycott of tobacco, which was heavily taxed, had been organized. Every evening as the Austrian military band started playing the Venetians would leave the Piazza. In mid-January came the Palermo rising. By the end of the month the Kingdom of Naples had been granted a parliament. On 8 February Charles Albert hurriedly granted Piedmont a constitution and five weeks later Pius IX followed his example for the Papal States. The Veneto and Lombardy were by this time under martial law; Paris had risen, then Vienna. In Venice tension heightened during March. On the 17th and 18th there were skirmishes in the Piazza, and on the 22nd Daniele Manin proclaimed the Republic of St Mark alive once more. The Austrians, much under strength and confused by reports from Vienna, capitulated immediately and the revolution was accomplished almost without bloodshed. Ruskin and his wife had to make do with Folkestone. From there Effie wrote to their mutual friend, Pauline Trevelyan: 'You know my husband's care for the *continent* and these changes at times dishearten him very much and he is constantly longing to be on the other side of the Channel . . .'[27] They were then joined by the old Ruskins for a visit to Salisbury, where the dull scenery and 'perfectly savage' architecture were two of several causes of irritation.[28] Effie told her family that her husband hated England and shrieked with horror at the mention of Scotland.[29]

Finally, in early August, France at least seemed quiet enough for a visit. In Normandy Ruskin was 'in his element among cathedrals and tumble-down houses',[30] and Effie learnt to sympathize with his 'unpatriotic longings for foreign lands'.[31] In the meantime reinforcements had enabled the Austro-Hungarian army under Radetsky to defeat first the Tuscans, then the Romans, and, in July, the Piedmontese.[32] Charles Albert, ever ambiguous in his support of Italian liberal aspirations, abandoned Lombardy to reoccupation by the Austrians. Ruskin paid close attention, admitting to his father that he thought 'Radetsky is so hard on the Milanese I begin to which [sic] he may have it in his turn please tell me any interesting news you have in London.'[33] The revolution nearer to hand, however, shocked and troubled him. Paris,

scarred by the unhappy traces of a slaughterous and dishonourable contest —
is about as deep and painful a lesson . . . as ever was read by vice in ruin . . . At
Rouen . . . the distress though nearly as great, is not so ghastly, and seems to be
confined . . . to the class of workmen. There seems, however, everything to be
dreaded both there and at Paris — and the only door of escape seems to be the
darkest — that which grapeshot opens. I do not see how another struggle for
pillage is avoidable — a simple fight of the poor against the rich — desperate
certainly — and likely to be renewed again and again . . . And yet . . . if there
were enough merciful people in France to soothe without encouraging them,
and to give them some — even the slightest — sympathy and help . . . the country
might still be saved.[34]

The worst effect of all, he told W.L. Brown, was 'the entire Atheism of
the Paris University'.[35]

To the destruction wreaked by restoration and modernization and
the corruption of the people by Romanism are added the effects of
atheism, revolution and the irresponsibility of the upper classes. In *The
Seven Lamps of Architecture* England is alerted to these continental
evils. She must guard against the pitfalls of Romanism, keep fidelity to
the English liturgy, obedience to English law, provide happy and useful
employment to avoid the 'horror, distress, and tumult which oppress
the foreign nations . . .' (VIII, 248-9, 255, 261, 268-9). But Ruskin had
'unpatriotic longings'. He is unconvincing in recommending Early
English as the national style. It is the 'safest choice' (VIII, 258), but it
is not described or analysed. Ruskin's preference is for Southern Gothic.
This is clear from the comparison between Giotto's bell-tower in
Florence and Salisbury Cathedral, a comparison unfavourable to
Salisbury (VIII, 188-9). It is, in embryo, the comparison between the
English cathedral and St Mark's in *The Stones of Venice*; but in the
later book more is implied than an architectural evaluation. For St
Mark's Ruskin is slightly apologetic in *The Seven Lamps*. The Venetian
church, 'though in many respects imperfect, is in its proportions, and as
a piece of rich and fantastic colour, as lovely a dream as ever filled the
human imagination' (VIII, 206). In 1849 Ruskin had not yet come to
appreciate Byzantine architecture fully. Venice achieves her greatness
by casting off the 'luxuriance' of Byzantine features; six years later
Ruskin was to call this the most 'definitely false' passage he had ever
written (VIII, 130-1 and n.). About Venetian Gothic, however, he has
no reservations. The Ducal Palace is 'the model of all perfection' (VIII,
111; see also 182-3), while of English building Ruskin writes:

all that we do is small and mean, if not worse — thin, and wasted, and insubstantial. It is not modern work only; we have built like frogs and mice since the
thirteenth century . . . How small, how cramped, how poor, how miserable in its

petty neatness is our best! how beneath the mark of attack, and the level of contempt! What a strange sense of formalised deformity, of shrivelled precision, of starved accuracy, of minute misanthropy have we . . . (VIII, 135-6).

Ruskin is attacking English architecture, not English religion, or morality, or her political system. He still wishes to avoid the question of the relations between art and religion (VIII, 40n.). Yet Ruskin had stated an intention to show 'how every form of noble architecture is in some sort the embodiment of the Polity, Life, History, and Religious Faith of nations' (VIII, 248). The formalized deformity and minute misanthropy of English building should then imply a moral judgement. Ruskin is not yet willing to make that judgement. He would consider it further in his next book.

II.3   1849-50

Bound in with *The Seven Lamps of Architecture* was a catalogue of Smith, Elder & Co.'s publications. One of them, announced as 'in preparation', was *The Stones of Venice*. It is possible that Ruskin considered that he had gathered enough material in 1845 and 1846, and that he meant to complete the book without returning to Venice. But it would have been unlike him if he had refused an opportunity to do so. During the spring and summer of 1849 events in Italy took a course which made a visit possible. At the same time the circumstances of his family life developed in such a way as to make one desirable. In April 1849 Ruskin left England for the Alps. His parents went with him, but not Effie, who remained with her family in Scotland. Ruskin was looking forward to 'a glorious campaign of sketching' among the mountains.[1] Meanwhile the military campaign in Italy was going well for the Austrians. John James Ruskin was glad to hear of it.[2] His son worried about some of the consequences. On 24 April he wrote to Effie:

> I am very anxious about Venice just now: if the blockheads stand out, it may be all destroyed. Brescia I am sorry enough for, though it was one of the Italian towns I could best spare: if they knock down Venice, I shall give up all architectural studies: and keep to the Alps: they can't knock down the Matterhorn.[3]

Ruskin is untroubled by the severity with which the Brescia rising had been put down, nor does he fear for the Venetians, whose turn had now come. The 'blockheads' stood by their decision to 'resist at any cost'. The siege began in early May and lasted until the end of August. Ruskin did not remain 'very anxious', even about the buildings, for the whole of those four months. The Alps gave him

> a curious sensation of being shut in by the hills from all the noise and wickedness of the world. I hear of the Vatican's being undermined and Bologna bombarded, as if it were no affair of mine; and am quite prepared to hear of the Grand Canal being filled up with the Doge's palace. One can't attain such equanimity as that anywhere but among the Glaciers.[4]

Occasionally he thought of his next book, but casually, looking to Effie for assistance:

> I had nearly forgotten to ask you, love, whether it would be very irksome to you as you read Sismondi to write *every word* that bears in the remotest degree on the interests or history — of Venice? as I want to get at all the facts of Venetian history as shortly as I can, when I come home. Note every *man* who is a Venetian, wherever he appears: and make references to the places distinctly in a little note book kept for the purpose.[5]

Ruskin was asking a lot of his wife. At least a quarter of the *History of the Italian Republics* bears directly or indirectly on Venice. Ruskin knew this, for he had been struggling with it sporadically for nine years now. But there were more serious reasons for bitterness between Ruskin and Effie. Their own disappointment in each other was now aggravated by tactless correspondence between their fathers. The Ruskins and the Grays took mutual offence, and Ruskin wrote some hard letters on the subject of Effie's character, conduct and mental health.[6] In a moment of calm between hostilities Ruskin wrote more considerately, asking Effie whether she had 'any plans or thoughts for next year'.[7] He told her that he had 'for some time wished to have a *home* proper'.[8] He did not assume that it would be in England. Switzerland seemed a possibility. Ruskin would not have thought of 'Poor Venice' at this time:

> I saw they were bombarding it last week. How all my visions about taking you there; and bringing you here, have been destroyed: Well, it might have been too much happiness to be good for me . . .[9]

This was at the end of June, when only the lagoon fort of Malghera was under fire. In July the Austrians began experimenting with bombs attached to balloons, which were meant to explode in the city itself. They had more success with cannons tilted upwards at forty-five degrees. This gave enough range to inflict some damage on certain quarters of the city, but not enough to make the Venetians give up. Cholera killed many more than did artillery.[10]

In August Ruskin went to Chamonix, leaving his bored and lonely parents to pass a 'dreary anxious time' in Geneva.[11] From there on 4 August John James Ruskin reported to his son that

> Venice still holds out & Shells had come near St Marcks but the workpeople were crying for Surrender as they said they must have Bread — so I think the Austrians are already there & no harm done . . .[12]

The Austrians were not there yet, and he may have been misinformed about the people crying for surrender. But it was famine, and the failure of Garibaldi to arrive with a relief force, that broke the Venetians. Towards the end of August arrangements for surrender were negotiated. Manin and the leaders of the republic went into exile. On the 27th Hungarian troops entered the city. On the 30th Radetsky was received in silence by all except the clergy, some of whom were welcoming. Of all the 1848 revolutions that of Venice had lasted the longest, been the least bloody, and had the strongest appeal to tradition. Not even *The Times*, which was not well disposed to the Italian cause, was pleased to see the end of the republic:

> From February, 1848, till the present hour, there has been no popular movement conducted with so much dignity and maintained with such unswerving decision as that of Venice . . . We know of no example in history of a State — for Venice isolated among her lagunes is a State — which after so long a period of prostration . . . has risen from its torpor with such good effect.[13]

What the Ruskins thought we do not know. By this time they were on their way home. Again resentment flared up when Effie asked Ruskin to go to Perth to fetch her. With some irritation he agreed.[14] There, in mid-September, she asked him to take her to Venice. Ruskin 'had need of some notes for the sketch of Venetian art' and so 'was glad to take her there'.[15] Whether or not the suggestion was a deliberate attempt on Effie's part to save her marriage is not evident,[16] but certainly the time and the place were right. The political obstacle had just been removed. They would be away from interfering parents. A doctor had advised Effie that a winter in the south would be good for her throat, which had been troubling her for some time. Unlike Swiss travel, an Italian journey would be what John James Ruskin described as 'her sort of tour'.[17] Charlotte Ker, who had arranged to spend the winter with Effie in London, agreed to come to Italy instead. And however much Ruskin underestimated the amount of work *The Stones of Venice* would involve, he could always use time there well. The only ones not delighted by the sudden decision were Ruskin's parents. His father later told him, 'The first news of you going so immediately away now for 6 months struck like a Knell on your mothers heart . . .'[18] But for their son's fame and happiness they could 'bear any privation'. So John James Ruskin gave his blessing: 'If you are well and able to do for Venice what I think you will I may say Go where Glory waits thee . . .'[19] Anxiously he saw them off on 3 October.

Partly in order to show Effie something of the mountains and partly in order to allow time for Venice to be cleansed of cholera the Ruskins and Charlotte stopped in the Alps on the way down. They spent the last few days of October seeing the sights in and around Milan, and then went on for a week in Verona. From there they left, in the second week of November, for Venice. They had to cross the lagoon by boat as the railway bridge, blown up during the siege, had not yet been repaired. They got good rooms in Danieli's, with views of the Piazzetta and campanile, and there they remained for the whole of their stay. They had intended to spend only about a month in Venice, and then move on to Pisa for the winter.[20] In fact they stayed in Venice until March.

It was a strange time to spend four months in Venice. Effie's long chattery letters and the few that survive of Ruskin's graver ones reflect the condition of the city during the six months after capitulation. Cholera does not seem to have been noticeable. It may have died out quickly as a result of the severe winter, the coldest since 1829.[21] There were at least three heavy snowstorms in January, and at one point the lagoon began to freeze over. Wood was expensive and the Ruskins invented indoor ball-games to keep warm including 'a kind of shell-practice' mimicking, no doubt, the most recent bombardment of Venice.[22] Some 'common necessaries of life' were in short supply.[23] There must have been great poverty. One of the two currencies issued by the republic was now useless; Effie saw it being publicly burnt.[24] The other was redeemed by the Austrians, but a tax was levied on residents in order to pay for it. Many were homeless.[25] The young men were conscripted and had to leave their families without means of support.[26] There must have been high unemployment. Two main sources of income had dried up at the beginning of the revolution and had not yet recovered. Almost no trade passed through Venice during 1848; the port did not begin to recover until 1851.[27] There were no tourists to employ guides, gondoliers and language masters.[28] With the exception of the consul and one or two eccentrics the English had dispersed and not yet returned.[29] The Ruskins were probably the first English travellers to arrive. M. Dal Niel, having enlarged and done up his hotel in 1845, was now eager to convert half of it into a private residence for the Ruskins.[30] It would certainly have been more profitable than allowing it to be filled with officers of the Austro-Hungarian army, who did not pay for their billets.[31] Palaces were to be had cheaply, as were the luxury goods, such as lace, for which Venice was famous.[32]

The retail trade must also have suffered from the absence of the nobility, who had tended to leave the city during the revolution. Many were now apparently afraid to come back, afraid not of the Austrians, but of the republicans.[33] Some did return for the Christmas and carnival festivities, but when it came to the point did not dare take part.[34] Certain kinds of social activities, such as attendance at the Fenice and the wearing of masks, had long been considered collaborationist.[35]

Radetsky tried to overcome this nervousness and promote fraternization by giving a regular military ball. He ordered that if the ladies did not come the officers should dance with each other.[36] But even this 'political measure', aimed at the weakest link in Venetian society, was not entirely successful.[37] The professional classes, who had furnished the leaders of the rising, remained distinctly cold, and the lower classes, it seems, openly hostile. It was not uncommon for soldiers to be stabbed on the streets at night.[38] Nor did a shared religion bring Austrians and Venetians together. Suspicions of the clergy's concilia- tory policy fomented anti-clericalism and reduced church attendance.[39] In the tense atmosphere the Austrians maintained an obvious military presence. They supervised the dealings of the civic authorities, and kept cannons trained on the Piazza.[40]

The Venice of the winter of 1849-50 affected Ruskin and his wife in different ways. Effie was not very interested in art, history or landscape. She went to see paintings and buildings occasionally, but tended to reproduce her husband's views of them, or refer her correspondents to Murray's *Handbook*.[41] She enjoyed her surroundings not for their aspect but because of the opportunities for activities such as excursions to the islands, picnics, wandering about intricate streets, even rowing. But Effie did 'like to see & know every thing' of what was going on around her.[42] This led her to see a great deal of life in Venice at the time. She was moved by the problems of individual Venetians with whom she came into personal contact, and made efforts to help.[43] But by conditions in general she refused to be greatly disturbed. 'The Lower population here are exactly like animals in the way they live . . .' Effie wrote in one letter.[44] Of the stabbings in the street she only said: 'such things are not pleasant to be happening every day'.[45] She claimed to have heard the political question discussed 'constantly';[46] one suspects that she overheard without entering deeply into conversation herself. In Milan on 28 October Effie had pronounced herself 'a thorough Italian' and against oppression,[47] but a week later began to modify her position. Radetsky was so kind and moderate 'that the Italians must be immense fools if they do not for the present take advantage of it'.[48] If Effie soon changed sides altogether, it was probably because of the company she kept — and was forced to keep, or suffer isolation. On the journey down Ruskin had written home for letters of introduction for her and Charlotte. This was useless, for there were 'few English' in Venice.[49] After four visits Ruskin still knew no one except his banker, and was not interested in enlarging his acquaintance. Fortunately Effie was independent and learnt to make her own way. If her husband would not come out to listen to the band or go to the opera, she would go with Charlotte, their valet-du-place and George Hobbes, their servant.[50] She even took to rowing on the Grand Canal, something which greatly alarmed her father-in-law. Effie was much stared at on the street, and sometimes followed back to the hotel. She quickly got used to it, and was pleased and flattered by the attention paid to her, but remained level-headed. Effie knew that, because of the political upheavals, circumstances were extraordinary. If she received compliments continually, it was partly (but only partly) because 'there were no other Ladies to be seen at present'.[51]

But after a month of this Effie began to get anxious to meet some people. She was fortunate. In mid-December she met a young, intelligent officer in the Hapsburg army, Paulizza, and soon afterwards the kind though irascible antiquarian Englishman, Venetian by adoption, Rawdon Brown. Between them they were to 'spoil & pet' Effie for the rest of the winter.[52] She was introduced into Austro-Hungarian circles. Most of the Italians she met had 'German' or Russian connections. Such contacts offered what Effie most desired, a 'glimpse of foreign manners'[53] and good social life. They were almost all titled or of high military rank or both. Some of them were perhaps rather eccentric. One did see some 'odd looking as well as odd acting people in this place', and 'a sprinkling of English morals would not be amiss'.[54] But Effie was adaptable, and soon 'astonished at nothing foreigners do, for their life & education is so different from ours . . .'[55] She herself was extraordinary, a great dancer, quick to roar with laughter, good at languages, especially German, and could do what she liked. Effie did not have the inhibitions of Charlotte Ker, who seemed to be always darning stockings and suffered from 'so painful a deficiency' in picking up languages.[56] If at times she behaved freely, at others she would impose English mores with a certain quaintness, as when she refused to admit male acquaintances to her opera box.[57] And though open and affectionate, Effie did not get too emotionally involved. She replied to Paulizza's letters without reading them, and Charlotte thought she must have 'a perfect heart of ice' to be so unaffected by his devotion.[58] In all Effie was an immense success, and became so expert on society in Venice that she could act as a guide to newcomers, and indeed to her husband. Ruskin was amazed at the experience of walking out with his wife:

> I never saw any thing like Effie — she sees the tips of people's shawls and the rims of their hats down a couple of streets and round a corner and is perfectly alive as she walks in St Mark's Place to every thing that is going on at St Giorgio Maggiore.[59]

On such occasions Ruskin could not remember who was who. In spite of prompting from Effie he greeted strangers and cut those he was supposed to know. This 'caused the liveliest astonishment to all and sundry in Venice'. They could not make up their minds whether he was 'very mad or very wise'.[60]

Ruskin had other things to think about. The 'notes for a sketch of Venetian art' had turned into 'a more detailed survey of the Italian Gothic than I ever hoped to have obtained'. He found 'the subject so intricate that I have forgotten or laid aside everything for it . . .'[61] One of the reasons why Ruskin had misjudged the amount of work involved so seriously was that he was historically ingenuous. His request that Effie do the necessary preparatory work illustrates his naivety. So do the scale and nature of the questions he asked his father during this winter. John James Ruskin was to report on where the funds for mediaeval churches came from, the composition of the workforce employed on them, how strong Byzantine influence on Venice had been, and even to make 'an enquiry into Mediaeval manners'. He was eager to be of use, but had to apologize for his slowness in fulfilling this last request: 'it is an enormously large subject'.[62] In Venice Ruskin had expected to find the dates of buildings conveniently set out somewhere (IX, 3). Instead he found that even estimates of the Ducal Palace varied by as much as a hundred years (X, 328-9). Rawdon Brown helped him 'in a thousand ways', taking him to libraries, introducing him to archivists, supplying information directly (IX, 459, n.). As is clear from the fact that he spent years trying to master Sismondi only, in the end, to delegate the task to his wife, Ruskin did not find conventional history study congenial. By the time *The Stones of Venice* was completed he had come to the conclusion that *'restored* history', described as 'abstracts, and reasoning, and suppositions, and theories', was of little value, that we should 'spend our time only in the examination of the faithful documents which . . . have been left, either in the form of art or literature, portraying the scenes, or recording the events, which in those days were actually passing before the eyes of men' (XI, 265). Here Ruskin is praising Brown's work as editor of Venetian ambassadors' reports, a selection of which he arranged to be published with Smith and Elder.[63] But Ruskin himself was not rejecting history books in favour of archive study. He was not prepared to 'chase a single doge through all the shelves of St Mark's library'.[64] He was, however, prepared to chase a moulding or a set of measurements through most of the churches and palaces of Venice. These were Ruskin's own 'faithful documents'. His trust in the veracity of the eyewitness is naive, and in his own writings imaginative interpretation takes the place of the despised 'reasonings, and suppositions, and theories' of others. Yet Ruskin's recognition of the status of architectural ornament as historical witness was a genuine contribution to scholarship. His appreciation had been evident in *The Seven Lamps of Architecture*. But it was the work of this winter in Venice that gave substance to the sentiment. In spite of extreme cold, Ruskin was out most of every day, drawing, measuring, making daguerreotypes, methodically gathering evidence at first hand. By the end of it

> Venice presented itself to me merely as so many 'mouldings', and I had few associations with any building but those of more or less pain and puzzle and provocation; — Pain of frost-bitten finger and chilled throat as I examined or drew the window-sills in the wintry air; Puzzlement from said window-sills which didn't agree with the doorsteps, or back of house which didn't agree with front; and Provocation from every sort of soul or thing in Venice at once, — from my gondoliers, who were always wanting to go home, and thought it stupid to be tied to a post in the Grand Canal all day long . . .[65]

Ruskin had set off from England with a list of fifteen subjects 'to be drawn at Venice . if possible . or daguerred.'[66] In fact he collected countless numbers. The notebooks he filled and his method of working have been described by Robert Hewison.[67] The notes he had so casually expected to complete in a month took the whole winter and were still not finished.

The work was hard, monotonous and technical. John James Ruskin reported that his son's letters were 'very uniform'.[68] In spite of some nervousness about continental dissipations, he probably preferred reading Effie's accounts of military balls. Perhaps because he himself had a weakness for such high society as was available in Venice, John James interpreted his son's avoidance of company as abstention in favour of a higher mission and a superior fame:

> I rejoice to see your sense of your more important station & calling & distinction as a Writer saves you from the Entanglements & poor attractions & frivolities of Foreign Society — & that by Gods goodness you are likely to move unscathed through Carnivals & all manners of Dissipation . . .[69]

Ruskin explained that he had misunderstood:

> You say I am kept by a sense of my position and calling out of Entanglement of foreign Society — but unhappily it is to me no entanglement at all. I most heartily wish I could feel as much interest & pleasure in seeing and talking to people as would enable me to receive from them the information which I might — or to do them the good in my power. But Operas, drawing rooms and living creatures have become alike nuisances to me. I go out to them as if I was to pass the time in the Stocks . . .[70]

There were one or two from whom Ruskin could 'receive . . . information'. He liked and admired Paulizza, who was an inventor as well as a soldier (he had devised the explosive-bearing balloons used in the aerial bombardment of Venice). But Ruskin did not speak German, and neither had he enough Italian to hold a conversation in that language.[71] In Rawdon Brown he found a friend and a father figure. But both Brown and his friend Cheyney, whom Ruskin met later, were 'of a different species from me — men of the world, caring very little about anything except Men'.[72] It was not just that Ruskin lacked curiosity about human affairs, he was positively repelled. Probably he did not, yet, wish to censure the drawing-rooms frequented by Effie directly.

With the population in general he had no such inhibitions. Effie reported that he refused to go into churches while services were in progress because of the people: 'John . . . finds them so filthy that he cannot bear to touch them or be amongst them . . .'[73] The 'filth' was partly metaphorical. As in 1845 disgust with living creatures was connected with his work. Daily it led him into situations which caused him to 'mourn over cannonshot, & quarrel with Carpenters . . . mutter and growl at the people'.[74] But unlike that of 1845 the muttering and growling of the winter of 1849-50 is complicated by distress and compassion. John James Ruskin wrote in reply to one letter 'By what you say — the sufferings of all Classes during the siege must have been awful . . .'[75] Ruskin had not needed to mix with people to learn of sufferings, as his answer shows:

> there can be little of the merriment of Xmas here — they have as you say, suffered much, and lost all, or nearly so; and the more I see of the town — and I have now explored almost every corner of it — the more my fixed impression is of hopeless ruin; fully concealed by scrabbles of whitewash — or by bad new brickwork — but ruin alike of palace and cot.[76]

Getting permission to draw window mouldings was complicated by letting and multiple occupation of palaces. In two months Ruskin had not once been 'admitted into a palace by the permission of its rightful owner'. The poorer quarters exhibited a more material squalor:

> In my walk to-day I passed through some of the outskirts of the city towards the mainland. I had little conception of anything so grass-grown or melancholy — all ruined walls — neglected patches of garden surmounted by rotten stakes, or heaps of refuse and plots of waste land — heaps and banks of kneaded mud or fallen walls — not even the picturesque nets of Italy to redeem it, the look was of the kind of place in the outskirts of London which are the shrines of Warren's blacking and Parr's pills . . .[77]

A week after writing this letter Ruskin wrote in his diary of another such walk, this time among the canals of Cannareggio towards the Fondamente Nuove:

> They are lonely and stagnant canals, bordered for the most part by the dead walls of gardens — now waste ground — or by patches of dark mud, with decayed black gondolas lying keel upmost, sinking into the putrid and black ground gradually; or by remnants of palace wall, never finished, of which the doors and the angle shafts alone remain. Farther on one comes to detached goups of low and filthy houses, with mud paths trodden hard between them; but through their dark alleys I saw the horizontal brightness of the lagoon sunshine and over the hard frozen snow made my way down to the shore.[78]

The entry concludes with a description of sky and water, the sunset catching the islands and the distant mountains. But the light and colour do not soften the filth and decay; both wretchedness and beauty are recorded with coolness and clarity and remain separate.

Ruskin had probably never explored any city so thoroughly before. His architectural investigations led him to observe much more of conditions in post-revolutionary Venice than Effie did. A long letter to W.L. Brown of 8 January 1850 shows that though Ruskin may not have known the names of the people walking in Piazza San Marco, he was more acutely aware of what was 'going on' there; the letter also shows that he was having difficulty in explaining what he saw.[79] Brown, now vicar of Wendlebury near Bicester in Oxfordshire, must have written to his ex-pupil pointing out the advantages of railways (which Ruskin had attacked in *Modern Painters* II). Ruskin replied at great length in an endeavour to make clear to Brown, and perhaps to himself, how the 'rutted and sometimes muddy road of one's wandering occupation' might lead one to adopt totally opposed views of the world. He begins by quoting Brown's own words back at him:

> 'I am one of those who always expect to find a reason for whatever *Is*' . . . *your* Philosophy is that we have attained this perfection — that things if they are wrong in one way are right in another — that there is a balance here and an equivalent there — that there is a Natural course of things, which has always its purpose and necessity — &c — : Mine is — or has lately begun more distinctly to be — that we are *all wrong* . . . advancing as fast as we can to a condition of misery which may make us a spectacle and a warning to all other Spiritual Creatures looking on . . . That is what I believe we are doing. — I look upon our engineering and screwing and wedging as just so much Bedlamism — You look upon it as all right and proper.
>
> But consider for a moment how your tranquil position and work in life influences your views of these things. Your theory is true in your own horizon.

Things in England — or at least — in the neighbourhood of Bicester — *are* I think
as well as they can be . . . and though sometimes at your quiet tea table you hear
of a Count or two being hanged in Hungary, or a politician or two stabbed in
Italy, the distance of the things makes it an agreeable excitement to you — and
you are ready to think it as one does past history — 'All right.'

But now come out of those Wendlebury green fields, and step out into my
gondola with me, and let me hear how you like the view from the middle of the
lagoon. There is St Mark's place on one side of you; it is full of people, with a
band of some 50 soldiers playing waltzes to them — a great many of them are
nearly starving; they are walking up and down in the sun to keep as warm as
they can — the others are there because they have nothing to do, or will do
nothing — but they would murder all the fifty soldiers who are playing waltzes
to them, if they could. On the other side of you there is a church with a Corinthian
portico, and in front of it a battery of six guns, bearing on St Mark's place in
order to keep the people who have nothing to do from murdering the 50 soldiers
who are playing the waltzes.

At the end of St Mark's Place you see St Mark's church. At the door of it you
will find a man selling dolls and children's toys, and another selling poultry, and
another selling holy pictures, and another selling wax models of the Nativity
with two shepherds — two donkeys and three wise men: Go in: and there is
much fiddling and trumpeting and burning of candles, there is a woman in the
corner praying to the black statue in the pink satin dress with the large fan: her
husband was turned out of the Arsenal five months ago in some new government
arrangement; having no work . . . he got disagreeably importunate, and was finally
refused — So he drew a stiletto and killed the Governor of the arsenal — wounded
his aide-de-camp — and himself — The man was carried out half dead, held up or
tied up for form's sake, and properly shot. The Governor was buried quietly: the
aide-de-camp's arm cut off at the shoulder — the wife is praying to the black
statue — the children have begged some half-pence from my wife and are now in
the porch of the church outside — the baptistry, playing at pitch and toss. There;
two of them have quarrelled, but they are too cowardly to fight it out; so they
blaspheme a little and toss it again.

Let us take a few strokes with the oar westward and we are between two rows
of palaces — of *Once* palaces at least — The first door on the left was an abbot's
— there is a lovely cloister inside — a bishop sculptured over the door in the act
of blessing — It belongs now to a vendor of marine stores — There is a noble
palace opposite; it is an hotel — or it was — there is nobody in it now but starving
lacquais de place — That next one is to let — it is eleven o'clock in the morning
— but the one servant who keeps it is in bed — you must come back again — A
little further on we come to another; there is a black ship with its yards in at
the windows — and a crane out of the gothic balconies — it is a coal warehouse
— the next looks like a ruin — but was never built — The family built their door,
and put their arms on it — Then went away through the great door which shuts
and no man opens — Here is one at last, freshly painted — an old one it is, too —

but is well whitewashed — that *is* 'all right' — it belongs to an opera dancer — Here is one — the loveliest of all — and in good order too — it was once the Doge Foscari's It was put in good order for an Academy — it is now a barracks and a regiment of Croats sleep in the drawing room — Turn we down this darker canal — towards the church tower with the smoke coming out of the top. The Italians admire steam engines as much as we do, but cannot afford to build chimneys — it is cheaper to use old church steeples; — a little further you come to another church — a ruin also — which is used as the No 100 of that quarter of the town: — Now we come out into the open sea — and can breathe again — and there are the Alps running along their blue horizon for two hundred miles: And all the blue of those 200 miles is studded with cities — and all those cities are like the one we have just left. Inhabited by a people *naturally* the sweetest — the kindest — the loveliest — the most thoughtful — the most mighty of the earth — a people full of fancy — and fire —.and affection — capable of all things — high couraged — high hearted — industrious — enduring — enthusiastic — devotional — a people living in a country full of all manner of natural blessings — a people now slothful — ignorant — incapable of *conceiving* such a thing as Truth or Honesty — Blasphemous — Murderous — Sensual — Cowardly — A people governed by another; which they hate, merely because they *are* governed by them — Governed severely because they can be no otherwise governed — and the People that govern them; temperate — thoughtful — welltrained — well taught — yet holding their national existence by a mere steel spring which one jar may break: — inflicting oppression automatically, as a nation, while individually they are kind and good: — and yet the best of them without a religion — despising the faith they are bred in — and — ignorant of any other . . .

Ruskin had not finished yet. From the inhabitants of the Veneto he moves to the Savoyard, 'languid and decrepit', the Swiss, 'ten thousand times more criminal and sensual', to the 'only hopeful island in the great ocean of Continental storm and foam'. England has liberty, strength, money, wit 'and all manner of means', all of which she invests in railways. Ruskin refuses to believe that she does so for benevolent reasons and, questioning those reasons, is led to some curious conclusions:

. . . *was* this indeed the magnificent purpose of our British Existences — *Was* it that we might be puffed — or projected — or twirled or twitched or whistled in so many seconds of time over the Menai Strait — that we set our noble engineers to so work. It was not. It was for nothing but to make money — it was pure gambling from beginning to end . . . I believe a man spends his money more worthily in God's eyes — who spends it to *buy* his own salvation — and I take the thing at its worst — than one who spends it only to get more — and to have more footmen — and finer plate — and a stall at the Opera, which were the objects of ninety-nine hundredths of the Makers of the Railroads — And as the motive of the thing is — so will its future honour be — So its Benefit.

Meantime the Cause of all this European misery — the Romanist Church — is festering on like a great smouldering candle, smoking all that comes within reach of it and we English might snuff it — or put it out — or do what we chose with it — if we could only agree how to hold the snuffers . . .

Ruskin ends by castigating internecine quarrelling between the Evangelical and High Church parties. In Venice he and Effie had the impression that the Catholic Church was so weak that the smallest effort on the part of Protestants would extinguish it finally.[80]

Apart from the faultiness of judgement here, there are obvious gaps in the arguments Ruskin puts to Brown. Nothing he has said in his description of Venice would suggest that the condition of the city is determined by her religion. Nor can the misery about to overtake his compatriots be traced to such a cause. Ruskin does not clearly identify what it is that will make us 'a spectacle and a warning'. It has to do with mechanization, speculation, the greed for money, and a materialistic style of life. Ruskin's harshest irony is directed against 'British Existences'. They are apparently guilty of a graver abuse of their resources than that typical of Romanism at its worst, the purchase of indulgences. If one judges by the 'motive of the thing', and this is what Ruskin is suggesting, England must expect a more terrible retribution than that which has fallen on the disorderly, superstitious continent. Yet the English are expected to launch a crusade against the Church of Rome and put Europe to rights. England remains the 'one hopeful island'. The adjective is not used ironically. Her liberty, her wealth and her strength are still appreciated. Ruskin is not yet ready to make a consistent and comprehensive attack on modern Protestantism or the cash nexus. Distaste for the productions of nineteenth-century English commerce had been clear since 1845. Now reactions begin to come together into something 'more distinct', a 'Philosophy' that 'we are *all wrong*'. Ruin and progress are juxtaposed. But they are not logically related. The descriptive parts of Ruskin's letter show great clarity, thoroughness and energy of observation. His deductions show uncertainty and confusion, the most daring challenges working at crossed purposes to the most deep-seated prejudices. Ruskin does not seem to have been aware of this. He ends by asking Brown to read his letter carefully, 'for I am planning and acting in accordance with the belief expressed in it'.

Ruskin, Effie and Charlotte left Venice in the second week of March, Effie with much regret, Ruskin 'almost relieved to be away from a place which gave him so much distress'.[81] They reached home in early May. *The Foundations*, the first volume of *The Stones of Venice*, appeared ten months later, in March 1851. As a whole, the book was to

be one of the most highly structured of Ruskin's works. By temperament he was inclined to the miscellaneous. Commentators have appreciated the orderliness and assurance of *Stones*.[82] Read as an exploratory
work, the book reveals confusions of thought similar to those in Ruskin's
letter to Brown of January 1850. Some, indeed, might be attributed to
too rigid organization. The Fall of Venice, like the Romanist Church in
the letter to Brown, is blamed for all distress. It is at once too simple
and too vague a concept to explain the city Ruskin observes so clearly.
Its application to modern England is also problematic.

'The Quarry', the first chapter of *The Foundations*, begins with a
comparison between the three maritime powers, Tyre, Venice and
England (IX, 17). The first is a total ruin, the second shortly to be so;
the third, at the height of her strength, is to take heed. Such analogies
are traditional, and Ruskin had precise authority for this one. Byron
had issued the same warning in the same terms in the fourth canto of
Childe Harold. Turner had drawn the sack of Tyre for the frontispiece
to *Liber Studiorum*. Ruskin himself, in Venice in 1845, had declared
'Tyre was nothing to this'.[83] Behind all these instances lies the description in *Ezekiel* 26 and 27 of Tyre, like Venice noted for wealth,
wisdom, beauty and empire, and the prophecy of despoliation as
punishment for having set herself up as God and for 'iniquity of traffic'.
But Ruskin does not make precise use of his text here, and does not say
of what England may be guilty. Rather he recognizes the difficulty of
definition by reviving an image of Venetian unreality. The city is 'a
ghost', so insubstantial 'that we might well doubt, as we watched her
faint reflection in the mirage of the lagoon, which was the City, and
which the Shadow'. Ruskin undertakes to 'trace the lines of this image',
which, in spite of the efforts 'of countless chroniclers, remains in vague
and disputable outline . . .' He then seems to modify this claim, avert-
ing his reader that the present inquiry 'will hardly render this outline
clearer'. Oddly, however, it will 'alter its aspect', and give him a 'clearer'
idea of Venetian character 'than he is likely to have gleaned from the
current fables of her mystery or magnificence' (IX, 18).

Such fables, those of Ruskin's childhood reading, conceived of
Venice as an oligarchy. In fact, Ruskin tells us, she was three hundred
years an 'agitated' democracy and six hundred an elective monarchy; it
was only during the last five hundred years that the monarchy was
reduced to 'spectral and incapable magnificence' by the aristocracy (IX,
19). But subsequent statements undermine both the chronology and
the characterization of the second and third of these periods. First the
aristocracy is referred to, pejoratively, as limiting monarchic power,
then, approvingly, as 'organizing itself, by its unity and heroism, into a
separate body' (IX, 20). First Ruskin describes its formation as complete in 1297, the date of the closing of the Grand Council to all but

members of listed families; then he seems to postpone its definition to 1453, when the Inquisition of State was introduced and 'her govern-ment takes the perfidious and mysterious form under which it is usually conceived' (IX, 19, 22).

One might imagine that Ruskin is offering his reader a time of 'good' aristocracy (1297-1453), followed by one of 'bad' aristocracy. This does not appear to be the case. The year 1297 does mark the completion of the 'Rise of Venice' and the beginning of Ruskin's most important period. This 'central struggle of her life' is not, however, a consistently virtuous time, being marked by 'her darkest crime . . . her most fatal war . . . her two noblest citizens' (IX, 20-1). Moreover as a period it stops short of 1453, for it ends with the death of one of these 'noblest citizens', Carlo Zeno, on 8 May 1418 (IX, 21). This gives Ruskin his date for the Fall of Venice. But again apparently precise chronology is put in doubt first by the statement that the *'visible'* fall occurs five years later, and then by the affirmation that the 'diminution of the prosperity of the state' coincides with 'the establishment of . . . oligarchical powers' (IX, 22), which could refer to either 1297 or 1453 but certainly neither to 1418 nor 1423. And since Ruskin proposes to show that constitutional developments are neither the cause nor the consequence of 'national enervation', it is not clear why he has pointed out this coincidence, or what he means by claiming that 'the decline of her political prosperity was exactly coincident with that of domestic and individual religion' (IX, 22-3). For if prosperity declines together with religion, why assert a connection with a change in government which is not supported by the dates given, and is in any case declared irrelevant? Ruskin offers no definition of 'political prosperity' other than to distinguish it from 'commercial prosperity', which continues throughout the fifteenth century (IX, 21-2). It seems to have to do with heroes, but with 'how they were trained', not with their names or positions. In fact Carlo Zeno does not figure in the book in any other context, and one might well look outside the logic of *The Stones of Venice* for an explanation of Ruskin's insistence on the Fall's taking place on an exact day, month and year. Richard Ellmann has suggested that counting back from Ruskin's birthday on 8 February 1819 gives 8 May 1818 as the date of his conception, making his mother's fall coincide with the five hundredth anniversary of the Fall of Venice.[84] This might be more helpful with interpretation of Ruskin's writings if he had kept to that date with any consistency. Yet he shifts ground twice more within this chapter. He says of the Venetians that 'for a thousand years they fought for life; for three hundred they invited death' (IX, 22-3). This would place the Fall at the end, not the begin-ning, of the fifteenth century. Later in 'The Quarry' he speaks of 'vital religion' as having expired some time between the birth of Giovanni

Bellini in 1423 and that of Titian in 1480 (IX, 31). Elsewhere in *The Stones of Venice* Ruskin finds the roots of the Renaissance (which should coincide with or follow the Fall) as far back as the fourth century (X, 370).

Outside *Stones* there are numerous other versions of the Fall. In 1845 Ruskin had thought Venice reduced to a state worse than that of Tyre in the space of four years.[85] In 1846 in *Modern Painters* II he blamed Canaletto for not having shown the beauty of Venice as she was 'before her fall', meaning the fall to Napoleon in 1797 (III, 213). In the same year, in revisions to *Modern Painters* I, it is implied that the city was already in ruins in Tintoretto's time (IV, 264). In the writings of 1876 Venice is, in *St Mark's Rest*, religious until the death of Carpaccio in 1520 (XXIV, 255), according to the Academy *Guide* did not abjure her religion 'in heart until after Tintoretto had painted the San Rocco "Crucifixion"' (XXIV, 155), in *Fors Clavigera* is said to have maintained good laws 'as long as there was a doge in Venice' (until 1797) and furnished her markets with good merchandise until 1845 (XXIX, 41). All of which shows that the Fall of Venice is not a chronological concept, and that far from being disciplined by 'the orderly flow of Venetian history',[86] Ruskin has, within a single chapter, created havoc with the sequence of political events.

It is obvious that Ruskin was not at all interested in the sequence of political events, although he was interested in political concepts and the exemplification of such concepts in the past. Much of his difficulty here seems to derive from an attempt to fit the two together before having thoroughly criticized received views of history in general and Venetian history in particular. Ruskin's contradictory versions of the aristocracy, for instance, are the product of an obligation to find a place for an inherited conception of Venetian government as 'perfidious and mysterious' which is at odds with his own strengthening impression of stern but responsible authority. Similarly he makes a gesture of respect for the view of Venetian ambitions as cynically commercial: 'the most curious phenomenon in all Venetian history is the vitality of religion in private life, and its deadness in public policy' (IX, 24). Piety is only manifest in instances of 'noble, individual feeling' or when there is no time to calculate expediency: 'the heart of Venice is shown only in her hastiest councils . . .' (IX, 24-5). In the Travellers' Edition of *Stones* Ruskin was to annotate this passage:

Yes: that is so, — but it *is* her heart, which was the main gist of the matter, — fool that I was not to understand! Venice is superficially and apparently commercial; — at heart passionately heroic and religious; precisely the reverse of modern England, who is superficially and apparently religious; and at heart, entirely infidel, cowardly, and dishonest.

By the time he wrote this, in 1879, Ruskin had rejected materialist interpretations of man and history. In 1850 he had doubts about both. He could offer the evidence of the 'heart', and already preferred to rely on it himself, but could not entirely dismiss that of 'public policy' as presented by 'realistic' historians. In 'The Quarry', therefore, Ruskin attempts to accommodate points of view not truly compatible with his own slowly clarifying convictions. The results are to be seen in chronological muddle, unsatisfactory equations between religious and political changes and equally unsatisfactory paradoxes such as this 'curious phenomenon' of the Venetian Senate giving way to piety when it did not have time for proper deliberation.

Of the same kind, but graver, was the difficulty of reconciling an ideal of Venetian Christianity with hostility to Catholicism. Ruskin had dealt with part of the question of the Romanist Church as raised in the letter to W.L. Brown in a pamphlet published three days after *The Foundations*. *Notes on the Construction of Sheepfolds* had first been intended for an appendix to *The Stones of Venice*, hence its strange title, which hardly indicated that it was a call to heal the divisions within the Church of England. It blamed Evangelical 'rudeness' and High Church 'superciliousness', but chiefly the latter, for the fact that three hundred years had passed since Luther 'and the Papacy not yet overthrown! Christ's truth still restrained, in narrow dawn, to the white cliffs of England and the white crests of the Alps . . .' (XII, 557). John James Ruskin was to lose some Irish customers and fear reprisals against his son when next in Venice because of statements such as these, though of course he agreed with them.[87] In one case he was the direct source. In 'Papal Power in Venice', the fifth appendix to *Stones* I, Ruskin reprinted a short essay on Catholic Emancipation written by his father in 1839, and contrasted Venetian resistance to Vatican pretensions with the 1829 English Parliament's uniquely 'impious and impolitic' concession of suffrage (IX, 423-4). Another appendix warns English travellers that the divine account book is recording their spending on ornaments and pictures, extra couriers and horses 'for show and magnificence', on sightseeing, ball-dresses and 'general vanities'; the total will be compared with the sum given to 'the struggling Protestant Churches of France, Switzerland and Piedmont' (IX, 473).

Such commentary does not amount to making the Romanist Church the 'chief cause of European misery', as Ruskin had done in the letter to Brown. The Fall is something more complicated than a single, foreign institution. But the two are closely related. The first cause of the Fall in *The Stones of Venice* is 'the peculiar degradation of the Romanist superstition' (IX, 44-5). Only as a result of this do there arise the 'two great divisions of adversaries', Protestantism and Rationalism, or the Renaissance (IX, 44). Ruskin's wish to argue the truly Christian nature

of Venice up until the fifteenth century and at the same time attribute
her fall to Romanist superstition was to test his ingenuity, especially
when it came to discussing Byzantine churches. The argument rests on a
sharp distinction between the faith of the early Venetians and 'Romanism
... since the separation of Protestantism from its side' (IX, 58).
Annotating 'The Quarry' in 1879 Ruskin was to ridicule his own
'sectarian ignorance' on this point:

> Protestantism (so far as it was still Christianity, and did not consist merely in
> maintaining one's own opinion for gospel) could not separate itself from the
> Catholic Church. The so-called Catholics became themselves sectarians and
> heretics in casting them out; and Europe was turned into a mere cockpit, of the
> theft and fury of unchristian men of both parties; while, innocent and silent on
> the hills and fields, God's people in neglected peace, everywhere and for ever
> Catholic, lived and died (IX, 58n.).

By 1879, however, Ruskin had outworn his allegiance to the religious
party in which he had grown up, a tie broken, he would sometimes say,
by hearing a sermon from a Piedmontese preacher,[88] a representative of
one of those 'struggling Protestant Churches' readers of *The Stones of
Venice* had been urged to support. He had not that freedom in 1850.
But experiences in Venice and the writing of the book itself would do
something to give Ruskin a less institutionalized view of religion, and
help him grow in sympathy for some forms of 'Romanist superstition'.
 The first volume was, however, taken up with preliminaries. The bulk
of *The Foundations* establishes general laws by which good architecture may be 'indisputably discerned' from bad (IX, 56). Only in the last
chapter does one enter 'The Vestibule', led from Padua down the
Brenta to the lagoon, though not allowed to enter the city (IX, 412-15).
It is an elaborate description, slow, emphatic, long drawn-out, insistent
on sensation and observation rather than association. Ruskin takes us
'through the dark gates of Padua' on what would seem to be a fabulous
adventure along 'the broad road leading towards the East'. He stresses
the natural fertility of the land, making it harvest time and extremely
hot, and the colours overpowering. Suggestions of abundance are mixed
with those of disease. The vine leaves are 'veined into scarlet hectic',
the grapes 'gloomy blue'. The river is especially sinister, being 'a muddy
volume of yellowish-grey water, that neither hastens nor slackens', and
having a strange eddy as if dragging something down. Against this
impression of heaviness and strength comes an image of horror, one of
the famous Brenta villas, 'a glaring, spectral shell of brick and stucco' in
'feverish sunshine'. On 'Another dreary stage' we find one of the older
villas

sinking fast into utter ruin, black, and rent, and lonely, set close to the edge of the dull water, with what were once small gardens beside them, kneaded into mud, and with blighted fragments of gnarled hedges and broken stakes from their fencing . . .

One recognizes the broken walls, rotting gondolas and putrid mud of Ruskin's walks of Christmas 1849. Equally unpicturesque is the scene in the inn at Mestre where 'peculiar', knotted bread is eaten off a dirty tablecloth. Outside there are a few poor buildings, a ditch and 'a close smell of garlic and crabs, warmed by the smoke of various stands of hot chestnuts', and porters quarrel about who is to get the job of taking the travellers' baggage. Realism alternates with fantasy as Ruskin revives romantic expectations only to frustrate them. Going to the quay we 'fancy' the water 'black with stagnation', find it is 'the black boats of Venice', and enter one

rather to try if they be real boats or not, than with any definite purpose, and glide away; at first feeling as if the water were yielding continually beneath the boat and letting her sink into soft vacancy.

From soft vacancy we are brought back to low banks 'of mud and rank grass', also unreal but rather tawdry: they seem 'as if they were dragged by upon a painted scene'. Monotonous progress is punctuated by the contrasting first sights of the Alps, 'the colour of dead rose-leaves', and the bastions of the fort of Malghera, as a result of the recent Austrian bombardment 'torn to pieces and staggering in ugly rents towards the water'. The 'rank grass' peters out into 'weedy shore', and instead of the open lagoon we see the railway bridge looking like a 'low and monotonous dockyard wall'. Rogers had described his journey from Padua 'in a wondrous Ark' in the course of which he had dreamed of bloody tyrants, passed boatloads of witty, mysterious Italians, and finally

> Gliding on,
> At length we leave the river for the sea.
> At length a voice aloft proclaims 'Venezia!'
> And, as called forth, she comes.[89]

Ruskin's journey is a criticism of Roger's approach. Ruskin's more complicated city is announced not by an enchanter but a black cloud:

Four or five domes, pale, and apparently at a greater distance, rise over the centre of the line; but the object which first catches the eye is a sullen cloud of black smoke brooding over the northern half of it, and which issues from the

belfry of a church.
  It is Venice.

The smoking belfry is the example of improvised industrialization
described in the letter to Brown, the church of San Girolamo, deconsecrated by the Napoleonic administration, now the main steam flour mill
in Venice. It is one of Ruskin's signs of 'European misery'.

II.4 1851-52

On 1 May 1851 Ruskin began work on the 'second part of . . . [his] Venetian Work' with the prayer 'May God help me to finish it to His glory, and man's good.'[1] He already had a reputation for not completing promised volumes (IX, xliii). Ruskin's father was anxious that he finish *Stones* and get back to *Modern Painters*, which had now been in abeyance for five years.[2] Though distressed at the prospect of another long absence John James Ruskin would therefore have been susceptible to his son's argument that 'I ought to finish my book & I cannot finish it properly but at Venice.'[3] For Ruskin had left 'portions of his subject unexplored',[4] and wanted to 'finish or retouch my descriptions on the spot'.[5]

Effie had been longing to go back ever since they had left fifteen months before. She and Ruskin left England on 4 August. After Alpine excursions with English friends whom they met on the way, they travelled quickly through Lombardy, arriving in Venice on 1 September. They were met by Rawdon Brown, with whom they stayed for a week while negotiating for an extra room in apartments they had leased in a palace on the Grand Canal. The arrangement to rent rooms from the owner, a Baroness Wetzlar, had been made through Rawdon Brown in the early summer.[6] As usual the Ruskins overstayed their time and when their lease expired in May had to move into a hotel in St Mark's Square. But for eight months they experimented with life in an establishment of their own in the most elite part of Venice. Ruskin and Effie had had in mind the possibility of taking a private house since November 1849, when John James Ruskin had unwarily suggested that it might be cheaper than living in hotels.[7] When he heard that they had immediately begun house-hunting he regretted having put this 'too Romantic idea' into their heads.[8] Both he and Margaret Ruskin doubted whether living near water, and especially 'the unsavoury waters of the narrow canals of Venice' were good for Ruskin's and Effie's 'relaxed constitutions'.[9] And even if they were, as Ruskin had previously claimed, 'gaining in Bodily Vigour' in Venice, would it either morally or religiously harmonize with your feelings or strengthen your minds or Character? . . . Mama deems it a duty to beseech of you to pause before you plunge too far into the fascinations of Continental Life — They never yet I fancy did much good to either man or woman — Woman especially . . . I cannot at once say I entirely approve of hiring House or Palace abroad yet — It sounds Byronish or Shelleyish . . . How few of our best men have dwelt in Foreign Land? — Gibbon is the most known after Byron & neither would we like you to resemble . . .[10]

Ruskin must have replied, indignantly, that he did not in the least resemble Gibbon or Byron.[11] But if John James Ruskin was terrified of his son's becoming an expatriate, it was because of the thought of permanent separation rather than because of the disreputable connotations. Carelessly, Ruskin now told him of his happiness in his Venetian palace:

for the first time in my life I feel to be living really in my own house. For I never *lived* at any place that I loved before — and have been either *enduring* the locality, or putting up with somewhat rough habitation — I never found myself settled for six months in any place that I liked.[12]

In the Casa Wetzlar he and Effie could arrange things to their comfort. Prepared, this time, for a Venetian winter, they laid hay under the carpets.[13] Besides the 'Cart-load' of luggage they had brought with them, they had more things sent out by sea, including wine, preserves and a fire-grate.[14] Keeping house brought glimpses of Venetian popular life. Effie told her mother that

you would think one kitchen held the whole parish sometimes. When I want to speak to Mary, who sits in an Inner room, I have to pass Nani, Annetta, Beppo, Carlo, the Priests, the Ironing woman, the Porter, his family, Nani's daughters, some of Annetta's children, George and his violin . . . and stray Gondoliers & women whom I never saw before . . . Nani makes them a great dish of Fish seasoned strongly with Garlic and the smell is something too dreadful if one happens to pass by the door . . .[15]

Clearly Effie had no chance of imposing domestic authority and fortunately seems to have been happy not to try. Mary, her maid, had some difficulty in adjusting at first. She complained of Venetian perversity in refusing to understand English, thought she was being insulted, and was for the first month 'very sulky'.[16] But the cheerful crowds in the kitchen must have endeared themselves to Mary in the end, for when she left Effie's service in 1854 it was because she wanted to return to Venice.[17] John's servant, John Hobbes (known as George to distinguish him from Ruskin), must also have formed friendships, for he became violently anti-Austrian.[18] Certainly the Ruskin servants formed closer ties with Venetians than did their employers. Having a private residence brought a change in status. Effie was no longer 'a mere Traveller' but a 'Venetian Lady'.[19] This did not mean that she mixed with Venetians. They were still 'not in society in Venice because they don't choose'.[20] During the carnival there were a few more masks to be seen than two years before, but they were hustled and insulted by the crowd.[21] But company of other nationalities was plentiful and lively. The English had now returned. Some, those who came in the early autumn, were tourists, 'with Murrays under arm'.[22] Some were 'bigotted Romanists', converts who insisted on trying to win over the Ruskins.[23] But there were others. Rawdon Brown's friend, Edward Cheyney, had now returned. Cheyney, whom the Ruskins had met in England, was apparently rather fierce, but proved kind and helpful.[24] Lady Sorell, widow of a former British consul, was perhaps the most useful.[25] It was she who launched Effie into the society that was her real element. Paulizza, her old friend and admirer, had died during the Ruskins' absence. But the Austrian, Hungarian, Russian and French aristocratic families who arrived in November for the winter season provided a round of evening gatherings in which unattached young army officers still predominated. Once again Effie was an outstanding success.[26] She now had no trace of sympathy with Italian or Venetian desires for independence. Effie was furious at hearing of the demonstrations of anti-Austrian feeling in England, pronounced Austrian contempt for Italians well deserved and took to wearing dresses in orange and black, the Austrian colours.[27] Her friends might be Catholic, but unlike the importunate English converts they were at least not enthusiastic in their Catholicism: 'Their only Religion is Honor and a strong feeling of love to the traditions of their families mixed with Moyen-Age sentiments of Chivalry and knowledge of the Art of War . . .'[28] Effie continued to admire even though these 'Moyen-Age sentiments' gave rise to some awkward situations. She had difficulties with two particularly persistent admirers, and a duel was fought over her.[29] Most embarrassing of all was the chain of events which led to Ruskin himself being challenged to a duel. Just as the Ruskins were about to leave Venice some jewellery of Effie's was stolen, and suspicion fell on an English officer serving in the Austro-Hungarian army. The incident fuelled bad feeling between the Venetian police and the hotel-owner on the one hand and the military and Austrian society on the other. The Ruskins were caught in the middle, permission to leave was withheld until the end of June, and as they passed through Verona a close friend of the suspected man challenged Ruskin to fight. The affair might have been even nastier, they thought, if they had not had the help of Brown and Cheyney.[30]

Brown had never approved of Effie's friends, whom he thought 'all such idiots and fools'.[31] But Brown was notoriously quarrelsome and changeable, perhaps 'mad and not accountable', and suspected Effie of carrying on an illicit relationship.[32] In fact she was enjoying being adored, and had some need of consolation, for the 'peculiar' Ruskins were being hostile again.[33] John James Ruskin came out with some 'extraordinary productions' in the way of letters criticizing her extravagance in clothes.[34] Effie, quite justifiably, had 'some times forebodings rather gloomy' at the thought of returning to England. She and Ruskin were to live in Herne Hill, a short distance away from the old Ruskins. Effie had no say in the domestic arrangements being made by her parents-in-law. Her husband announced that he *never intended as long as they lived to consult . . .* [her] on any subject of importance'.[35] His kindness and tolerance of her way of life was only a measure of the distance between them. This shows in the terms in which he wrote of her to his father:

> Bad people — or people in a bad state — can only be benefited by Kindness — or letting alone — (unless they come to that pitch of badness that they must be punished for the sake of society — I don't mean that Red Republicans are to be won by kindness — or mended by letting alone). Therefore I am always either kind or indifferent to Effie — I never scold — simply take *my own way* and let her have hers . . .[36]

Of 'Badness' of both kinds Ruskin saw a great deal between September 1851 and June 1852, though it was not always clear where the dividing line lay, and even issues involving the more criminal forms of Badness gave Ruskin some trouble in formulating his judgements. In one case red republicanism, indecency and desecration of beauty manifested themselves in combination. Ruskin cited as an instance of Italian character, 'a curious Hybrid between the Fox and the Pig', the use of the five bricked up arches of the Ducal Palace arcade as a urinal:

> Since the Austrians came back, some order has been attempted with this abuse and I was delighted to see four large tablets put up in these arches, with 'E' vietato di lordare sotto pena di multa.' In a week after they were put up, I saw some marks on these tablets — and on going up to them — I found them scribbled over with black pencil — with 'Morte all' Austria' written between the words.
>
> This may I think be considered as very nearly typical of the character of modern Italian republican agitation. They rage against Austria because she will not let them — against their own palaces.[37]

But the forces of evil did not always range themselves so neatly. In its own way the Austrian military presence defiled the city: 'I get very angry every time I pass the guns in St Mark's Place.'[38] The military presence was massive and obvious. Everywhere had 'the look of fortification'; Croat soldiers were installed even in the convents. Ruskin's reaction was strong enough to make him once declare sympathy with the radicals.[39] The use of lotteries to raise money for the government was also 'inexcusably wrong'. In a letter to Samuel Rogers Ruskin said that there was no

> more melancholy sight than the fevered and yet habitually listless groups of the poorer population gathered in the porches of St. Mark's, and clustered about its pillars, not for any religious service, but to wait for the declaration of the prize tickets from the loggia of Sansovino.[40]

The religious issue complicated political judgement even further. Since 1846 Ruskin had been struggling with the problem of the apparent connection between the wrong religious principles and the right artistic principles, the fact that only Catholicism seemed to produce good art (see pp. 66-7). Now he came up against another misalliance, the apparent link between the right religious principles and the wrong political principles, and vice versa. The authoritarian, Catholic Austrians repressed Protestant endeavours in Italy, while in Hungary Kossuth's rebels were largely Protestant. Ruskin wished the confusion could be resolved:

> what a pity it is that we cannot get Protestants and Radicals separated. I don't know a cleverer trick of the Devil, since the world began — than getting Protestant energy, at this moment — confounded, in Austria and Italy with red republicanism, and Popery identified with peace . . .[41]

Racial, religious and political prejudices were at crossed purposes, making Ruskin take first one side and then the other on the issues dividing Europe.

In *The Stones of Venice* Ruskin was to take the Austrian side against Italian republicans and English liberals (XI, 254-5). But he never shared Effie's warm partisanship with the Austrians. When not working he rowed or walked on and around the Fondamente Nuove, where people did not gather.[42] It was not only a question of withdrawing physically. Ruskin probably attended more social functions than he had during the winter of 1849-50. But his stance was always that of an observer, not a participant. He described these occasions carefully for his father, indicating sometimes neutrality, sometimes approval, sometimes disapproval, never involvement. Ruskin went with Effie up the campanile to watch the arrival of the young Emperor and Radetsky. Afterwards he compared them to 'a great white baboon and a small brown monkey'.[43] On another occasion the population of Venice was asked to meet the Emperor at the station and accompany him down the Grand Canal to St Mark's. Ruskin allowed his gondola to stay alongside the imperial boat to protect him from some men of hostile aspect, but unlike Effie and the gondolier, he was not excited by being so near Hapsburg royalty.[44] When Radetsky gave a ball in Verona Ruskin looked on with mild pleasure as Effie was presented to and made a fuss of by the Marshall, and approved of the arrangements for the entertainment of the guests; they included a library where he could look at books.[45] Ruskin's attitude was an extension of his attitude to Effie herself. Because the Austrians did not do much that was 'inexcusably wrong', at least in comparison to the red republicans, he regarded them with a mixture of kindness and indifference.

But Ruskin's calculated refusal to censure is almost as damning as his violent but erratic abuse of Romanists or radicals. It contained an element of despair which was not present when he was giving voice to righteous fury. Ruskin had been angry enough in 1845 to compare himself to Timon of Athens in his hatred of man. But he had not shown signs of the resignation which begins to appear in his letters to his father at the beginning of 1852. 'The more I watch the world — the more I feel that all men are blind and wandering — I am more indulgent to their sins — but more hopeless ...'[46] he wrote on 9 January. A week later he declared that after *Stones* and *Modern Painters* he would go back to geology and 'leave the world to darkness'.[47] On 7 February he contrasted the English with 'Italians'; the former were disagreeable in society but pleasant at home, the latter agreeable in society but 'would be unbearable in private life':

> Here — it is the apples of Sodom dust inside; with us cocoanuts — milk inside — and a monkey face and rough shell outside. But I don't intend to live on the shell any more.[48]

The next day Effie wrote home that Ruskin was refusing to write to a family friend to congratulate him on the birth of a son:

> He says he has no friends and that he never will have any and that the world and every body in it are all going wrong but that he is right, and then he sits and writes such accounts to Mr R — of the state of society both here in Venice and in London and thinks himself an excellent judge, although he knows no one and never stirs out.[49]

On 20 February Ruskin wrote to his father of the

> degradation into which the operatic amusement is sinking the European mind — First you have every possible means of excitement ... then, the people ... take this excitement every night — till it ceases to be an excitement ... one evil

reacting on another, the final result of the general corruption is still unseen – and to come.[50]

Ruskin's obsession with Renaissance aristocrats in pursuit of pleasure in *The Stones* clearly derives from his reaction to the 'state of society' directly observed in Venice in 1851-52.

Ruskin's declaration that he had not and never would have any friends seems petulant and self-pitying, yet he had reasons for loneliness and depression. From home he had news of the deaths first of his 'earthly Master', Turner, in December [51] and then, in February, of Samuel Prout.[52] For some weeks after Turner's death Ruskin suffered from a shaky hand and sleeplessness.[53] Sorrow over the death of the man was aggravated by worries about what was happening to the paintings and drawings. Ruskin had been named one of the executors of the will, and wondered if he should not drop his work and come home. John James Ruskin anxiously asked for instructions and passed on alarming stories about the machinations of dealers and the other executors.[54] To grief over Turner was added grief over Tintoretto. When Ruskin heard of a plan to restore the *Paradise* in the Ducal Palace, he told his father that it would be worse to him than the death of Hallam had been to Tennyson: 'Men are more evanescent than pictures yet one sorrows for lost friends – and pictures *are* my friends. I have none others.'[55] Ruskin felt he was losing friends daily. He could not 'stir a foot without seeing somebody destroying something'.[56] He doubted whether the Ducal Palace would stand five years more.[57] Ruskin had casts made of the capitals and of sculptures on St Mark's, but failed in efforts to get the National Gallery to buy two Tintorettos.[58] He began to envy the scientist, whose work progresses; with the art critic ' "All his *thoughts* perish".'[59] In Venice Ruskin was cut off from the only living artists in whom he could see a future, the pre-Raphaelites. He did not, apparently, write to them, or to anyone but his father.

John James Ruskin was not always the most reassuring of correspondents. He was not in good health, and this made him more than usually nervous.[60] Directly and indirectly, he exerted pressure on his son this winter. Strongest of all was the pressure generated by the pain of '*not seeing you*'.[61] For a while there was talk of the old Ruskins coming out to the continent, perhaps to Switzerland, which they preferred to Venice.[62] But Margaret Ruskin's sight was failing, and John James feared incompatibility with Effie, of which they already had experience.[63] He feared interrupting his son's work, for that might have worse consequences: 'There is one thing we are very anxious for – to have you finish your work at Venice in the first place not to have to go back . . .'[64] In the meantime he fussed over secondary matters, probably a way of expressing the same anxiety. Ruskin was exceeding his allowance,[65] he did not keep to his travelling schedule, and so missed letters from home.[66] Both parents worried about the unhealthiness of Venice,[67] and John James Ruskin tormented himself especially with the idea of his son drowning himself in the lagoon. He understood that gondola accidents were not uncommon, especially if one indulged in 'what is called Horse-play',[68] which Ruskin was hardly likely to do. Warnings about the dangers of Venetian dissipation or allowing himself to be ensnared by Jesuits and Black Romanists were also somewhat unnecessary.[69] Margaret Ruskin was reported 'sighing at night' when she heard that her son was not going to church on Sundays, though she was placated when told that it was because there was no English church in Venice.[70] It is not surprising that Ruskin was at first reticent on the matter of his religious doubts. These he had confessed to his lifelong Oxford friend, Henry Acland, in the spring of 1851.[71] In the first three months of 1852 they seem to have built up 'until I felt myself on the very edge of total infidelity'.[72] Of this Ruskin said nothing to his father until he had resolved the crisis by deciding to 'act as if the Bible were true'. This apparently satisfied John James, who preferred to avoid self-examination in religious questions. He answered his son that 'Speculation is useless', and described himself as having 'physically, morally, spiritually lost all frankness & freedom of speech on any subject . . .'[73]

On the progress of the literary work, however, John James Ruskin was kept up to date, for he was now in effect his son's agent, editor and general manager. Again there was some friction here, for old Mr Ruskin did not like some of the tendencies that had emerged during recent years. The expensive folio series of *Examples of the Architecture of Venice* was incurring heavy losses, and he advised that publication be suspended.[74] Thinking of *Pre-Raphaelitism* and *Notes on the Construction of Sheepfolds*, John James warned against pamphlets, which 'are, as I told you, coining your Brains into a bad Currency . . .'[75] Now Ruskin seemed set on a still more ephemeral style of publication, and on venturing outside the field in which he was 'invulnerable', that of art.[76] In March Ruskin submitted for his father's approval three letters intended for *The Times*, one on election, one on taxation, one on education.[77] This third letter was to John James Ruskin's liking, and he advised adapting it for an appendix to *The Stones of Venice*. But the first two alarmed him. Within nine days of receiving them John James wrote six long letters setting out his objections.[78] He found that the first smacked of universal suffrage, even though the proposal was for each man's vote to be given different weight according to his age, position and wealth. The second was on the right lines, but showed ignorance of the facts. Free trade had been the subject of debate among experts for many years, and Ruskin had arrived on the scene too late and ill-equipped. The letters were polemical, and would expose both father and son to ridicule, which would be suicidal. Living in Venice Ruskin was no doubt misinformed about his country: 'you are not likely to know any thing of England that can be hid by foreign governments but when she does evil . . .'[79] Above all John James Ruskin was

> painfully & nervously sensitive about your appearing outré or utopian on fields where very small Knights of the pen could meet you & being clad in more practicable Armour might discomfit you — I cannot in my present state of nerves bear to see you attacked on subjects where your opponents might prove your Schemes utterly impracticable & every thing of this sort is so open to ridicule . . . I want you to read all Burkes Political Works — He was practical, imaginative — then philosophical . . . Ed[d] Burke subdued every grand Idea cast down every lofty Imagination — & tried all by the test of Practicability . . . In Moral Machinery — *Results* are the Test . . .[80]

Ruskin and his father may well have argued about 'Practicability' before. In May 1851 Ruskin had told Henry Acland that the object of *Notes on the Construction of Sheepfolds* was 'to direct men's thoughts, as far as I could, to the discovery of the reasons why what is right should be Impracticable'.[81] The three letters intended for *The Times* ask the same question in other contexts and, as John James Ruskin realized, it was pertinent to the book in progress:

> The Humility before God which you so beautifully touch on in early Venetian Character & Loftiness of purpose & spirit before man — Strict Integrity — Stern Honesty & purity of motive — if you can innoculate the Multitude with these, high & low — you would improve the House of Commons — & in no other way.[82]

If, in *The Stones of Venice*, Ruskin would often 'touch on' the Venetian virtues, but only occasionally draw from them lessons directly applicable to England, it may have been partly due to discouragement from his father. In later life he would show no hesitation about 'appearing outré or utopian'. St George's work would defy the limitations of 'Practicability', and even common notions of what the word meant. But in his early thirties Ruskin was not yet ready to take on all the forces of pragmatism.

John James Ruskin certainly exerted influence on another aspect of *The Stones of Venice*. He had recently collected his son's verses into an edition for private circulation, *Poems: J.R. Collected 1850*, resigning himself to the fact that there would be no more. The eloquence of *Modern Painters* II had offered consolation, brought Ruskin esteem. John James had also been pleased by the first and last chapters of *The Foundations*, but the rest he found 'tedious & heavy', as did others.

W.H. Harrison and his family had 'had less pleasure in your 1st Vol. Stones than in any of your Works . . .'[83] Another letter from Ruskin's father reported the view of George Smith, his publisher, that 'no *technical* Works are popular or sell — *Modern Painters* is the *selling* Book   I can as one of the public quite comprehend this — Your powers of writing are so fine that we grudge to have them cabind cribbed confined — We want you, pen in hand not Trowel . . .'[84] He hoped that *Stones* II would make up for this. Ruskin's ability to 'draw sermons out of stones' was marvellous; with the addition of 'some Turner gleam of Venice to be given in your word painting — It will be a book indeed . . .'[85] But the drafts of chapters sent home for inspection in the course of the winter often disappointed him. In the first version of the approach to St Mark's,

> the very truth of your description deprives me of pleasure by making me actually see what I so heartily feel to be decidedly unpleasant — from the *Jars of pickles all the way past Vinegar Cruets — Stale apple Fritters — Sausages — Crumbs* — to distress me — yet I see you put them as foils.[86]

These too realistic particulars could be cut out, and were, as was a quantity of material on tombs to which John James Ruskin expressed 'repugnance'.[87] But against his criticisms of 'the spirit of too minute antiquarian discussion'[88] Ruskin took a firmer stand:

> I am sorry you are not at all interested in my antiquarianism — but I believe you will like the book better when you see it finished — at all events, it would be foolish to abandon the labour of two whole years, now that it is just approaching completion. I cannot write anything but what is *in* me and interests me. I never could write for the public — I never *have* written except under the conviction of a thing's being important, wholly irrespective of the public's thinking so too — and all my power, such as it is, would be lost the moment I tried to catch people by fine writing. You know I promised them no Romance — I promised them Stones. Not even bread. I do not *feel* any Romance in Venice. It is simply a heap of ruins, trodden under foot by such men as Ezekiel describes 21, 31: and *this* is the great fact which I want to teach: To give Turneresque descriptions of the thing would not have needed ten days' study . . . at all events, I must work out my purpose now it is gone so far.[89]

Three days after writing this letter Ruskin relented enough to admit that there would be 'some pieces of colour — description which will give you pleasure'.[90] In the book he would, however, use them in ways that reinforce his 'antiquarianism'. Colour, beauty and romance must be picked out from amidst the 'heap of ruins' trampled by men like those in Ezekiel's prophecy against Jerusalem, 'brutish men, and skilful to destroy'.[91]

Ruskin had first seen Venice under this dual aspect in 1845. But in 1845 Ruskin had seen the destruction of Venice in terms of both ruin and modernization. This second element is missing from, or given very little weight in, *The Stones of Venice*. It is also comparatively absent from his letters and diaries. 1845 was the peak of an economic boom. Since then, as a consequence of the revolution, Venice had lost the gains of those years. In 1849-52 there was probably not much actual improvement going on. So to some extent Ruskin's silence on the matter accurately reflects the depression. But there is also a sense in which it is a matter of choice. In June 1852 he wrote to Rogers:

> I fear that now there is but one period of beauty or honour still remaining for her. Perhaps even this may be denied to her, and she may be gradually changed, by the destruction of old buildings and erection of new, into a modern town — a bad imitation of Paris. But if not, and the present indolence and ruinous dissipation of the people continue, there will come a time when the modern houses will be abandoned and destroyed, St. Mark's Place will again be, what it was in the early ages, a green field, and the front of the Ducal Palace and the marble shafts of St. Mark's will be rooted in wild violets and wreathed with vines. She will be beautiful again then, and I could almost wish that the time might come quickly, were it not that so many noble pictures must be destroyed first (XI, xxvii-xxviii).

The Fall, which in *The Stones of Venice* is seen as having its inevitable conclusion in the submersion of the city (something Ruskin did not foresee in a literal sense), is therefore a matter for wishful thinking. It is preferable to the prospect of a 'bad imitation of Paris'. Hence a certain grace is conceded to Venice. Paradoxically, a certain grace is also conceded to the 'modern town'. The flourishing nation has time to learn from the example of ruin. In 1860 Ruskin changed his mind on this point. After that date modern British 'prosperity' is explicitly stated to be worse than any Venetian loss of prosperity, and the true destruction of Venice is identified with her 'resuscitation'. That is already implied here, in the fear that Venetians may deny their city an honourable death. But the argument stops short of its logical conclusion, cut off by the negative associations of the 'indolence and ruinous dissipation' on which reabsorption into nature depends. Ruskin's dislike of the products of modern industry is as yet emotional; he has not the logical instruments needed to criticize the industriousness itself. But in the writing of the second and third volumes of *The Stones of Venice* he would go a long way towards acquiring them.

The second volume of *Stones*, *The Sea-Stories*, appeared in the spring of 1853. At the end of volume I Ruskin had left his traveller in the middle of the lagoon. He begins 'The Throne', the first chapter of *The Sea-Stories*, by considering the kind of situation in which he finds himself:

> In the olden days of travelling, now to return no more, in which distance could not be vanquished without toil, but in which that toil was rewarded, partly by the power of deliberate survey of the countries through which the journey lay, and partly by the happiness of the evening hours, when from the top of the last hill he had surmounted, the traveller beheld the quiet village where he was to rest, scattered among the meadows beside its valley stream; or, from the long hoped for turn in the dusty perspective of the causeway, saw, for the first time, the towers of some famed city, faint in the rays of sunset . . . (X, 3).

This is an archaic version of the continental tour, a sentimental picture of travel as Ruskin remembered it prior to the coming of the railways which have removed the 'toil' from overcoming distance, cancelled the rewards of overnight stops in remote villages, and spoiled the approaches to legendary cities. Appropriately, Ruskin raids the writings and readings of his youth for imagery to describe the old approach to Venice. In 'Velasquez the Novice', his unfinished novel of 1836, the party experiences 'a slight feeling of disappointment' at the first sight (I, 543). In 'The Throne' the traveller feels 'slight disappointment'. In *Childe Harold* Byron 'saw from out the wave her structures rise'.[92] In 'Velasquez' Venice rises 'as if summoned out of the deep' (I, 543). In 'The Throne' we find 'the strange rising of its walls and towers out of the midst, as it seemed, of the deep sea . . .' (X, 4). In Ruskin's poem of 1846, 'La Madonna dell'Acqua', the shrine of the 'lone Madonna' stands in a sea which is threatening, for one can hear 'deep-mouthed surf', but in the sunset the water becomes 'the burning floor/Of ocean' (II, 227-8). Other features of the scene include 'breezes bleak', 'the wild seaweed', and a 'faint storm-bird'. In 'The Throne' the shrine is replaced by the 'lonely island church' of San Giorgio in Aliga standing in a sea of potentially 'bleak power' now calmed to 'a field of burnished gold'. There is also a 'salt breeze', 'white moaning sea-birds' and 'masses of black weed' (X, 4). In the 'Venice' section of Samuel Rogers's *Italy*, 'No track of men, no footsteps to and fro,/Lead to her gates.'[93] In 'La Madonna dell'Acqua', 'No footsteps fret the pathway to and fro'. The traveller of 'The Throne' enters Venice by 'untrodden streets' (X, 6). The disturbing incongruities of the voyage down the Brenta with which *Stones* I had closed are not present. Expectations are gratified in a climactic passage down the 'bright vista' of the Grand Canal, under the Rialto Bridge, 'shadowy', 'adamantine', and 'moonlike', to the 'silver sea' where the Ducal Palace, 'flushed with its sanguine veins, looks to the snowy dome of Our Lady of Salvation'.

If, at this point, Ruskin employs more than usually highly-coloured language and allows the sexual reference common in traditional praise of Venice to come near the surface, it serves as a warning that he has been indulging his reader. With such stimulus,

> it was no marvel that the mind should be so deeply entranced by the visionary charm of a scene so beautiful and so strange, as to forget the darker truths of its history and its being. Well might it seem that such a city had owed her existence rather to the rod of the enchanter, than the fear of the fugitive; that the waters which encircled her had been chosen for the mirror of her state, rather than the shelter of her nakedness; and that all which in nature was wild or merciless, — Time and Decay, as well as the waves and tempests, — had been won to adorn her instead of to destroy, and might still spare, for ages to come, that beauty which seemed to have fixed for its throne the sands of the hour-glass as well as of the sea (X, 6-7).

Ruskin reveals the magical city to be the product of historical ignorance, ignorance of the beginnings of Venice as well as of her end. Yet he only does so after having given the most eloquent example of the kind of 'Turner gleam' his father wanted. And by making this journey take place 'In olden days' Ruskin gives justification for cherishing that vision in memory. For although at that unspecified time visitors might have seen 'the darker truths' if they had looked for them, there is a sense in which the '*visible*' fall had not yet taken place. Ruskin speaks of the 'last few eventful years' as having changed 'the face of the whole earth', Venice and her 'noble landscape of approach', more than the previous five hundred.

The strictly contemporary traveller is not allowed the vision permitted to a previous generation. If in a hurry and willing to 'shut his eyes' he may retain it, but his doing so is shown to be escapist, foolish and feeble:

> They, at least, are little to be envied, in whose hearts the great charities of the imagination lie dead, and for whom the fancy has no power to repress the importunity of painful impressions, or to raise what is ignoble, and disguise what is discordant, in a scene so rich in its remembrances, so surpassing in its beauty. But for this work of the imagination there must be no permission during the task which is before us. The impotent feelings of romance, so singularly characteristic of this century, may indeed gild, but never save, the remains of those mightier ages to which they are attached like climbing flowers; and they must be torn away from the magnificent fragments, if we would see them as they stood in their own strength. Those feelings, always as fruitless as they are fond, are in Venice not only incapable of protecting, but even of discerning, the objects to which they ought to have been attached. The Venice of modern fiction and

drama is a thing of yesterday, a mere efflorescence of decay, a stage dream which the first ray of daylight must dissipate into dust. No prisoner, whose name is worth remembering, or whose sorrow deserved sympathy, ever crossed that 'Bridge of Sighs,' which is the centre of the Byronic ideal of Venice ... the most conspicuous parts of the city have been so entirely altered in the course of the last three centuries, that ... Henry Dandolo or Francis Foscari ... would not know in what part of the world they stood, would literally not recognise one stone of the great city ... The remains of *their* Venice lie hidden behind the cumbrous masses which were the delight of the nation in its dotage; hidden in many a grass-grown court, and silent pathway, and lightless canal, where the slow waves have sapped their foundations for five hundred years, and must soon prevail over them for ever. It must be our task to glean and gather them forth, and restore out of them some faint image of the lost city; more gorgeous a thousand fold than that which now exists, yet not created in the day-dream of the prince, nor by the ostentation of the noble, but built by iron hands and patient hearts, contending against the adversity of nature and the fury of man, so that its wonderfulness cannot be grasped by the indolence of imagination, but only after frank inquiry into the true nature of that wild and solitary scene, whose restless tides and trembling sands did indeed shelter the birth of the city, but long denied her dominion (X, 7-9).

Ruskin offers a series of opposed alternatives. One must choose between prettiness and strength, discernment and feeling, flowers and fragments, the imagination or truth. The argument of *The Stones of Venice* is built on the dichotomy between past and present, and the magnificence of the old city cannot be perceived if one confuses the two in a romantic haze. Yet Ruskin's own romantic inheritance is clearly shown. The feelings of romance may be 'impotent' as regards preservation or historical truth, but Ruskin has just shown how powerful they can be in determining experience. These feelings, like creepers on overgrown ruins, 'must be torn away'; yet, oddly, 'they ought to have been attached'. And though 'this work of the imagination', the repressing of painful impressions, is denied, the emphasis is perhaps on 'this work', for it is the 'indolence of the imagination' which cannot grasp the true wonderfulness of Venice. Merely to reproduce the 'Byronic ideal', as Ruskin himself had once done, required no creative effort; one will be required to resurrect the true city.

What Ruskin proposes, moreover, has much in common with what it is meant to replace. Instead of the 'stage dream' we are offered something scarcely more tangible, 'some faint image of the lost city'. In place of one Venice we shall another 'more gorgeous a thousand fold', in place of dreaming princes, heroes with 'iron hands and patient hearts'. Nor was to emphasize a need for inquiry to break with Romantic tradition, for it was the Romantics who had revived an interest in

Venetian history. Though Ruskin had undertaken original research on a scale and of a kind his predecessors had not contemplated, many of his enquiries begin where they had ended. It was not so much that Byron was ignorant, but that he did not use his studies consistently (X, 8n.). Much of Ruskin's work consists of literal investigation of the grounds of impressions which earlier generations had found fascinating but not taken the trouble to explain. The gondola had enchanted many; Ruskin gives account of its structure, the mechanics by which it is propelled, the reasons for the 'gondolier's cry'.[94] Byron was attracted by 'crumbling palaces'; Ruskin gathers fragments from 'many a grass-grown court, and silent pathway and lightless canal'. If Byron preferred the melancholy Venice of ruins to 'when she was a boast, a marvel, and a show',[95] Ruskin rejected the 'cumbrous masses' of her pleasure-seeking dotage in favour of the adversities of her birth, like the poet is drawn to the prospect of the 'slow waves' prevailing over her stones, and makes melancholy a characteristic of all Venetians up to the final stage of her Fall. It was with those Renaissance and eighteenth-century travellers who cared nothing for the aspect of Venice, or who came only for entertainment, that Ruskin had nothing in common. This he was to draw attention to in *Praeterita*, thirty years later (XXXV, 294-5). In 1853 he did not 'think it necessary' to point out his affinity with Byron, though he was to do so both in his autobiography and in the *Stones* Epilogue of 1881 (XXXV, 150-1; XI, 233).

But Ruskin misrepresented himself when, in *Praeterita*, he said that at the time of writing *Stones* he 'felt exactly as Byron did, in every particular' (XI, 233). Since writing the first volume, which had partially admitted the Byronic version of the oligarchy, he had come to realize that it conflicted with his own political views. This would have been made apparent by reading James Fenimore Cooper's *The Bravo* in 1852. On 2 March Ruskin wrote angrily to his father of 'common novel sentiment about Venice' and Cooper's 'ridiculous' novel in particular: 'The republicanism and abuse of the Venetian government are also so absurd that it may be worth while taking notice of them in a short note, as I daresay this book is an authority with Americans about Venice.'[96] John James Ruskin agreed that *The Bravo* was a 'disagreeable book' and went further: 'No American can *feel* Venice I am sure . . .'[97] Perhaps because Americans are thus declared hopelessly lost, Ruskin makes no mention of *The Bravo* in *The Stones of Venice*. But it is the political outlook expressed by Cooper that is under attack when he states that 'No prisoner, whose name is worth remembering, or whose sorrow deserved sympathy, ever crossed that "Bridge of Sighs" which is the centre of the Byronic ideal of Venice . . .' Like Cooper, Byron had idealized the victims of the old republic; Ruskin would idealize its representatives. The centre of Byron's Venice was the bridge leading to the prisons; the centre of Ruskin's Venice would be the palace where judgement was passed.

It is not until the end of *The Sea-Stories*, however, that the reader is taken to this centre. The Venetian achievement is to be seen as the creation not of luxurious nobles but of heroes of a more primitive, Anglo-Saxon stamp. In preparation Ruskin sends the traveller on a series of journeys to the periphery. The first is into the lagoon and prehistory:

> in order to know what it was once, let the traveller follow in his boat at evening the windings of some unfrequented channel far into the midst of the melancholy plain; let him remove, in his imagination, the brightness of the great city that still extends itself in the distance, and the walls and towers from the islands that are near; and so wait, until the bright investiture and sweet warmth of the sunset are withdrawn from the waters, and the black desert of their shore lies in its nakedness beneath the night, pathless, comfortless, infirm, lost in dark languor and fearful silence, except where the salt runlets plash into the tideless pools, or the sea-birds flit from their margins with a questioning cry; and he will be enabled to enter in some sort into the horror of heart with which this solitude was anciently chosen by man for his habitation. They little thought, who first drove the stakes into the sand, and strewed the ocean reeds for their rest, that their children were to be the princes of that ocean, and their palaces its pride; and yet, in the great natural laws that rule that sorrowful wilderness, let it be remembered what strange preparation had been made for the things which no human imagination could have foretold, and how the whole existence and fortune of the Venetian nation were anticipated or compelled, by the setting of those bars and doors to the rivers and the sea (X, 13).

The first task set the imagination is to remove the city altogether. Ruskin describes a landscape of Creation, without light, heat or sound. The features are minimal, sand and salt water, barely distinguishable one from another. The first Venetians, like the first men, must struggle against natural adversity. Though unaware, they are a chosen people of God. His mysterious ways with geology have prepared this site on the margins of the world for a city that is to be its centre. From this 'throne' Venice would 'gather and give forth, in world-wide pulsation, the glory of the West and of the East, from the burning heart of her Fortitude and Splendour!' (X, 15.)

The second chapter, 'Torcello', takes the traveller a little nearer the 'burning heart'. Again he is sent out into the empty, desolate lagoon at the end of the day, but at the end of this voyage is a pastoral scene:

> The cattle are feeding and resting upon the site of the city that they left; the mower's scythe swept this day at dawn over the chief street of the city that they

built, and the swathes of soft grass are now sending up their scent into the
night air, the only incense that fills the temple of their ancient worship. Let us
go down into that little space of meadow land (X, 19).

The mower is no fantasy, for the grass in the square of the old city was
in fact cut for hay. But Ruskin has made him into an archaic, semi-
allegorical figure, and made him go before we arrive. There are therefore no people, and Torcello appears to have been reabsorbed into
nature. We approach by a 'scarcely traceable foot-path' between broken
fences and flowering hedges, and find at the end a group of buildings
so modest that 'whatever sin it may have been which has on this spot
been visited with so utter a desolation, it could not at least have been
ambition' (X, 20). Since Ruskin offers no other sin in explanation of
ruin, Torcello remains unsullied. It is therefore the perfect place to
begin the reconstruction of Venice as a Christian state. The first stage
relies on a reading of the Cathedral as having

evidently been built by men in flight and distress, who sought in the hurried
erection of their island church . . . a shelter for their earnest and sorrowful
worship . . .(X, 20).

As Ruskin noted in 1879, 'A great deal of this talk is flighty, and some
of it fallacious . . .' The Cathedral was not hurriedly erected. Founded
in the seventh century, it was added to and decorated over the next five
hundred years, and in any case no stone building could be improvised
in such a place. Ruskin certainly knew this, but preferred to imply that
the first thought of the refugees fleeing from the Huns ravaging the
mainland was to build a church. As a whole, therefore, the Cathedral
expresses

the deep sorrow and the sacred courage of men who had no home left them
upon earth, but who looked for one to come . . . the actual condition . . .
exactly typical of the spiritual condition which every Christian ought to
recognise in himself . . . (X, 21).

Particulars bear out this principle, the purity of the Christianity of the
men of Torcello. The brightness inside indicates their looking to religion
for comfort, not 'for threatenings and mysteries' (as do Romanists, is
the implication) (X, 26). The absence of worldly imagery shows their
freedom from earthly ambition. The raised seats for the clergy symbolize
their true and original function as 'bishops or *overseers* of the flock of
God' (X, 25). Being without decoration or comfort, the trappings of
power, these stone benches are 'sternly significative of an episcopal
authority which in the early days of the Church was never disputed . . .'
(X, 34). The prominence given to the episcopal throne is a reminder to

modern Protestants that 'in the minds of all early Christians the Church itself was most frequently symbolised under the image of a ship, of which the bishop was the pilot' (X, 34). The accumulated evidence identifies the men of Torcello, and hence the first Venetians, with the early Christians. By the end of the chapter Ruskin is able to make a yet more daring identification and from this draw far-reaching conclusions. For these men

> looked upon each other as the disciples did when the storm came down on the Tiberias Lake ... And if the stranger would yet learn in what spirit it was that the dominion of Venice was begun, and in what strength she went forth conquering and to conquer, let him not seek to estimate the wealth of her arsenals or number of her armies, nor look upon the pageantry of her palaces, nor enter into the secrets of her councils; but let him ascend the highest tier of the stern ledges that sweep round the altar of Torcello, and then, looking as the pilot did of old along the marble ribs of the goodly temple-ship, let him re-people its veined deck with the shadows of its dead mariners, and strive to feel in himself the strength of heart that was kindled within them, when first, after the pillars of it had settled in the sand, and the roof of it had been closed against the angry sky that was still reddened by the fires of their homesteads, — first, within the shelter of its knitted walls, amidst the murmur of the waste of waves and beating of the wings of the sea-birds round the rock that was strange to them, — rose that ancient hymn, in the power of their gathered voices:
>
> THE SEA IS HIS, AND HE MADE IT;
> AND HIS HANDS PREPARED THE DRY LAND (X, 34-5).

At such points Ruskin's command of rhetoric is such that one scarcely notices the manoeuvering of historical argument. Yet it is important, for on this argument depends his version of the Rise of Venice. Ruskin has ignored the island's secular buildings, a few of which still stood. His omission reinforces the suggestion that the founders of the city, like Ruskin himself, concentrated all their energies on a religious building. By means of the ship and sailor metaphor he emphasizes similarities between the religion of Torcello and early Christianity, and associates the construction of the island city, and hence the construction of Venice, with the foundation of the Church itself. Ruskin has telescoped the several centuries that passed between the flight from the mainland and the completion of the Cathedral, even to the point of suggesting that the roof was put on before the fugitives' original homes had finished burning. By closing this chronological gap, he compresses the time of exile and destitution and the time of empire and dominion into one historical concept. Whereas Byron stood upon the Bridge of Sighs and repeopled Venice with doges, senators, military leaders, prisoners and merchants, Ruskin stands behind the altar of a church and repeoples the city in microcosm with mariners, the heirs of the apostles themselves. He has demilitarized, decommercialized and desecularized the greatness of Venice.

Effie Ruskin did not experience Venice in the late 1840s and early 1850s as a 'heap of ruins'. In order that the reader of *Stones* shall do so, Ruskin has kept him away from contemporary Venetian life. For, as he admits at the beginning of the third chapter, 'Murano',

> In the centre of the city there are still places where some evidence of vitality remains, and where, with kind closing of the eyes to signs, too manifest even there, of distress and declining fortune, the stranger may succeed in imagining, for a little while, what must have been the aspect of Venice in her prime (X, 36).

Such blending of ancient and modern endangers the double vision of the core of Venice as at once heart of splendour and source of disease. Ruskin sends his traveller through a 'belt of ruin' on the north of Venice where the signs of death are obvious. One of the poorest parts of Venice, this was where Ruskin had observed the broken walls, rotting gondolas and putrid mud on his walks to the Fondamente Nuove in the winter of 1849-50. Opposite the quay is the cemetery built under the Napoleonic administration on the ruins of the church of San Cristoforo della Pace. Ruskin points out the paradox: 'the modern Venetians have replaced the Peace of the Christ-bearer by the Peace of Death . . .' (X, 37). Once out on the water the 'power of Nature' displaces the 'folly . . . the misery, of man'. The 'pure' clouds are orderly, 'rank beyond rank', the lagoon reflects 'the towers of cloud above', while the towers of distant villages are 'poised apparently in the air' (X, 38-9). Then harmony is broken by the cloud of smoke from the Murano glass furnaces, the man-made cloud being the reverse of the natural one. The village, from afar 'like so much jewellery', is ruinous when seen close at hand. Within Murano, things do not reflect each other, but conflict. The fishermen do not care for their fourteenth-century windows or Verona marble. The oaths of people selling fish and fruit defy the injunctions against swearing stencilled on the walls. The distinction between past life and present death then becomes slightly blurred, as poverty provokes more sympathy for living Venetians than is usually shown in *Stones*. We 'may not regret' the smoke from the furnaces, for it is 'one of the last signs left of human exertion'. The population of Murano has life 'more than is usual in Venice'. We see cottages, 'hardly knowing if there be more cheerfulness or melancholy in the way the sunshine glows on their ruinous but white washed walls' (X, 39-41). Ruskin seems to acknowledge some loss of orientation in describing the boat as 'seized by a strong green eddy'. We 'let ourselves drift', are

'whirled' into the right canal, and arrive 'somewhat giddy' at the
Cathedral of Saints Maria and Donato. Here confusion must be resolved.
The Cathedral is 'encumbered with modern buildings', 'utterly defaced';
only 'fragments' are 'precious' (X, 41-2). It is not important to the
argument of the book to separate the ancient from the less ancient, but
it is essential to distinguish between ancient and modern. So while
Ruskin has not cared to date the parts of the Cathedral of Torcello, he
takes trouble with that of Murano, assembling evidence to show that
'none of these truly ancient fragments can be assigned to a more recent
date than 1140' (X, 42-5). They therefore date from well before the
Fall.

Ruskin's description of the first series of fragments, the border of
marble triangles around the exterior of the apse (X, 49-58), is relaxed
and confident, as is all discussion, in *The Stones of Venice*, of decoration with abstract design or sculpture of natural subjects. But the
history of the Cathedral and the mosaics inside do present interpreta-
tive problems, for they involve matters of tradition and doctrine of a
distinctly Catholic nature. In 'Torcello' Ruskin had offered a pre-
Catholic version of Venetian Christianity, but had still had to apologize
to the 'Protestant beholder' for the great mosaic of the Madonna (X,
27). As a 'Protestant beholder' himself, Ruskin was having less
difficulty in appreciating such images than he perhaps ought. Embarrass-
ment seems to be indicated by the lengths he goes to both abuse and
excuse the stories associated with the Cathedral of Murano:

> The legends of the Romish Church, though generally more insipid and less varied
> than those of Paganism, deserve audience from us on this ground, if on no other,
> that they have once been sincerely believed by good men, and have had no
> ineffective agency in the formation of the existent European mind. The reader
> must not therefore accuse me of trifling . . . (X, 42).

Twenty years later the fact that something had been 'believed by good
men' would be the best possible reason for reverence, not a justification
for paying attention. Even here, however, it is clear that Ruskin is
attracted by the miracle which led to the founding of the church, the
tradition behind its particular feast and the tales of competitive acquisi-
tion and discovery of relics (X, 42-5). As he states in an appendix on
'Idolatory', he already did not 'like to hear Protestants speaking with
gross and uncharitable contempt even of the worship of relics . . .' (X,
452n.).

Elaborate preparations are made for admiration of the mosaic of the
Madonna. Ruskin first describes the scene inside the church on the day
before a feast. It is barely possible to make the figure out among the
panelled columns, stucco roses, cherubs, 'dirty hangings . . . dim pictures

on warped and wasting canvas; all vulgar, vain and foul . . .', or to pay attention amidst the shouting of 'the tribe of beggars who were assisting the sacristan with their wisdom respecting the festal arrangements' (X, 62-3). We are made to 'quit the church' and told that

> If we return to-morrow we shall find it filled with woful groups of aged men and women, wasted and fever-struck, fixed in paralytic supplication . . .
>
> We return, yet once again, on the following day. Worshippers and objects of worship, the sickly crowd and gilded angels, all are gone; and there, far in the apse, is seen the sad Madonna standing in her folded robe, lifting her hands in vanity of blessing. There is little else to draw away our thoughts from the solitary image (X, 64-5).

It is impossible, then, to see the Madonna in the context of contemporary worship. The effect is to dissociate her from modern Romanism. From here Ruskin can pass to energetic defence of the old religion:

> The whole edifice is, therefore, simply a temple to the Virgin: to her is ascribed the fact of Redemption, and to her its praise.
>
> 'And is this,' it will be asked of me, 'the time, is this the worship, to which you would have us look back with reverence and regret?' Inasmuch as redemption is ascribed to the Virgin, No. Inasmuch as redemption is a thing desired, believed, rejoiced in, Yes, — and Yes a thousand times . . . there is first the broad division of men into Spirit worshippers and Flesh worshippers; and then, of the Spirit worshippers, the farther division into Christian and Pagan, — worshippers in Falsehood or in Truth . . . Balance well the difference between those who worship and those who worship not; — that difference which there is . . . between the calculating, smiling, self-sustained, self-governed man, and the believing, weeping, wondering, struggling, Heaven-governed man . . . For that is indeed the difference which we shall find, in the end, between the builders of this day and the builders on that sand island long ago. They *did* honour something out of themselves; they did believe in spiritual presence . . . were content to pass away in nameless multitudes, so only that the labour of their hands might fix in the sea-wilderness a throne for their guardian angel (X, 66-8).

Uncharitable though Ruskin is, as yet, towards modern Catholics, a passage such as this does indicate growing independence of religious forms and institutions. Only two years before, in 1851, he had told Henry Acland that his own faith was held together only 'by the old Evangelical formulae'.[98] In *Notes on the Construction of Sheepfolds* 'Christ's truth' had been confined to the strongholds of Protestantism (XII, 558). Nothing here is precisely in conflict with this, for the old Madonna worshippers are still 'worshippers in Falsehood'. But the distinction between false and true is given less importance than the difference between Flesh and Spirit. Ruskin had conceived of this 'broad division' during the early spring of 1852. It may have helped him with a solution to religious crisis.[99] Later crises would lead him to redraw the divisions. Ruskin would then include among the faithful many of those modern Catholics who are here excluded, come to believe in a 'guardian angel' himself, and deny the right of many Protestants to call themselves Christians. Ruskin does not do this in 'Murano'. He leaves us with a contrast between two images of the Virgin, one a gaudily painted doll, the other the 'blue vision upon the inner dome' (X, 68). Both are symbols of Mariolatry, and do not call the Protestant reader to question. But there are signs that he may be criticized. Though Ruskin does not say who is the 'calculating, smiling, self-sustained man', one of 'those who worship not', he seems to have something in common with the imaginary reader who has smugly challenged the rightness of regret for the old Venetian religion.

Ruskin had taken care to prepare his stranger for his first sight of the city of Venice, of Torcello and Murano. The approach to St Mark's is the last and most orchestrated of his approach journeys. As usual attention is first to be given to some other object, in this case the English cathedral, the quasi-natural edifice in the midst of neat houses and shaven grass where the canon's children walk with their nurse-maids:

> Think for a little while of that scene, and the meaning of all its small formalisms, mixed with its serene sublimity. Estimate its secluded, continuous, drowsy felicities, and its evidence of the sense and steady performance of such kind of duties as can be regulated by the cathedral clock; and weigh the influence of those dark towers on all who have passed through the lonely square at their feet for centuries, and on all who have seen them rising far away over the wooded plain, or catching on their square masses the last rays of the sunset, when the city at their feet was indicated only by the mist at the bend of the river (X, 80).

What we are to think is not clear. Even if we did not know, from other sources, that Ruskin disliked the neatness of English houses, however old, and was so little attracted to English Gothic cathedrals that he had only studied one, and that without enthusiasm (see VIII, 6, 136), there would still be ambiguities. The serene but gloomy and somewhat threatening sublimity of the cathedral does not quite 'mix' with the small formalisms, and yet Ruskin says it does. The tranquil, tidy way of life suggested is, like that Ruskin attributed to Wendlebury in his letter to Brown of 1850, 'All right' (see pp. 81-2). If there is irony in such comment it is not made explicit or explored. In The Seven Lamps Ruskin had compared Salisbury unfavourably with Giotto's campanile, but thinking of them as specific buildings, and without local, social context (VIII, 188-9). Evaluation did not implicate a whole way of life.

Here the anonymous cathedral is a national monument, and to denigrate that, or suggest discontinuity between it and its surroundings, between ancient heritage and contemporary life, would have been to go further in criticism of England than Ruskin was at this stage prepared to go. The dangers of being misunderstood were many, as Ruskin knew. His father had reported that a reviewer in *Blackwood's Magazine* 'wonders what Religion you are'.[100] He himself had suspected him of supporting universal suffrage, and hinted that he was showing 'Byronish or Shelleyish' tendencies (see pp. 93, 99). More recently John James Ruskin had told him of a conversation with the Rev. Dr George Croly:

> Dr Croly was grandly eloquent . . . in denouncing you & me — He says you *abandon* the *finest Country in the World — live abroad* & *are literary* which three things or say two errors will make you an unhappy man for Life . . .[101]

Still uncertain about the evils of modern England, Ruskin sees those of modern Venice as glaringly obvious. So far he had presented the fallen state of the city under conditions of squalid decay, desolate ruin and picturesque discord.[102] In the centre it appears under the guise of raucous vitality. The Calle San Moisè is packed with people, noisy, turbulent, the buildings squashed together, the shops dark inside, the cheap furniture of Mariolatry jumbled up with the cheap goods for sale among them 'certain ambrosial morsels . . . too ambiguous to be defined or enumerated' (X, 81). The ambiguity of these morsels was John James Ruskin's contribution (see p. 101). If the description suggests jovial Latin disorderliness rather than disgust he must take some responsibility. The alley description as published is nevertheless a strong enough foil to what happens as the traveller enters the Square, when picturesque houses fall back and 'there rises a vision out of the earth' (X, 82). From the sublime through the picturesque Ruskin has come to the beautiful. The Gothic cathedral had 'rugged sculpture and confused arcades', the Calle San Moisè 'inextricable confusion of rugged shutters', but St Mark's offers 'confusion of delight' (X, 79, 80, 83). It is a 'treasure-heap' of infinitely various precious materials and subjects, but all its elements are deliberately and significantly organized, 'fantastic and involved', 'all twined together into an endless network', 'inter-woven', 'a continuous chain of language and of life' (X, 82-3). The English cathedral was worn down by rain, covered in lichen, its top is lost among the dark birds. In the alley a fig tree 'escapes' over a wall. In St Mark's art dominates, imitating nature both in the subject matter of its imagery and in the effects suggested. The sculptures are of leaves, fruits, blossoms and birds; shadow recedes across the marbles like the tide across sand, the crests of the arches break like spray.

But while the English cathedral is drastically altered by time and nature, life around it follows well regulated, unchanging patterns. It is the Venetian church that has 'stood unchanged for seven hundred years' but has no function whatever, for the people 'pass by it alike regardlessly' (X, 84). These miscellaneous 'lounging groups of English and Austrians', 'vendors of toys and caricatures', middle-class Venetians reading 'empty journals' in the cafés, unemployed workers 'basking in the sun like lizards', the cursing, gambling, snarling, sleeping children, 'every heavy glance of their young eyes full of desperation and stony depravity' are the figures Ruskin had described in his disturbed and hopeless letter to Brown, those who had led him to conclude that 'we are going *all wrong*' (X, 82, 84). They are at best idle, at worst miserable and revolutionary, a 'sullen crowd . . . which, if it had its will, would stiletto every soldier that pipes to it' (X, 84). They desire perpetual change, whether in the form of new waltzes, newspapers, or new governments. From above the scene 'the images of Christ and His angels look down upon it continually' (X, 85). To emphasize this difference between shifting present and the eternal truths of the past Ruskin takes us into the church by the quieter Baptistry door and points to the discrepancy between the message of the mosaics and the noise of the band outside: 'to be baptized with fire, or to be cast therein; it is the choice set before all men . . . Venice has made her choice' (X, 87-8).

It was relatively easy to apply the distinction between past and present to the irreligious crowd in the Piazza and the façade of the church, for the people ignore the building. It is more difficult to dispose of the worshippers inside. The reader cannot be sent away to return another day, as in the case of Murano, for St Mark's is always full, and of people praying earnestly. St Mark's has more 'effect on the minds of the people' than any other of the 'renowned shrines of Romanism'. To break the continuity between Byzantine and modern Catholicism, Ruskin declares the 'nobler characters of the building' not responsible for 'fostering a devotional spirit', here equated with 'super-stition' (X, 89-90). The people's fervour is due only to the 'stage properties' of music, dim lighting, incense and votive offerings (X, 90-1). Though also used in the past, these devices were

> not employed alone . . . the torchlight illumined Scripture histories on the walls, which every eye traced and every heart comprehended, but which, during my whole residence in Venice, I never saw one Venetian regard for an instant (X, 91).

Thus Ruskin alienates all modern Venetians from their church and is enabled to answer the question raised by the comparison between the English cathedral and St Mark's:

while, therefore, the English cathedral, though no longer dedicated to the kind of services for which it was intended by its builders, and much at variance in many of its characters with the temper of the people by whom it is now surrounded, retains yet so much of its religious influence that no prominent feature of its architecture can be said to exist altogether in vain, we have in St. Mark's a building apparently still employed in the ceremonies for which it was designed, and yet of which the impressive attributes have altogether ceased to be comprehended by its votaries. The beauty which it possesses is unfelt, the language it uses is forgotten; and in the midst of the city to whose service it has so long been consecrated, and still filled by crowds of the descendants of those to whom it owes its magnificence, it stands, in reality, more desolate than the ruins through which the sheep-walk passes unbroken in our English valleys; and the writing on its marble walls is less regarded and less powerful for the teaching of men, than the letters which the shepherd follows with his finger, where the moss is lightest on the tombs in the desecrated cloister (X, 91-2).

In allowing that the English building is 'at variance . . . with the temper of the people' Ruskin suggests perplexities about his own country. But, since he does not subject the English temper to the same scrutiny applied to Piazza San Marco, they remain vague. Paradox and Wordsworthian imagery cover uncertainty and bring England out of the comparison with credit.

The fact that English tourists would find in *The Stones of Venice* support for belief in British superiority was one of the reasons why Ruskin subsequently deplored its influence. For their refusal to register the criticisms of England the book also contains he would blame his readers. The distinction between modern and ancient worship left Ruskin free to discuss the colour and carving of St Mark's 'altogether without reference to its present usefulness . . .'[103] It was no part of his purpose to ignore its past usefulness, and discussion of this brings Ruskin close to criticism of his own national church. For the mosaics of St Mark's are clearly didactic, and raise the problem that had been troubling Ruskin for several years. He had 'never yet met with a Christian . . . perfect and right before God, who ever cared about art at all', for 'all truly great religious painters have been hearty Romanists' (X, 124, 125). Ruskin offers two explanations for this. The 'ordinary Protestant Christian mind', failing to perceive 'those deeper characters of it which are not Romanist, but Christian', turns to bad art produced by 'those who believed neither Catholicism nor Protestantism, but who read the Bible in search of the picturesque' (X, 126). This merely suggests that the beholder has been deceived by the artist, though does not explain why all artists since the Reformation have been irreligious. Ruskin's next point, however, is that the modern demand for perfection in art has led to the sacrifice of iconographic tradition and simple religious expression: 'Ever since the period of the Renaissance ... the truth has not been accredited; the painter of religious subject is no longer regarded as the narrator of a fact, but as the inventor of an idea' (X, 127). This comes close to saying that the modern (Protestant) Christian, infected by the (atheistic) Renaissance, does not himself believe that the events depicted by a painter of a Biblical subject actually took place. Evidently realizing this, Ruskin adds a note explaining that 'I do not mean that modern Christians believe less in the *facts* than ancient Christians . . .' In the Travellers' Edition of *Stones* he annotated this note: 'I ought to have meant it though, and very sternly.'

In 1853 Ruskin was more concerned to point out what St Mark's had in common with Protestantism. The mosaics of the Basilica are a pictorial representation of the Bible, and were therefore essential in the days before printing. Having read them as such Ruskin expects his traveller to

> look with some change of temper upon the gorgeous building and wild blazonry of that shrine of St. Mark's. He now perceives that it was in the hearts of the old Venetian people far more than a place of worship. It was at once a type of the Redeemed Church of God, and a scroll for the written word of God (X, 140).

With a greater appreciation of the true function of St Mark's will come stronger condemnation of the people in the square outside. Ruskin ends, as he had begun, with 'the long perspective of St. Mark's Place'. There men gathered from all over the world 'for traffic or for pleasure', while above them the church testified to heavenly riches and judgement to come:

> And when in her last hours she threw off all shame and all restraint, and the great square . . . became filled with the madness of the whole earth, be it remembered how much her sin was greater, because it was done in the face of the House of God, burning with the letters of His Law. Mountebank and masquer laughed their laugh, and went their way; and a silence has followed them, not unforetold; for amidst them all, through century after century of gathering vanity and festering guilt, that white dome of St. Mark's had uttered in the dead ear of Venice, 'Know thou, that for all these things God will bring thee into judgment' (X, 141-2).

Ruskin knew that St Mark's had been 'built upon various models and at various periods' (X, 143). This he states at the beginning of his fifth chapter 'Byzantine Palaces'. He also, of course, knew of recent alterations. But in *The Stones of Venice* Ruskin makes the Basilica witness against the present by having 'stood unchanged for seven hundred years'. A Byzantine palace partly used as a tobacco deposit testifies to the same effect but in another way. The Fondaco dei Turchi

> is a ghastly ruin; whatever is venerable or sad in its wreck being disguised by attempts to put it to present uses of the basest kind. It has been composed of arcades borne by marble shafts, and walls of brick faced with marble: but the covering stones have been torn away from it like the shroud from a corpse; and its walls, rent into a thousand chasms, are filled and refilled with fresh brick-work, and the seams and hollows are choked with clay and whitewash, oozing and trickling over the marble, — itself blanched into dusty decay by the frosts of centuries. Soft grass and wandering leafage have rooted themselves in the rents, but they are not suffered to grow in their own wild and gentle way, for the place is in a sort inhabited; rotten partitions are nailed across its corridors, and miserable rooms contrived in its western wing; and here and there the weeds are indolently torn down, leaving their haggard fibres to struggle again into unwhole-some growth when the spring next stirs them: and thus, in contest between death and life, the unsightly heap is festering to its fall (X, 145).

A photograph of the building before its restoration in the 1860s con-firms the state of decay. Yet others could still see the Fondaco dei Turchi as 'a picturesque ruin' (X, 144n.). Ruskin's insistence on the horror of its condition shows how far he had come, since the early 1840s, in criticizing that point of view. It also illustrates the warning he had given his readers at the beginning of this volume, that to be charmed by dilapidation makes one blind to the fragments. Although Ruskin's hostility to modern Venice sometimes leads him to adopt narrow arguments, it also involved the sacrifice of easier pleasures and was a condition of growing perceptiveness.

Even in their desolation, the Byzantine palaces of the Grand Canal seem remote from the abandoned city of Torcello. Ruskin reminds us of the link with sorrowing Christianity on which his interpretation of Venetian beauty depends:

> Such, then, was that first and fairest Venice which rose out of the barrenness of the lagoon, and the sorrow of her people; a city of graceful arcades and gleaming walls, veined with azure and warm with gold, and fretted with white sculpture like frost upon forest branches turned to marble. And yet, in this beauty of her youth, she was no city of thoughtless pleasure. There was still a sadness of heart upon her, and a depth of devotion, in which lay all her strength (X, 171).

For this sadness Ruskin gives Biblical authority. The disks of green serpentine and purple porphyry on the façades of these palaces are like the shields which, according to Ezekiel, the men of Tyre hung on the city walls.[104] Other Old Testament texts confirm that 'love of bright and pure colour' shows the 'seriousness of the early Venetian mind' (X, 172). This was the gift Byzantine Venice passed on to her sixteenth-century painters (X, 172, 175-6). In speaking of Titian and Tintoretto, Ruskin temporarily gives up the role of prophet delivering sentence of deserved doom on the city and mourns her loss:

> I do not wonder at what men Suffer, but I wonder often at what they Lose. We may see how good rises out of pain and evil; but the dead, naked, eyeless loss, what good comes of that? . . . stranger than all, the whole majesty of humanity raised to its fulness, and every gift and power necessary for a given purpose, at a given moment, centred in one man, and all this perfected blessing permitted to be refused, perverted, crushed, cast aside by those who need it most . . . these are the heaviest mysteries of this strange world, and, it seems to me, those which mark its curse the most. And it is true that the power with which this Venice had been entrusted was perverted, when at its highest, in a thousand miserable ways: still, it was possessed by her alone . . . (X, 177-8).

It was in such a mood that Ruskin, early in 1852, wrote to his father of coming to see 'mistake' rather than sin, as the cause of misery.[105] In the letter he had compared himself to Shakespeare in this respect. In the book it is 'That mighty Landscape . . . that mighty Humanity . . . the great Manhood . . . that mighty Mythology' of Tintoretto that brings Ruskin to take a less censorious view of the Fall of Venice (X, 178-9).

It is not clear how much of *The Stones of Venice* Ruskin wrote on the spot, but in the correspondence of the winter of 1851-52 there is no mention of a general chapter on Gothic being sent home for editing. Ruskin was certainly thinking of the difficulty of defining the style while in Venice, but it seems likely that much of Chapter VI, 'The Nature of Gothic', was written after his return to London. The characteristics of Gothic are classified as 'savageness', 'changefulness', 'naturalism', 'grotesqueness', 'rigidity' and 'redundance'. As one critic has pointed out, they are 'more relevant to the Gothic of the north than to that of Italy'.[106] Elsewhere in the book Ruskin locates Venice in the middle of a bare, hostile expanse, and gives her inhabitants the heroic virtues needed to overcome adversity. In 'The Nature of Gothic' he describes the whole southern part of Europe in terms of heat, brilliance, ease and fertility (X, 186). It is in the north that we find the

> out-speaking of the strong spirit of men who may not gather redundant fruitage from the earth, nor bask in dreamy benignity of sunshine, but must break the rock for bread, and cleave the forest for fire . . . (X, 188).

If Ruskin does not say where Venice is in his verbal map of the continent it is because he is not concerned with her here. He does go some way towards passing the same kind of judgement on England that he has passed on Venice. The southern city betrayed her own peculiar inheritance, colour, seriousness, pure faith. The servility England now imposes on her labour force betrays the Gothic virtues and feudal responsibilities. But the analogy is not precise. However strongly Ruskin condemns English manufactures, building and conditions of work, he proposes no English equivalent of the Fall. Whereas in Venice the difference between one piece of sculpture and another indicates the moral collapse of society, in England this is not necessarily the case. The instinct 'which makes us desire that our house windows should pair like our carriage horses' negates the Gothic 'changefulness'. Yet Ruskin

would not impeach love of order: it is one of the most useful elements of the English mind; it helps us in our commerce and in all purely practical matters; and it is . . . one of the foundation stones of morality. Only do not let us suppose that love of order is love of art (X, 205).

In his discussion of 'rigidity' Ruskin speaks of

the moral habits to which England in this age owes the kind of greatness that she has, — the habits of philosophical investigation, of accurate thought, of domestic seclusion and independence, of stern self-reliance and sincere upright searching into religious truth . . . (X, 242-3).

In Ruskin's later writings commerce and 'purely practical matters' would not appear in a category separate from that of art. 'England in this age' would then be allowed no 'kind of greatness' and no praise accorded to such progressive 'moral habits' as those mentioned here.

Ruskin never meant his definition of Gothic to represent a model to be imitated. In his ideal residence, the Venetian Gothic palace, the rough essences of Gothicness are modified almost out of existence. It is so gracefully decorated that some reminder is needed of the fact that

these refined and richly ornamented forms were used in the habitations of a nation as laborious, as practical, as brave, and as prudent as ourselves; and they were built at a time when that nation was struggling with calamities and changes threatening its existence almost every hour (X, 311).

The heroic, Anglo-Saxon virtues of Venice do not find direct expression in this architecture, but her Christian faith does. The religious symbol over the main doorway of every palace is a public confession of belief.

Comparing this openness with Anglican reticence, Ruskin goes further in criticism of his own church than he had so far:

> It seems to be only modern Protestantism which is entirely ashamed of *all* symbols and words that appear in anywise like a confession of faith ... let us look to it, whether that strong reluctance to utter a definite religious profession, which ... we conclude to be modesty, or fear of hypocrisy, or other such form of amiableness, be not, in very deed, neither less nor more than Infidelity; whether Peter's 'I know not the man' be not the sum and substance of all these misgivings and hesitations ... (X, 325).

Other direct comparisons between ancient Venice and modern England arise out of Ruskin's examination of 'the building which at once consummates and embodies the entire system of the Gothic architecture of Venice, — the DUCAL PALACE' (X, 327). Ruskin had made enormous claims for this building both as 'the central building of the world' (IX, 38) and as the centre of his book. In a letter of 26 April 1852 he told his father:

> The fact is the whole book will be a kind of great 'moral of the Ducal palace of Venice,' and all its minor information will concentrate itself on the Ducal palace and its meaning ... And so I shall give many a scattered description of a moulding here and an arch there — but they will all be mere notes to the account of the Rise and fall of the Ducal palace, and that account itself will be subservient to the showing of the causes and consequences of the rise and fall of Art in Europe.[107]

To describe the rest of *The Stones of Venice* as 'mere notes' to this last chapter seems disproportionate. Byzantine church building had usurped some of the attention Ruskin had thought to concentrate on secular Gothic when he had begun the book, and as the centre of Venice St Mark's rivals the Ducal Palace. But it is probably true that of all Venetian buildings the Palace was the one for which he had most lasting affection and which was the most constant and interesting source of moral teaching.

Because the dating of the Fall of Venice depends on the chronology of the Ducal Palace, Ruskin sets out the stages in its history at length, making unusual use of written evidence. Much of it came from chronicles and decrees in the St Mark's Library, then housed in the council chambers of the Palace. In making use of these Ruskin was helped by Brown's friend Giambattista Lorenzi, an ex-Arsenal worker, now sub-librarian. Lorenzi had a special interest in these documents, and Ruskin thought them in themselves 'singularly illustrative of the Venetian character' (X, 329). The wording of one, for instance, showed that 'piety towards God, and justice towards man, have been at least the nominal purpose of every act and institution of ancient Venice' (X, 337n.).

That the Venetian state had in fact been founded on piety and justice would be shown by a reading of the sculptures. This is possible because the chronicles show that 'The history of the Ducal Palace . . . begins with the birth of Venice', that is the establishment of a seat of government on the island of Rialto. Political and architectural history also coincide in that in 1301, four years after the closing of the Grand Council, work was begun on a new council chamber, the first addition in a Gothic style. Thus, 'as the Byzantine Palace was, in its foundation, coeval with that of the state, so the Gothic Palace was, in its foundation, coeval with that of the aristocratic power' (X, 340). Ruskin approves of both, interpreting the absence of rebellion against the formalization of oligarchy as 'an expression, by the people, of respect for the families which had been chiefly instrumental in raising the commonwealth to such a height of prosperity'. Other than to emphasize that the first Venetians were exiles, Ruskin had so far offered no pre-Fall version of the secular side of ancient Venice. In this notion of responsible despotism he gives the outlines of a political ideal to be offered in exchange for the 'Byronic ideal'. Ruskin draws attention to the prisons, a 'range of apartments . . . comfortable rooms with good flat roofs of larch, and carefully ventilated', in order to 'clear the government of the accusations so constantly made against them, by ignorant or partial historians, of wanton cruelty to prisoners' (X, 342). But 'the energy of aristocratic power, and of the Gothic style' work in harmony for only a brief period. In 1423 begins the demolition of the surviving façade of the Byzantine palace:

> That hammer stroke was the first act of the period properly called the 'Renaissance.' It was the knell of the architecture of Venice, — and of Venice herself . . . A thousand palaces might be built upon her burdened islands, but none of them could take the place, or recall the memory, of that which was first built upon her unfrequented shore. It fell; and, as if it had been the talisman of her fortunes, the city never flourished again (X, 352).

The Renaissance, then, cuts the nation's links with her ancestral virtues, though it is not explained what is meant by 'the city never flourished again'.

One may suspect Ruskin's general statements about Venetian political history. But in reading the kind of evidence with which he was most at ease he is scrupulous and convincing. The largest part of Ruskin's account of the Ducal Palace is taken up with

1 *Venezia Coronata per l'erezione del gran Ponte sopra la Laguna il giorno 11 Gennaio 1846* (The Coronation of Venice by the erection of the Great Bridge across the Lagoon, 11 January 1846), lithograph by G. Kirchmayer (Museo Correr, Venice). The date is that of the formal opening of the bridge; it was already complete when Ruskin arrived in Venice on his third visit in 1845.

2 Danieli's Hotel, ex-Palazzo Dandolo, by unknown photographer (Conway Library, Courtauld Institute, London), probably mid nineteenth century. The photograph shows the façade painted to look like marble as described by Ruskin in a letter to his father of 10 September 1845. Ruskin stayed at Danieli's in 1835, 1841, 1849-50 and 1872.

3 Fondamenta del Battello, Cannaregio, photograph by C. Naya (Ditta Oswaldo Böhm, Venice), probably mid nineteenth century. Ruskin describes conditions in such areas of the city in letters and diary entries of the winter 1849-50 and in the third chapter of *Stones* II.

4 St Mark's Square with the military band and Austrian and Hungarian troops, by unknown photographer (Museo Correr, Venice), c. 1860. Both Ruskin's father and his wife enjoyed this daily feature of life in Venice under Austrian occupation. Ruskin himself comments on the suppressed tension in such a scene in his letter to W.L. Brown of 8 January 1850, and uses it for ironic contrast in his description of St Mark's in the fourth chapter of *Stones* II.

5 The Church of San Girolamo, Cannareggio, drawing by Giovanni Pividor (Museo Correr, Venice). Deconsecrated under the Napoleonic administration, San Girolamo was converted into a stream flour mill by Federico Oexle in 1842. Without mentioning it by name, Ruskin uses it as an example of improvised industrialisation in his letter of 8 January 1850, and the smoke from its steeple/chimney is the chief element in the traveller's first sight of Venice at the end of *Stones* I.

6 South-west corner of the Ducal Palace, by unknown photographer (Conway
Library, Courtauld Institute, London), second half of the nineteenth century.
This corner of the Palace was the headquarters of the Austrian corps of guards.
The cannons, whose function was to control events in St Mark's Square, made
Ruskin 'very angry' every time he passed them, he told his father in a letter of
16 November 1851.

7 Drawing of lottery tickets, St Mark's Square, photograph by C. Naya (Ditta Oswaldo Böhm, Venice), late nineteenth century. Ruskin describes the event in his letter to Samuel Rogers of 23 June 1852, condemning the government-run lottery as a covert and immoral form of taxation.

8 Torcello, photograph by C. Naya (Ditta Oswaldo Böhm), late nineteenth century. In the second chapter of *Stones* II Ruskin alludes to the old town square as virtually a farmyard. Restoration work, begun in 1906, has since altered the appearance of the bell-tower, Cathedral and Santa Fosca.

9 The Fondaco dei Turchi, photograph by C. Naya (Ditta Oswaldo Böhm), early 1860s. In the fifth chapter of *Stones* II Ruskin describes this 'ghastly ruin', in part inhabited, in part used as a tobacco deposit. Tobacco was a state monopoly — hence the Hapsburg eagle hanging from the centre arch.

10 The Fondaco dei Turchi, photograph by C. Naya (Ditta Oswaldo Böhm), after its restoration by Federico Berchet for the Municipality in the 1860s. During the latter part of the century it housed the Correr Museum.

11 The first Academy bridge, photograph by Muster (Ditta Oswaldo Böhm), probably early twentieth century. This bridge, built by the Fonderia Neville in 1854, was replaced by the present wooden structure in 1932. The reader of the *Guide to . . . the Academy* is instructed to remove this bridge by means of 'charity of imagination'.

the course of divinity and of natural history embodied by the old sculptor in the great series of capitals which support the lower arcade of the palace; and which, being at a height of little more than eight feet above the eye, might be read, like the pages of a book, by those (the noblest men in Venice) who habitually walked beneath the shadow of this great arcade at the time of their first meeting each other for morning converse.[108]

For their iconography these fourteenth-century capitals on the sea side of the Palace are compared with Dante, Giotto and Spenser, for their art and meaning with the fifteenth-century imitations on the Piazzetta side. The latter almost always lack sternness and subtlety, or omit some essential Christian symbol. The faces of the children carved on the fourth of the earlier series are

> full of youthful life, playful, humane, affectionate, beaming with sensation and vivacity, but with much manliness and firmness also, not a little cunning, and some cruelty perhaps, beneath all; the features small and hard, and the eyes keen. There is the making of rough and great men in them. But the children of the fifteenth century are dull smooth-faced dunces, without a single meaning line in the fatness of their stolid cheeks; and, although, in the vulgar sense, as handsome as the other children are ugly, capable of becoming nothing but perfumed coxcombs (X, 388).

Ruskin's evaluations of Venetian Renaissance character are not uniform. He condemns the Solomon angle in comparison to the Adam and Eve and Noah angles because it expresses the Renaissance spirit of 'firm confidence in its own wisdom' (X, 359). Yet Ruskin shows confidence in that wisdom. The capital beneath the Solomon sculpture shows justice personified and seven 'acts of justice or good government, or figures of lawgivers':

> It is the assertion by that government of its belief that Justice only could be the foundation of its stability, as these stones of Justice and Judgment are the foundation of its halls of council. And this profession of their faith may be interpreted in two ways. Most modern historians would call it, in common with the continual reference to the principles of justice in the political and judicial language of the period, nothing more than a cloak for consummate violence and guilt; and it may easily be proved to have been so in myriads of instances. But in the main, I believe the expression of feeling to be genuine. I do not believe, of the majority of the leading Venetians of this period whose portraits have come down to us, that they were deliberately and everlastingly hypocrites. I see no hypocrisy in their countenances. Much capacity of it, much subtlety, much natural and acquired reserve; but no meanness. On the contrary, infinite grandeur, repose, courage and the peculiar unity and tranquillity of expression which come of sincerity or *wholeness* of heart ... (X, 427-8).

Over the next twenty years Ruskin would grow in confidence in the mode of interpretation for which he shows preference here. But in *The Stones of Venice* he is attempting to show correspondence between the ideal and the practical, and therefore makes efforts to explain the evidence offered by 'Most modern historians'. Ruskin claims that if these leading Venetians failed to apply the principles of justice it was the fault of the 'Romish Church'. Rather than accept that secret trials were 'a confession of sinister intentions', he asks whether it was not 'the result of an endeavour to do justice in an age of violence? — the only means by which Law could establish its footing in the midst of feudalism'. The view of feudalism implicit here is relatively 'enlightened', and severity is not presented as a general principle but as a necessary expedient. Ruskin does, however, make an extreme suggestion about its relevance to the nineteenth century. Thinking of the tenants' rights movement in Ireland and episodes of violence against landlords, he asks whether Irish juries might not 'justifiably desire to conduct their proceedings with some greater approximation to the judicial principles of the Council of Ten?' The question recalls a remark in John James Ruskin's paper of 1839 on Catholic Emancipation, a paper reprinted in the fifth appendix to *Stones* I. It was John James's view that a 'stern republic' was necessary to deal with a Catholic population, though the 'mild sway of constitutional monarchy' might be adequate for a Protestant people (IX, 424). Ruskin, meanwhile, was speculating about educational principles effectable only by a government with 'an authority over the people of which we now do not so much as dream' (XI, 263). The old Venetian republic offered elements for a definition of such an authority.

In the capitals of the Ducal Palace Ruskin had found images of civic justice equivalent to the promise of heavenly justice represented by St Mark's. His closing panegyric to the Ducal Palace is not addressed to the ideas it embodies, but to the Renaissance paintings its great rooms contain. These pictures

made their walls as precious as so many kingdoms; so precious, indeed, and so full of majesty, that sometimes when walking at evening on the Lido, whence the great chain of the Alps, crested with silver clouds, might be seen rising above the front of the Ducal Palace, I used to feel as much awe in gazing on the building as on the hills, and could believe that God had done a greater work in breathing into the narrowness of dust the mighty spirits by whom its haughty walls had been raised, and its burning legends written, than in lifting the rocks of granite higher than the clouds of heaven, and veiling them with their various mantle of purple flower and shadowy pine (X, 438-9).

It is a comparison with nature implying both opposition and analogy between the mountains and the building Ruskin loved best.

In March 1851 Effie Ruskin had written to Lady Trevelyan of the forthcoming pamphlet, *Notes on the Construction of Sheepfolds* predicting that 'you will not like it'.[109] Lady Trevelyan, whose sympathies were Puseyite, indeed thought that Ruskin might have kept his 'quarrel with the Pope' to himself,[110] but they remained friends nevertheless. By September 1853 Ruskin was able to write to her expressing different expectations:

> I am heartily glad you like the second volume of Stones: I am nearly sure you will be pleased with the third — which is more general in its subjects — & perhaps Cardinal Wiseman will like it too — as there is plenty of abuse of the reformation in it . . .[111]

The third volume, *The Fall*, appeared that autumn. It was certainly 'more general in its subjects', for it traces the vast 'change in the European mind' which has led from the gorgeous architecture of the Middle Ages to the mean buildings of nineteenth-century London (XI, 4). The Renaissance, the chief conductor of that change, is examined for its 'abstract *nature*', rather than as a Venetian historical phenomenon (XI, 90-114). Venice is a rich source of examples, such as the series of tombs which illustrate the growth of 'pride of life', one of the main characteristics of the Renaissance (XI, 5). At the end of each chapter Ruskin returns to Venice to lament progressive moral collapse. But compared to *The Sea-Stories, The Fall* is less concerned with the city as a unit, and more with the condition of Europe with special reference to England.

It is here that 'abuse of the reformation' comes in. In Chapter II, 'Roman Renaissance', Ruskin traces the consequences of the corruption of Catholicism in reaction to which came the separation from the Church of two forces, 'one tending to Reformation, the other to Infidelity' (XI, 121-2). The latter stands aside while the struggle between Protestantism and Romanism proceeds, a struggle equally damaging to both. Protestants lost all 'beloved custom and believed tradition', nurtured 'habits of disbelief, the self-trusting, rashly-reasoning spirit' which led to sectarianism, the English Revolution and the killing of the king (XI, 123, 126-7). Faith is weakened, becomes vulnerable to the onslaught of revived pagan culture and 'Paganism again became, in effect, the religion of Europe' (XI, 132). And since in nineteenth-century England, 'the Pagans are nominally and fashionably Christians', they undermine the efforts of the 'small body' of true Christians, even to the point of triumph in the institutions of education (XI, 132-3). Here Ruskin comes near to equating the condition of modern

Protestantism with that of modern Romanism, and the state of England with that of Venice. But in the end he does not do so:

> I believe that in a few years more we shall wake from all these errors in astonishment, as from evil dreams; having been preserved, in the midst of their madness, by those hidden roots of active and earnest Christianity which God's grace has bound in the English nation with iron and brass. But in the Venetian those roots themselves had withered; and, from the palace of their ancient religion, their pride cast them forth hopelessly to the pasture of the brute. From pride to infidelity, from infidelity to the unscrupulous and insatiable pursuit of pleasure, and from this to irremediable degradation, the transitions were swift, like the falling of a star (XI, 133-4).

Of this 'insatiable pursuit of pleasure' Ruskin had given little illustration. In Chapter III, 'Grotesque Renaissance', he sends his reader to the Church of Santa Maria Formosa. On the base of the bell-tower is 'A head, − huge, inhuman, and monstrous, − leering in bestial degradation, too foul to be either pictured or described, or to be beheld for more than an instant . . .' (XI, 145). This image of lust is all the worse because it defiles a place where an ideal concept of marriage was celebrated. Up until the middle of the tenth century it had been the custom to have 'but one marriage day for the nobles of the whole nation':

> Imagine the strong bond of brotherhood thus sanctified among them, and consider also the effect on the minds of the youth of the state; the greater deliberation and openness necessarily given to the contemplation of marriage, to which all the people were solemnly to bear testimony; the more lofty and unselfish tone which it would give to all their thoughts. It was the exact contrary of stolen marriage. It was marriage to which God and man were taken for witnesses, and every eye was invoked for its glance, and every tongue for its prayers (XI, 139).

Although this usage was abandoned after the abduction of the brides by pirates in 943, betrothal continued to be a matter for public congratulation, and the rescue of the brides remembered yearly in the Festa delle Marie. This festival culminated at the Church of Santa Maria Formosa on 2 February, the feast of the Purification of the Virgin and the anniversary of the 'one marriage day'. The date was already of special significance to Ruskin, for it was his parents' wedding day. In 1866, thirteen years after the publication of *Stones* III, he was to propose to Rose La Touche on that day, and keep it as a festival ever afterwards.

Effie Ruskin, on the other hand, was to make a choice not dissimilar to that of 'stolen marriage'. Six months after the appearance of *The Fall* she left her husband, instituted proceedings for annulment, and married the pre-Raphaelite painter John Everett Millais. Ruskin had ignored his wife during their time in Venice, and was personally indifferent to her social pleasures. But Effie does have some connection with *The Stones of Venice* in that the Fall is associated with gathering for the purposes of enjoyment and, in its last stage, with the gathering of foreigners. In 'Grotesque Renaissance' it is Doge Foscari who, in 1423, sows the 'seeds of death' by beginning his reign with a year of feasting (XI, 195). Long after that date, however, Ruskin sees in the Venetian character 'an intense earnestness both in their pursuit of commercial and political successes, and in their devotion to religion . . .' (XI, 193). Signs of this he finds in sixteenth-century ambassadors' dispatches shown to him by Rawdon Brown, and in Venetian portraits. For while in the rest of Italy painters idealized their subjects, the Venetian artist was himself 'in some degree frivolous or sensual', but was forced to 'rise to unapproachable sublimity when his subject is a member of the Forty, or a Master of the Mint' (XI, 194). Seriousness survives 'up to the close of the seventeenth century'. Only then does Venice succumb to utter dissipation:

> as once the powers of Europe stood before her judgement seat, to receive the decisions of her justice, so now the youth of Europe assembled in the halls of her luxury, to learn from her the arts of delight (XI, 195).

Ruskin probably had in mind such travellers as Lady Mary Wortley Montagu, whose letters he had read shortly before coming to Venice in 1849, and the young Grand Tourist of the *Dunciad*, for the works of Pope had been his evening reading in Venice in the winter of 1851-52.[112] That the city still functioned as a place of amusement for visitors from many parts of Europe Ruskin knew from observation of his wife and his friends, the representatives of the Hapsburg Empire and its allies.

Because of the two winters in Venice, the 'sketch of Venetian art' first projected had grown into a work of such scope that Ruskin experienced 'something burdensome in the vast breadth of the subject'.[113] It is hardly surprising that in tackling such a subject he should at times show uncertainty. This is perhaps most evident in the fourth and last chapter of *The Fall*, the 'Conclusion' in which Ruskin draws the moral for England. For having shown that since the seventeenth century 'no resuscitation has taken place, nor does any for the present appear possible', Ruskin exempts modern England from that judgement:

> That modern science, with all its additions to the comforts of life, and to the fields of rational contemplation, has placed the existing races of mankind on a higher platform than any that preceded them, none can doubt for an instant;

and I believe the position in which we find ourselves is somewhat analogous to that of thoughtful and laborious youth succeeding a restless and heedless infancy. Not long ago, it was said to me by one of the masters of modern science: 'When men invented the locomotive, the child was learning to go; when they invented the telegraph, it was learning to speak.' He looked forward to the manhood of mankind as assuredly the nobler in proportion to the slowness of its development. What might not be expected from the prime and middle strength of the order of existence whose infancy had lasted six thousand years? And indeed, I think this the truest, as well as the most cheering, view that we can take of the world's history (XI, 196-7).

The optimism is not out of character. But Ruskin's acceptance of scientific and industrial innovation as grounds for hope in the future is at odds with the main tendency of the book, which is to look to the past. It is certainly at odds with his writings after 1860, when what was a tendency in this book became a general principle.

The Stones of Venice was to be received in ways that did not gratify this older Ruskin. In the Preface to the 'New Edition' of 1874 he lamented the fact that it had promoted the imitation of Venetian Gothic while its 'best teaching' had been ignored. Reluctant to republish the book, Ruskin wrote in a draft of this Preface that he was now doing so 'merely for my own gain' (IX, 13n.). Though this rudeness to his readers did not appear in the published version, he took the opportunity to attack them in the Travellers' Edition, issued under his own control in 1879-81. In 'Castel-franco', the strange Epilogue to this edition, Ruskin describes travellers to Venice as part of the crowd in St Mark's Square, not surveying from a distance. They read *The Stones of Venice*,

helped always through the tedium of the business by due quantity of ices at Florian's, music by moonlight on the Grand Canal, paper lamps, and the English papers and magazines at M. Ongania's, with such illumination as those New Lamps contain — Lunar or Gaseous, enabling pursy Britannia to compare, at her ease, her own culminating and co-operate Prosperity and Virtue with the past wickedness and present out-of-pocketness of the umquhile Queen of the Sea (XI, 231-2).

The English are now considered 'a people set wholly on the pursuit of the same pleasures which ruined Venice, only in ways as witless as hers were witty'. Even so, Ruskin felt some further explanation was needed for their having praised the style of the book while

nobody praised the substance, which indeed they never took the trouble to get at; but, occasionally tasing its roughness here and there, as of a bitter almond put by mistake into a sugarplum, spat it out, and said, 'What a pity it got in.'

If *The Stones of Venice* was read in this way it is perhaps because the 'roughness', criticism of modern England, does occur 'here and there', and it is not clear what 'pursy Britannia' has in common with the corruption and misery of Venice. Such extreme degradation as that of the 'madness of the whole earth' in St Mark's Square or the 'ghastly ruin' of the Fondaco dei Turchi might seem all too easy to avoid. But what had not been learned from the warning of a Venice in decay, Ruskin hoped might yet be understood from the teachings of her virtuous time. He closes 'Castel-franco' with a description of the divinely-inspired election of a Doge, used in *St Mark's Rest* (XXIV, 271-2), the oath of the Confraternity of St Theodore from *Fors Clavigera* 71 (XXIX, 64), and the vision of a 'golden city' offered in the final volume of *Modern Painters* (XI, 242-5).

Such lessons, however, belong to another phase in Ruskin's Venetian work and in Ruskin's life as a whole. He had first visited Venice, in 1835, as an adolescent. When he completed *The Stones of Venice*, in 1853, he was still only 34. The book was written out of the varied experiences of six journeys to Venice spread over seventeen years of Ruskin's youth and early maturity. Another seventeen years were to pass before he visited the city again. When he did so, in 1869, he was aged 50. In the interval Ruskin came to think of himself as an old man.

III   The Ideal of Venice

III.1 1869

At five o'clock on the afternoon of 9 May 1869 Rawdon Brown was to be at Venice station to meet Ruskin off the train from Verona. That morning Ruskin looked back on his long absence from Venice and wrote 'I don't know how the seventeen years have passed.'[1]

They had begun with a household upheaval. Effie's leaving Ruskin in 1854, the charge of impotence on which divorce proceedings were based, her remarriage in 1855, caused scandal. Mutual friends divided on the issue, but this was not of Ruskin's choice. He certainly did not allow it to interrupt his work. In 1856 *Modern Painters* III and IV appeared. They were deliberately looser in structure than anything Ruskin had written previously, and ironic in tone. These two volumes represent only a small portion of Ruskin's production during the 1850s. He wrote for the Arundel Society (*Giotto and his Works in Padua*, 1853-54, 1860), taught at the Working Men's College in Red Lion Square (from 1854), drew up drawing manuals (*The Elements of Drawing*, 1857; *The Elements of Perspective*, 1859), helped with plans for the Oxford Museum of Natural History building (from 1856), arranged the drawings in the Turner Bequest for the National Gallery (1857-58), tried to guide the work of individual artists (Rossetti, John Inchbold, J.W. Brett), gave evidence before parliamentary committees (National Gallery, 1857; Public Institutions, 1860) and lectured to associations, art schools and public meetings throughout Britain. Not all of these addresses were published at the time, but those that were filled three volumes; *Lectures on Architecture and Painting* (1854), *The Political Economy of Art* (1857) and *The Two Paths* (1859). Annually from 1855 to 1859 Ruskin wrote *Notes on the Royal Academy* criticizing the latest exhibition. These guides, like the other work of this decade, were part of an attempt to influence public taste directly, to intervene in the production and distribution of a national art. The publication of the fifth and last volume of *Modern Painters* in 1860 marks the end of that attempt and the beginning of Ruskin's attack on English capitalism.

Ruskin went abroad twice during this period, but avoided Venice. It took him a long time to recover from the work for *Stones*. In 1857

Charles Eliot Norton, the Harvard academic who had lately become
Ruskin's friend, was touring Italy. Ruskin wrote to him in praise of
Verona, with abuse of Rome and of Venice with mixed feelings:

> I went through so much hard, dry, mechanical toil there, that I quite lost,
> before I left it, the charm of the place. Analysis is an abominable business . . . I
> have got all the right feeling back now, however; and hope to write a word or
> two about Venice yet, when I have got the mouldings well out of my head —
> and the mud. For the fact is, with reverence be it spoken, that whereas Rogers
> says: 'There is a glorious city in the Sea,' a truthful person must say, 'There is a
> glorious city in the Mud.' It is startling at first to say so, but it goes well enough
> with marble, 'Oh Queen of Marble and of Mud.'[2]

It seems that Ruskin needed to eliminate the experience of those two
long winters in order to be able to 'write a word or two about Venice
yet'. Inspiration could be found in Venetian painting elsewhere. In the
Louvre in 1849 Ruskin had found in Veronese a 'conception of
humanity' as sublime as, and more gorgeous than, that of Tintoretto.[3]
Leaving the Alps for Paris in 1854 he spoke of it as his habit to 'go
straight to Paul Veronese — if I can — after Chamouni'.[4] In 1858
Ruskin again travelled in Switzerland, and after to Turin to work in the
Galleries. This time he was led to compare Veronese's power not with
the mountains that represented the supreme art of God, but with a
bigoted sermon by a Waldensian preacher, and other representatives of
'Protestantism clumsily triumphant'.[5] The use made of Venice in
Modern Painters V reflects this experience and the fact that 1860 was a
turning point. Venetian painting is used to illustrate a kind of mind
'wholly realist, universal, and manly'(VII, 296). And though the worldly,
human concerns of these artists kept them from landscape, Ruskin was
not sure that this was to be regretted. Turner goes to nature as a refuge
from an infernal, industrial England which is the 'furnace of the world
. . . a field of fierce volcanoes' (VII, 425). In the chapter 'The Two
Boyhoods' Ruskin describes the ideal City, the Venice of Giorgione's
youth:

> A city of marble did I say? nay, rather a golden city, paved with emerald. For
> truly, every pinnacle and turret glanced or glowed, overlaid with gold, or bossed
> with jasper. Beneath, the unsullied sea drew in deep breathing, to and fro, its
> eddies of green wave. Deep-hearted, majestic, terrible as the sea, — the men of
> Venice moved in sway of power and war; pure as her pillars of alabaster, stood
> her mothers and maidens; from foot to brow, all noble, walked her knights; the
> low bronzed gleaming of sea-rusted armour shot angrily under their blood-red
> mantle-folds. Fearless, faithful, patient, impenetrable, implacable, — every word
> a fate — sate her senate. In hope and honour, lulled by flowing of wave around

their islands of sacred sand, each with his name written and the cross graved at his side, lay her dead. A wonderful piece of world. Rather, itself a world (VII, 374).

Not since 1843 had Ruskin written with such unmixed praise of Venice. This is his only version of the city not written out of recent experience, and it was probably necessarily so. This Venice is the product of Ruskin's forgetting, a place of the imagination, perfect, self-enclosed, 'itself a world'. Against this heroic, 'golden city' is set a London mean, littered and tumultuous from which the boy Turner gathers scraps of beauty and adventure but whose foulness remains with him all his life (VII, 377). The terms of the comparison between England and Venice as presented in *The Stones of Venice* are quite reversed. Instead of the traveller gathering the fragments from among the ruins of Venice, Turner must search out glimpses of colour among the rubbish of London prosperity. The confrontation is direct. It is not a case of England in her greatness taking warning from Venice in her weakness. Both are taken at their prime, in full enjoyment of their powers, and the power of England is shown to be deadly.

The Catholicism of Renaissance Venice was a Church 'gorgeous, harmonious, mysterious; — a thing which had either to be obeyed or combated, but could not be scorned' (VII, 381). Turner finds a form of religion

discreditable — discredited — not believing in itself: putting forth its authority in a cowardly way, watching how far it might be tolerated, continually shrinking, disclaiming, fencing, finessing; divided against itself, not by stormy rents, but by thin fissures, and splitting of plaster from the walls. Not to be either obeyed, or combated, by an ignorant, yet clear-sighted youth! only to be scorned. And scorned not one whit the less, though also the dome dedicated to *it* looms high over distant winding of the Thames; as St. Mark's campanile rose, for goodly landmark, over mirage of lagoon. For St. Mark ruled over life; the Saint of London over death; St. Mark over St. Mark's Place, but St. Paul over St. Paul's Churchyard (VII, 383).

Ruskin is not refering just to 'Protestantism . . . triumphant' here. The subject of Turner's mythological paintings, the English religion of death, is the religion of monetary asceticism and mortifying labour. The dragon of the Hesperides, 'Crowned with fire, and with the wings of bat', is born of covetousness or malignity and secretness. He is the 'British Madonna' of capitalism: 'In Athens, we have the triumph of Pallas; and in Venice the Assumption of the Virgin; here, in England, is our great spiritual fact for ever interpreted to us — the Assumption of the Dragon' (VII, 408). Compared with the horrors of such triumph, the old 'European misery' seems insignificant. Spiritual destruction is no longer equated with physical destruction. Ruskin had seen the last of Giorgione's frescoes ten years before, but

> though that scarlet cloud ... may, indeed, melt into paleness of night, and Venice herself waste from her islands as a wreath of wind-driven foam fades from their weedy beach; — that which she won of faithful light and truth shall never pass away ... from the lips of the Sea Sybil men shall learn for ages yet to come what is most noble and most fair; and, far away, as the whisper in the coils of the shell, withdrawn through the deep hearts of nations, shall sound for ever the enchanted voice of Venice (VII, 439-40).

The passage is prophetic of Ruskin's own future work. He would yet show what men could learn from Venice. But for the moment he had other, more analytical work to do. Shortly after issuing *Modern Painters* V Ruskin went to Switzerland and wrote the four papers on wealth, *Unto this Last*. Three more sets of essays on economic and social subjects followed: 'Essays on Political Economy' (1862-63), *Sesame and Lilies* (1865), *The Crown of Wild Olive* (1866).

Frequently, during the early sixties, Ruskin sought refuge in the Alps, even tried to make a home there. He would have liked to 'shut eyes and ears' he told Rawdon Brown. Asked why, Ruskin told him: 'In my own country, for the noise and smoke; in others, for the cries and blood.'[6] There had been 'cries and blood' enough in Italy of recent years, the years that had brought the unification of all Italy, with the exception of Rome and the Veneto, under the crown of Piedmont-Sardinia. Ruskin may have been persuaded to the Italian cause by Elizabeth Barrett Browning. In 1859 he wrote bitter letters to the newspapers about the

> twenty thousand men or thereabouts lying, at this time being, in the form of torn flesh and shattered bones, among the rice marshes of the Novarese, and not one jot of our precious Protestant blood gone to the signature ... Not so much as a corononer's inquest on those dead bodies in the rice fields — dead men who must have been murdered by somebody ... your twenty thousand ... are made rice manure of, and you think it is all right (XVIII, 538).

Ruskin also had personal reasons for not going to Venice. He told Rawdon Brown that it would make him 'too sad' with memories of youth.[7] More important, perhaps, was Ruskin's love for Rose La Touche. She exerted a pull in the opposite direction from that of the 'world' glorified in *Modern Painters* V. In February 1860 Ruskin had written:

her father — staunch Evangelical of the old school — does not believe in Greek
... she pets me as she would a panther that kept its claws in — always looking
under the claws to see that the velvet is all right & orthodox. She petted me
yesterday, up, or down — (I don't know which) — to such a point that when
I began drawing in the evening I found I didn't like the Venetians — but could
only look at Angelico ...[8]

There had, Ruskin told Harriet Beecher Stowe that summer, 'never ...
been anything in any other part of the world like Venetian strength
well developed'.[9] Rose, so frequently ill, never had that kind of robust-
ness. When Ruskin spoke of 'the Venetians' he meant Titian and
Tintoretto, Veronese and Giorgione. He had not yet discovered the
earlier, gentler painter, Vittore Carpaccio.

In 1862 Ruskin took Edward Burne-Jones and his wife to Italy and
sent them on to Venice by themselves while he stayed in Milan studying
Luini. It may have been then that Burne-Jones told him of Carpaccio.
Ruskin would not be convinced until he had seen his paintings for
himself but he may have been curious. A year later comes the first sign
of a willingness to visit Venice. Ruskin writes to Rawdon Brown of
taking

a little bachelor's den, for a permanency of a cupboard to put things away in,
with a marble balcony to the window, somewhere on the Grand Canal or by the
Ponte dei Sospiri quarter — the only one for me, wherever I live, now. I should
not be ever much at Venice, my health requiring hill air, but I should like to
find my own door opening to me when I come.[10]

It did not come to anything, and now the Alpine project also foundered.
Though Denmark Hill did not draw him, it needed him. Early in 1864
John James Ruskin died. For the next two years Ruskin stayed nearer
his mother. Joan Agnew, Ruskin's cousin, came to live with them.
Ruskin's only contact with Venice was through Brown and Lorenzi,
the archivist. For four years he contributed money for the publication
of Lorenzi's collection of documents relating to the Ducal Palace.[11]

In 1866, however, Ruskin made a real attempt to return to Venice, if
only because he needed a diversion. On 2 February Ruskin proposed to
Rose La Touche. She asked him to wait three years, in which time she
would be twenty-one, and Ruskin fifty. Shortly after that occasion,
Constance Hilliard, Pauline Trevelyan's fourteen-year-old niece, came to
stay at Denmark Hill. In about the middle of March Ruskin put to her
aunt

a plan which is a little for her — & a great deal for myself. For I want a little
change too now — and I'm so horrid that I can't bear myself alone any more —

and I wouldn't go, alone anywhere: but I just want to run to Venice & back in about six weeks, to look at a Titian or two — and Con's got to be very fond of my cousin Joan — and I should like to have them both with me . . .[12]

His next letter shows the reasons for getting away becoming more urgent:

I hope we *shall* be able to manage it somehow: for though I get on pretty well, I can't take any exercise here — and I believe I need change more than I know: and besides, Rosie's going away on 2nd April — and I'm afraid I shall be very bad, — so manage it for me if you can, or I shall be moping about deserted Grosvenor Street — which would'nt be as healthy as Venice . . .[13]

Though seriously ill, Lady Trevelyan decided that she and her husband would join the party, and they set off at the end of April. Two weeks later, at Neuchatel, she died. Ruskin, who had thought to surprise Brown by the visit, wrote to tell him that they could not come further south, and to explain an allusion to Rose in some previous letter:

I may perhaps be able to tell you about her some day — perhaps never; — at present she is still suffering from the effects of long illness, and does not like to talk seriously of anything, least of all of anything likely to give pain either to her parents or to me, and she knows she can't please both. So she stays my child pet, and puts her finger up if ever I look grave. But they won't let her write to me any more now, and I suppose . . . I shall settle down to — fifteenth-century documents, as you've always told me I should.[14]

Even such mild versions of his relationship with Rose seem to have 'pained' Rawdon Brown, and Ruskin probably told him little more.[15] But he was not about to 'settle down' to archive work. More than ever he was engaged in combat. His war was of a different kind from the one fought on the continent that summer. The Italians were disgraced by Austria, but their allies the Prussians won, and the Veneto was handed over to Italy. In October 1866 Ruskin agreed with Lily Armstrong that

Yes; it is nice that Venice is free from the Austrians, but Venice and all Italy, are still enslaved to an emperor they know not of, and there is no hope for them till they have broken *his* yoke asunder — cast *his* cords from them — For as *our* true monarch is not Victoria but Victor-Mammon — so their's is Victor — ah — *not* Emmanuel — but Belial.

'To vice industrious — but to nobler deeds
Timorous and slothful.'

And the only idea of the Venetians, in regaining what they imagine to be liberty — is not to recall the Toil of Venice — by which she Rose — but the Pleasures by which she Perished.[16]

Ruskin began fighting his war against Victor-Mammon in increasingly direct fashion. In 1867 he wrote the letters to the workman, Thomas Dixon, which were published as *Time and Tide*. Ruskin wondered whether he should not give up art and science altogether, but did not want to.[17] He therefore tried to do everything. In 1868 Ruskin served on the Committee for the Relief of the Unemployed, but found it 'like threading many needles not in a line (and some restive) with a thread fluffy at the end . . .'[18] He lectured from Dublin to Abbeville. He began a study of wild flowers, *Proserpina*, and by March 1869 was writing a book on Greek myths, *The Queen of the Air*. Ruskin was overworking and feeling 'much torn by various dispositions to work in fifty ways at once'.[19] Then suddenly, at the end of April, he 'referred printers and everybody' to Charles Eliot Norton, who was in London at the time, and rushed off to Verona.[20] There from May until August Ruskin worked mainly on the Scaliger and Castelbarco tombs he had always loved. He had two assistants to help him. He took with him Arthur Burgess, the impoverished young engraver who was helping Ruskin with *Proserpina*, and summoned from Florence John Wharlton Bunney, his pupil from the Working Men's College days of the mid-1850s. This company did not make Ruskin feel less lonely.[21] But he did find a new enthusiasm. He would dam the lateral valleys of the Alps, prevent flooding and stop erosion. Only a few days after he had arrived there he was writing excitedly about

> my great plan . . . to turn the entire valley into a safe and fruitful and happy region.
>
> Now, nothing in mere farming or gardening would interest me enough to keep my mind engaged in work in the open air; but here is a motive, and an employment which will last to the end of my days.[22]

Ruskin visited Venice three times from Verona, staying about four days on each occasion.[23] He went partly in order 'to see my old friend Mr. Brown, whom also I haven't seen for seventeen years'.[24] But the paintings were as important. Ruskin told Joan that he was 'happy here at Venice in looking at my favourite old pictures, and shall hope every year to do good work on them, and on Italy'.[25] He was 'full of good hope about this place'.[26] By chance Ruskin ran into Holman Hunt, and they went together to the Tintorettos in the Academy San Rocco. Ruskin read out passages from *Modern Painters*, and was surprised to find how good they were. In San Rocco he had scaffolding put up and did some drawing.[27] Ruskin was

> made very thoughtful by this review of Tintoret — after so many — seventeen years . . . And I am so anxious at least now to spend my last ten years well —

and so puzzled what to choose out of the much I can do that no one else can — Tintoret or Turner — neither of them visible to any one but me — nor the colours of architecture — nor of skies. And life so short at best.[28]

In Venice Ruskin gathered together aspects of his past. Among other things about which he quarrelled with Norton at this time was Byron, whom Norton had called insincere. Ruskin, writing from Verona, contradicted him fiercely, and added:

If he were only at Venice, now I think we should have got on with each other. It is very wonderful to me to be either in Venice, or here. Such a Dead World — of other people's lives and one's own.[29]

On other days he seemed to enjoy nostalgia, and put aside thoughts of work remaining to be done: 'I am enjoying Venice very much, however, as a rest. I have not thought it so beautiful since I was a boy.'[30] From this date remembrance would be an important aspect of Ruskin's experience of Venice, as in his thought and work as a whole. In a new sense the city was 'Such a Dead World', for part of his own past was buried there. But memories would be used creatively, and in combination with diversifying interests.

Even these three brief visits from Verona brought new contacts. On 13 May Ruskin told his mother of having met, through Rawdon Brown, Giberto Borromeo. He said that he had made 'great friends' with this Milanese prince and Italian patriot.[31] This was an exaggeration, but on the way home Ruskin visited Borromeo in Milan and was delighted by his collection of paintings.[32] Ruskin's command of the language was never good enough to permit close friendships with Italians, and he was not interested enough to overcome the obstacle. But in future he was to have more contact than previously, if only because people occasionally sought him out. It appears that at some point during Ruskin's time in Verona in 1869 he was approached by the Venetian scholar, later director of the Correr Museum, Nicolò Barozzi, and asked to give permission for a translation of *The Stones of Venice*.[33] This seems to have come to nothing, not surprisingly given Ruskin's reluctance to re-issue the book in England. But such an incident is a sign of the beginnings of an influence in Italy and in Venice in particular, and this was to have consequences for Ruskin himself at a later date. Another meeting was of greater immediate interest to him. Carlo Blumenthal, Ruskin's banker in Venice during the *Stones* time, had some informed knowledge of the management of the lagoons.[34] He referred Ruskin to an engineer associated with the construction of Venetian aquaducts, and they discussed the Alpine valley project. Ruskin reported excitedly to

Norton that the erosion of the mountains was directly related to the age-old problem of the lagoons:

> For 1200 years, the Venetians have been fighting vainly with the Brenta and its slime. Every wave of it is just so much gold, running idly into the sea, and dragging the ruin of kingdoms down with it. Catch it when it first falls, and the arid north side of the Alps would be one garden . . .[35]

Norton evidently thought it all mad, as he did many of Ruskin's ideas.[36] Yet this ambitious project for harnessing the river system of north eastern Italy and transforming the Alps was 'only the beginning of an even bigger one for making people old-fashioned'.

In 1869 Ruskin could not anticipate what form this bigger plan would take, or that land management would come to play a smaller part in his 'making people old-fashioned' than a Venetian painter he had previously neglected. On 13 May he wrote to Edward Burne-Jones to make a confession:

> My dearest Ned, — There's nothing like Carpaccio! There's a little bit of humble-pie for you! Well, the fact was, I had never once looked at him, having classed him in glance and thought with Gentile Bellini, and other men of the more or less incipient and hard schools, — and Tintoret went better with clouds and hills. I don't give up my Tintoret, but his dissolution of expression into drapery and shadow is too licentious for me now. But this Carpaccio is a new world to me . . . (IV, 356).

It would take Ruskin several years to investigate this 'new world'. The days spent in Venice in 1869 produced no immediate, concrete results. But it did re-establish acquaintance with the city, uncover a new source of teaching, and open the way for a new phase in Ruskin's Venetian work. It could not begin immediately, for he had to prepare for a new task in England. On 5 June in Verona Ruskin had heard of the offer of the Slade Professorship at Oxford.[37] By early September he was back in England. William Cowper-Temple must have congratulated him with a degree of glee that was misjudged. Ruskin wrote determinedly: 'I'm *not* going to be kept in England by this thing . . . I am not going to make Oxford a main business of my declining life.'[38] Oxford would take up more of his energy than this might suggest, but in a sense Ruskin was right. The University was to be one of many businesses, and it would certainly not keep him in England.

III.2 1870

Ruskin gave his Oxford inaugural *Lectures on Art* in February and March 1870. While preparing them he wrote to Joan

> The lectures are coming nice; though they're giving me sad trouble — and, in fact, I oughtn't to be teased to talk any more at my time of life, but should be left to paint snail-shells — and live in a big one . . .[1]

On 7 January Rose La Touche had passed him without speaking, and Ruskin had entered a large cross in his diary.[2] Later he heard from her again, but still needed to get away. This spring the plan which had failed in 1866 would be carried out. Ruskin would take Joan, Constance and Mrs Hilliard to Italy. He would also take his gardener, David Downes. Perhaps Ruskin wanted his opinion on bridling Alpine rivers, for it was Downes who was to supervise the Hinksey diggings.

Ruskin and his party crossed the Channel on 27 April. On the way down Ruskin wrote to Rawdon Brown of being 'very weary of England and her ways':

> I want a place, almost anywhere — minute enough for an ant like me to manage — that I may call 'home' and I want it to be somewhere on the south side of the Alps — that I may reach Venice and Milan easily and that I may in such feeble and slow way as I can — work towards my thought of the final management of the Alpine rivers.[3]

Ruskin thought Borromeo might let him have a field to build a cottage on. This came to nothing, as did his river project, in which Ruskin already shows less confidence than the year before. Nothing could be done now, at any rate, for his mother's health was poor, and he could not leave her long. Ruskin managed, however, to spare a month for Venice. Brown and Cheyney, it seems, helped entertain Joan and the Hilliards. In a note of 30 May Ruskin thanked him: 'My people . . . very happy with you & Mr Cheyney today', and asked about arranging to see glass-blowing and gondola building.[4] Another warned that 'the ladies have a design on you to day'.[5] Ruskin got on with his work in the meantime. He examined, and began copying details from the Carpaccio paintings in San Giorgio degli Schiavoni.[6] As yet, however, Carpaccio had not taken over Ruskin's Venetian interests and Tintoretto dominated. Ruskin 'resolved to give my five autumn lectures at Oxford on *one* picture, Tintoret's Paradise. It will be rather too large, than too narrow, a subject.'[7] He had intended to take the girls to see Alpine roses after Venice, and then visit Charles Eliot Norton, who had taken a villa near Siena. But on 20 June Ruskin wrote:

I have changed my purpose, suddenly . . . for many reasons, chiefly the danger of losing hold of what I have just been learning here, it is better for me not to stay in Italy, but to go home quietly and write down what I have got — else I should learn too much, and get nothing said (XXXVII, 8).

The party travelled quickly down through the towns of Tuscany to Siena and back to England. On the way through Switzerland Ruskin seems to have had regrets: 'I feel that I have left Italy too soon for my purposes, and I must come back in the autumn for a few weeks.'[8] He did not do so, nor did he give the whole of his Oxford course on the *Paradise*. Ruskin's subject for the Michaelmas term was Greek and Florentine sculpture as illustrated by coins. He ended the academic year, however, with a long and controversial lecture on *The Relation between Michael Angelo and Tintoret*. It places both painters in an age of compromise in which men search for justifications for not obeying precepts of conscience.[9] Between 1480 and 1520 'the deadly change' occurs (XXII, 83), and four evils are substituted for four right principles:

Ill work for good.
Tumult for Peace.
The Flesh of Man for his Spirit.
And the Curse of God for His Blessing (XXII, 87).

These changes are perpetrated by Titian, Raphael and Michelangelo, but chiefly by Michelangelo. Tintoretto, who comes after them,

himself alone nearly as strong as all the three, stands up for a last fight; for Venice, and the old time. He all but wins it at first; but the three together are too strong for him. Michael Angelo strikes him down; and the arts are ended (XXII, 83).

Tintoretto fights for Venice, and is helped by the conditions Venice accords her painters. Like Bellini and Titian before him he is

happily protected by his subordination to the Senate. Raphael and Michael
Angelo lived in a world of court intrigue . . . Tintoretto and Titian . . . practically
lived as craftsmen in their workshops, and sent in samples of their wares, not to
be praised or cavilled at, but to be either taken or refused (XXII, 88-9).

Once more Venice is used to castigate another nation. Even in a fallen
age Venice stands higher than Florence, and Florence implicates Oxford,
for Ruskin had made it his duty in this lecture to comment closely and
scornfully on the Michelangelo and Raphael drawing collections in the
Ashmolean Museum.

Ruskin was already engaged in organizing art collections of his own
choice for the University. They are highly idiosyncratic, apparently
miscellaneous assemblies of drawings and copies, some by well-known
artists, many more by the growing number of Ruskin employees and
disciples. Among them are a number of plant illustrations copied from
a fifteenth-century herbal in the Marciana Library in Venice. Between
1873 and 1877 an artist by the name of Caldara made these and other
drawings of plants and flowers for Ruskin.[10] Those placed in the
Oxford Series were offered in contrast with the 'English fault of
mechanical precision instead of design' (XXI, 231). The concentration
on isolated, often finicky detail is characteristic of much of Ruskin's
later work. It is a special characteristic of the few Venetian fragments
used in Oxford lectures and collections that they point a negative
lesson. In two senses Venice was an alternative rather than a comple-
ment to the university town. One of Ruskin's reasons for going to
Venice in 1870 was that he needed a refuge from Oxford. The same is
true of the journeys of 1872 and 1876-77. And, as one Ruskin scholar
has remarked, 'the Venetian work was . . . uniquely detached from
Oxford'.[11] It was perhaps appropriate that Ruskin should draw more on
Greek and Florentine culture for his Professorship, however eccentric
his tenure proved to be. Venice, rare among Italian cities in having no
university tradition, had functioned as a concrete model of stateman-
ship, commercial and social relations for many in the past. Ruskin
would make more plentiful and positive use of Venetian sources in his
'practical' teaching, and in connection with an English city quite
different from Oxford.

III.3 1872

In January 1871 Ruskin issued the first number of *Fors Clavigera: Letters to the Workmen and Labourers of Great Britain*. It announced Ruskin's refusal to 'put up with this state of things, passively ... an hour longer' (XXVII, 13), 'this state of things' being a condition of prosperity which reduced many to starvation and crime. *Fors* appeared each month for seven years, and sporadically from 1880 to 1884. Through it Ruskin founded the St George's Fund, a 'National Store' intended as the antithesis of the National Debt. The St George's Company, later renamed the Guild of St George, was to increase this store by acquiring land and establishing communities independent of a capitalist economy and modern manufacturing methods, each with its own school. Odd bits of property were acquired, and a few individuals did try to carry out Ruskin's strange instructions. A special connection was formed with Sheffield, and at Walkley, nearby, the St George's Museum was created. This was Ruskin's most concrete 'achievement' as Master of the Guild.

But the pamphlet through which he conducted the Guild's business and propounded its principles for the best part of thirteen years contains some of his greatest writing and interpretation. The loose, serial form suited Ruskin's temperament and teaching, which was exemplary and cumulative rather than discursive. In Letter 14, the number for February 1872, he described the character of *Fors* as consisting of:

> first, as it may seem to me needful, commenting on what is passing at the time, with reference always to the principles and plans of economy I have to set before you; and then collecting out of past literature, and in occasional frontis-pieces or woodcuts, out of past art, what may confirm or illustrate things that are for ever true (XXVII, 250).

For 'what is passing at the time' Ruskin drew on newspaper reports, correspondence received, his daily experience. He could make connections between the most trivial phenomena and the 'principles and plans of economy'. Ruskin was never hampered in this respect by being abroad. Even in his late twenties he had proved a remarkable observer of foreign cities and of Venice in particular. By the 1870s he had clearly worked out principles by which to interpret what he saw. But if Ruskin would speak of contemporary Venice merely because he happened to be there, the relationship between the ancient city and illustration of 'things that are for ever true' was not casual. In Letter 8, that of August 1871, Ruskin stated that the children of St George's schools were to know 'the history of five cities: Athens, Rome, Venice, Florence, and London' (XXVII, 143). That there was no distinction between these imaginary children and readers of *Fors* Ruskin implicitly acknowledges in Letter 18, of June 1872:

> with the history of the five cities, I wish you to know also the opinions, on all subjects personally interesting to you, of five people who lived in them; namely, of Plato, Virgil, Dante, Victor Carpaccio (whose opinions I must gather for you from his paintings, for painting is the way Venetians write), and Shakespeare (XXVII, 314).

When Ruskin wrote this he was in Pisa with a number of friends and relations. Like that of 1870, the Italian tour of 1872 was undertaken mainly for personal reasons. Ruskin had suffered a terrible illness the previous summer. Relations with the La Touche family were bad as a result of Effie's having given Mrs La Touche her version of Ruskin's character. He was able to do little in Oxford during the academic year 1871-72. In December Ruskin's mother died. He decided to give up Denmark Hill and move what he could to Lancashire. There Ruskin had, on impulse, bought the house on Coniston Water, Brantwood. By spring 1872 he again needed a refuge, but repair and furnishing of Brantwood was not complete. Ruskin's cousin, Joan Agnew, had married Arthur Severn the year before. The Severns too were waiting for their house, Ruskin's old childhood home on Herne Hill, to be made ready. Ruskin proposed to take them abroad. Constance Hilliard and her mother were also invited, as was a young artist protegé, Albert Goodwin. The six of them set off in mid-April, travelling south by the Ligurian Riviera and Tuscany to Rome, where Joan was to be introduced to her father-in-law, Joseph Severn. The 'great event' of the tour, however, was to be Venice.[1] They arrived on 22 June and stayed at Danieli's. Connie took swimming lessons, perhaps in one of the floating pools anchored in the Basin of St Mark's. Goodwin and Arthur Severn made drawings of Venetian scenes. Ruskin made visits to the Academy and Ducal Palace, and then got down to gathering the 'opinions' of Carpaccio from the paintings in the School of San Giorgio degli Schiavoni. Ruskin now had an assistant permanently on the spot. J.W. Bunney had moved, or been sent, from Florence to Venice in 1870, and was to remain there with his family until his death in 1882.

He had arranged beforehand for scaffolding to be erected in the School, so Ruskin must have intended to examine the pictures in detail. In other respects, however, working conditions were not ideal, and he seems to have spent only four days in San Giorgio.[2] Within two weeks of arriving in Venice Ruskin had quarrelled badly with the Severns. The dispute was probably with Arthur rather than with Joan, and may have been partly caused by Connie.[3] Joan and her husband left for home alone. Ruskin then seems to have quarrelled with the Hilliards.[4] The party was a large one, they had been together for over two months, and there had already been disagreements over arrangements at Sestri and Rome.[5] But the underlying cause of anxiety was Rose. She was then staying in London with the novelist and poet, Ruskin's friend and hers, George MacDonald. The MacDonalds persuaded Rose to agree to see Ruskin, and wrote to Venice pressing him to return immediately. Ruskin at first refused, telling them to bring Rose to Switzerland. The MacDonalds replied by telegram: "'We dare move no farther.'"[6] Ruskin wavered, making arrangements to go, cancelling them for fear of spoiling the holiday, then, in the end, giving in.[7] He rushed Goodwin and the Hilliards away from Venice on 13 July and arrived in London a fortnight later. Briefly, there was calm between Ruskin and Rose; but she was now seriously ill.

Directly and indirectly, *Fors Clavigera* reflects the tensions of these three weeks in Venice. Being an omnivorous work, quite free of limitations of subject matter or obligations to unity of tone, it was perfectly adaptable to sudden changes in the mood or circumstances of its author. Even interruptions could be made use of. Ruskin took up Letter 19 on 23 June, the day after arriving in Venice, announcing that he could not

> write this morning, because of the accursed whistling of the dirty steam-engine of the omnibus for Lido . . . the dirty population of Venice, which is now neither fish nor flesh, neither noble nor fisherman; — cannot afford to be rowed, nor has strength nor sense enough to row itself; but smokes and spits up and down the piazzetta all day, and gets itself dragged by a screaming kettle to Lido next morning, to sea-bathe itself into capacity for more tobacco (XXVII, 328).

Three weeks later articles were to appear in Italian newspapers protesting about these comments. A reader from Wales, it seems, forwarded the extract to the *Gazzetta d'Italia*, and from there three Venetian papers, *Il Tempo*, *Il Rinnovamento* and *La Stampa* took up the matter.[8] The contributor of one article felt provoked enough to offer physical violence, but none of them had any notion of who Ruskin was. Quite naturally, the insult was interpreted as a simple expression of contempt for foreigners by a superior and ungrateful English tourist of unusually bad temper. In fact Ruskin was simply treating Venetians as he would the people and individuals of any country, including and especially his own. So offensive is much of Ruskin's 'commenting on what is passing at the time' that it is remarkable that the Whistler libel suit of 1877 was the only legal action to be brought against him.

Ruskin did enjoy making mischief, but his purposes were serious. As he explained at the beginning of Letter 20, 'Benediction', he had not simply 'lost . . . [his] temper, and written inconsiderately' in calling the Lido steamer 'accursed' (XXVII, 334). The discussion of blessing, cursing and swearing that follows is an investigation of their meanings in Biblical and classical texts. Repeatedly Ruskin interrupts his 'main' text to record the intrusion of the world outside his hotel room. First comes the noise of a steamer engine, quite out of proportion to the boat's size and function, then the cries of a boy selling a 'black mess' of rotten, unripe figs on the quay in front of the Ducal Palace. Ruskin, moved by his face, 'so open, and sweet, and capable it was; and so sad', gives him money without taking fruit, and the boy is puzzled:

> he little thought how cheap the sight of him and his basket was to me, at the money; nor what this fruit 'that could not be eaten, it was so evil,' sold cheap before the palace of the Dukes of Venice, meant, to any one who could read signs, either in earth, or her heaven and sea (XXVII, 336).

Finally, in dramatic and frightening demonstration of the 'intervals of time in modern music', Ruskin allows his commentary on Isaiah to be punctuated and brought to a halt by the roars and whistles of the ten smoking steamers lying between the quay and the Church of San Giorgio Maggiore (XXVII, 341-2), among them the Lido ferry, the Capo d'Istria, and a vast English ironclad.

It is characteristic of Fors Clavigera that topics are introduced in one letter and taken up again later, sometimes years later. The meaning of the boy fig-seller to 'one who could read signs' is not given fully until 1877, when Ruskin was next in Venice. The implications of going to the Lido by steamer are expounded in Letter 42, the number for June 1874. Here Ruskin reprints and translates an article from an issue of Il Rinnovamento which had appeared during his stay in Venice two years before (XXVIII, 93-4, 104). The tone of the article reflects the spirit of the paper's name, 'renewal'. It describes passengers crowding on to the deck of the boat until one complains of suffocation, the eighteen-minute trip to the Lido and the arrival at 'La favorita', the new bathing establishment. The fast passenger service had in fact been introduced expressly to serve this recent development. The Rinnovamento correspondent is much impressed by the rapid change. What was 'only a few months ago still desert and uncultivated' has been made into a 'site of delights' with 'Long alleys, grassy carpets, small mountains, charming little banks, solitary and mysterious paths'. For entertainment after bathing there is 'an immense salon' with orchestra of which the 'artists are all endued in dress coats, and wear white cravats. I hear with delight a pot-pourri from *Faust* . . . all honour to the brave who have effected the marvellous transformation.' For Ruskin this 'marvellous transformation' is an opportunity for some marvellous sarcasm and a lesson in economics (XXVIII, 95). The new park is a 'Conquest, you observe also, just of the kind which in our *Times* newspaper is honoured always in like manner, "Private Enterprise." ' Ruskin's alertness to this first step in the exploitation of the Lido, shortly to become one of the most fashionable tourist resorts in Europe, is typical of the capacity for observation and interpretation which makes Ruskin highly unusual among travellers. Whatever his intentions in coming to Venice he does not use the place to escape from critical consciousness. The city is subjected to the same analysis as that applied to England, and the same processes are found to be at work. Against both stands the testimony of history. Ruskin describes the conquest of the Greek islands by individual Venetian merchants as an example of 'the private enterprise of dead Venice, that you may compare it with that of the living' (XXVIII, 97). Regular readers of *Fors* would recognize these young adventurers of the thirteenth century as examples of the type of noble robber elsewhere represented by the *condottiere* Sir John Hawkwood and the pirate Sir Francis Drake. Open looting is, in the code of *Fors Clavigera*, the diametric opposite of the concealed stealing which is the lending of capital at interest. Similarly Ruskin's readers would recognize the boy selling rotten figs as one of a number of child victims of degrading labour, and the *Capo d'Istria* as one of many infernal machines driven by steam, gas or electricity, which pollute nature and are dangerous to those who use them. By recurrent reference to the example and elucidation of one example by means of another Ruskin constructs a special mythology illustrating the contest between good and evil.

St George, the soldier-saint for whom the Guild was named, is another such figure, the type of Christian chivalry. But Ruskin did not make use of the work done in 1872 on Carpaccio's St George series in San Giorgio degli Schiavoni until several months after leaving Venice, and even then his treatment is brief. In Letter 26, the number for February 1873, he merely shows that, unlike the designer of the current British pound note, Carpaccio painted his saint as if he really were fighting a dragon (XXVII, 475). Ruskin had more and more urgent things to say of Carpaccio's 'opinions' on another saint, St Ursula. She is the subject of the second half of Letter 20, 'Benediction', written in Venice on 5 July 1872. Ruskin speaks of having seen Carpaccio's paintings of the saint's life in the Academy in 1869, but no doubt he had looked at them again on his visit to the Academy a few days before. He concentrates on the *Dream of St Ursula*, the picture of the Princess asleep with the angel appearing to her to tell of her mission and martyrdom. But of the angel's message Ruskin has little to say here. Instead he describes the room, reading its furniture, flowers, books and 'beautifully wrought' objects as signs of Ursula's character and 'the kind of life she leads'. Each detail expresses 'the evident delight of her continual life. Royal power over herself, and happiness in her flowers, her books, her sleeping, and waking, her prayers, her dreams, her earth, her heaven' (XXVII, 344-5). The princess-dreamer is the precise opposite of two American girls Ruskin recalls seeing in the train from Venice to Verona in 1869, offered here as 'specimens of the utmost which the money and invention of the nineteenth century could produce in maidenhood'. Miserable and agitated, these girls fidget in the dust and heat, pick at French novels nearly reduced to rags, suck lemons first ground to pulp by rubbing them with sugar lumps and take no notice at all of a landscape with Shakespearean associations that should 'touch the hearts and delight the eyes of young girls' (XXVII, 345-6). Ruskin was writing on the day he received MacDonald's telegram urgently calling him back to England to see Rose. In St Ursula he describes an ideal of girlhood and at the same time an image of his hopes of the moment. In *The Arrival of the Ambassadors*, the painting which precedes the *Dream* in Carpaccio's series, Ursula's betrothal is contemplated:

> a prince of England has sent to ask her in marriage; and her father, little liking to part with her, sends for her to his room to ask her what she would do. He sits, moody and sorrowful; she, standing before him in a plain housewifely dress, talks quietly, going on with her needlework all the time (XXVII, 347).

By the time Ruskin came back to Venice, four years later, Rose was dead. His reading of these pictures alters accordingly.

III.4 1876-77

Ruskin often saw himself as trying to salvage something from the past. Since 1845 there had been the public battle which he described in 1874 as the 'fierce, steady struggle to save all I can every day, as a fireman from a smouldering ruin, of history or of aspect'.[1] Ruskin had recently agreed to republication of *Modern Painters* and *The Stones of Venice*. This meant having to unpack things he had 'laid by carefully' in his mind, only to find them 'all mouldy and moth-eaten when I take them out' (XXXVII, 111). In May 1875 Rose La Touche died. A few months later Ruskin began thinking of a summer in Italy the following year. This too he saw in terms of ruin:

> It is very strange to me to feel all my life become a thing of the past, and to be now merely like a wrecked sailor, picking up pieces of his ship on the beach. This is the real state of things with me, of course, in a double sense — People gone — and things. My Father and Mother, and Rosie, and Venice, and Rouen — all gone; but I can gather bits up of the places for other people.[2]

Sometimes he went further, daydreaming once more of a new life in Italy.[3] He would go with Charles Eliot Norton and 'take a pleasant little suite of rooms in Florence or Venice — and we'll economize together, and think together — and learn together — and perhaps — even Hope a little together before we die . . .'[4] Throughout the winter and spring plans remained vague. By May 1876 Prince Leopold and Rawdon Brown were pressing him to bring out a selection of pieces from *The Stones of Venice*, as he had promised in the 'New Edition' two years earlier.[5] This provided Ruskin with an official reason for going to Venice, and later with an excuse for continued absence from Oxford.[6] In the new *Stones* most of volume I was to be omitted, volume III expanded, and to replace the old plates, 'I will make new drawings, giving some notion of my old memories of the place, in Turner's time.'[7] Although Ruskin warned him that they would probably disagree, it seems that Norton was to be allowed a hand in this apparently tranquil project. Norton and also Brown no doubt wished to steer Ruskin along safer, more scholarly lines, while he was thinking of even more didactic,

151

Carlylean work.[8] In the meantime a more personal reason for going to Venice had emerged. At some time in the early summer Professor Charles H. Moore, a friend and colleague of Norton at Harvard, visited Brantwood.[9] Ruskin was to find that Moore was 'as fond of Carpaccio as I'.[10] He must have already had an interest, for they made an appointment to meet 'in Carpaccio's Chapel' in the autumn.[11] This gave Ruskin a deadline to which he felt 'bound by most religious promise'.[12]

Leaving Brantwood at the end of July, Ruskin went first to inspect new Guild properties, and then set off for Venice. He crossed the Channel on 24 August and travelled rapidly through France and Switzerland. At Geneva he learnt that in Venice he would find James Reddie Anderson, the Oxford pupil who was to work on Carpaccio's iconography.[13] In Milan Ruskin stopped to look at paintings in the Brera Gallery, among them two Carpaccios. The first allowed him to vent some of his bitterness against the University. The doctors in *The Preaching of St Stephen* were 'a complete assembly of highly trained Oxford men as far as expression went; but with more brains'. Another, *The Presentation of the Virgin in the Temple*, warned him that if he had let Rose go in this life he must not do so in Heaven also. With such 'curious lessons' coming from Carpaccio Ruskin was clearly not going to be able to concentrate on *The Stones of Venice*, with which he felt 'very languid and disgusted'.[14] From Milan he took the train on 7 September to Venice, where Rawdon Brown was waiting at the station to take him to comfortable and expensive rooms in the Grand Hotel.[15] Ruskin was not at this stage planning to stay long in Venice, for he meant to be back in Oxford in November.[16] But he repeatedly postponed his departure, and as he did so tried to reduce his expenses. First he negotiated a reduced rent, then he moved into new, presumably cheaper rooms in the same hotel, and then in February transferred to a tavern, the Calcina.[17] This was on the Zattere, the port area, convenient for the Academy, apparently frequented by writers and artists (XXIV, xxxv). The Calcina was certainly not smart. Rawdon Brown was 'very contemptuous'.[18]

During the early weeks, however, Ruskin enjoyed his luxury and especially his balcony overlooking the Salute.[19] Thirty-five years earlier he had described the view as 'enough to raise one from the gates of death'.[20] Now Ruskin relived aspects of his early experience of Venice. He found 'much more beauty than I used to' when doing the 'technical work of the *Stones*'.[21] The city was 'less injured' than he had feared.[22] He felt no painful associations:

I'm not miserable here, as every body else in Italy. The sea and boats are still sea and boats – the pictures are still pictures, and I have the sense of home without that of loss, for I had not my father and mother much with me here.[23]

Ruskin gave time to friends and acquaintances, to some with tolerance, to others, especially Moore, with pleasure.[24] He rowed on the lagoon in the late afternoons and grew stronger.[25] Occasionally he walked in the Piazza by moonlight.[26] Every day he watched sunrise and sunset. Until early October the weather was steadily warm and clear. Ruskin described the effects in dramatic language. They were 'sweet' or 'terrible', 'intense', 'tremendous', 'fearful', 'marvellous', 'glorious'.[27] Colours were high and strong, and seem oppressive at times. One sunset was

> at first feeble, but ending in a blaze of amber passing up into radiant jasper colour. Cirri inlaid in the blue, quite stupendous in beauty of form and fullness of colour all over, not touched on edges, but jasper fleeces, salmon-colour just raised the least towards rose, and filled with light; painted on the purest blue, but always like paint. San G[iorgio] Maggiore one glow; dark masts of ships against it in west unspeakable, but all passing so fast, and night in a moment.[28]

So far Ruskin had denied a sense of ruin and loss, but here the light and colour pass 'so fast'. In statements such as 'beauty, in the dying Venice, felt more than ever', beauty seems inseparable from death.[29]

But as yet he was healthily energetic and confident. Although the bright weather kept him outside and away from writing, the rest of his work went well during September.[30] The thought of so much work done in Venice in the past reassured him.[31] He could write playfully of the new *Stones*,

> which will have all the 'eloquent' bits in the second and third volume served up like pickled walnuts, in sauce of a very different flavour — perhaps brandy cherries would be a better symbol of what I hope the book will be.[32]

In fact he was putting off concentrated work on the book. Ruskin described his day in a letter to Norton.[33] He translated from Plato, read Venetian history, made drawings on the Grand Canal. Copying from Carpaccio took up the largest part of his time. His subject was not one of the St George pictures 'in Carpaccio's Chapel', but *The Dream of St Ursula* in the Academy, first the whole picture in miniature and then details.[34] Moore was making a study of the saint's head in the same painting. In a private room in the Galleries they worked together for an hour or so every morning, and then Ruskin would have 'a couple of hours tête-à-tête'. Afterwards he read 'any vicious book I can find to amuse me — to prevent St. Ursula having it all her own way'. Defiant of the very quality that held him to St Ursula, her other-worldliness, he enjoyed even Casanova's *Memoirs*.[35]

Ruskin's light-heartedness did not last. By the end of September he was beginning to feel 'the sorrow and horror of Venice very hard on me'.[36] A week later he started getting into difficulties with his St Ursula copy. He became increasingly obsessed with problems of minute detail and subtle colour.[37] During October Ruskin found it impossible to write down all the thoughts coming to him, and began to panic in the old way about time passing without showing results.[38] He realized he would 'have to stop all the winter — and it's dull in evening — and the work incessant — the hours have only 35 minutes, I think'.[39] He wrote of Venice 'I die with her.'[40] Ruskin tried to persuade Joan Severn, and later Albert Goodwin, to come out and be near him.[41] As he told Carlyle, 'I am so very lonely now, missing the father and mother more and more every day, and having no more anything to look forward to here, but the gradual closing in of all . . .[42] He had been over-optimistic about taking up Venetian history again:

> my old unfinished work, and the possibilities of its better completion, rise grievously and beguilingly before me, and I have been stretching my hands to the shadow of old designs and striving to fulfill shortcomings, always painful to me, but now, for the moment, intolerable.[43]

On 30 November Ruskin pronounced 'all Venice nothing to me, or a mere grief'.[44] Walking around the city he saw great 'distress among the poor'.[45] If there was any future, it was not here: 'I'm very unhappy in my work here. I don't want to write about Venice, now, but about Sheffield . . .'[46] He thought his work useful, but did not enjoy being useful: 'I'm only doing lots of good, and I'm very miserable.'[47]

Ruskin thought he knew what would make him happy. All the time he had been copying Carpaccio's St Ursula and writing about her in *Fors Clavigera* he had been thinking much of joyful visions (XXVIII, 736). He wished to believe in her:

> there she lies, so real that when the room's quiet — I get afraid of waking her!
>   How little one believes these things, really! Suppose there is a real St Ursula di ma, — taking care of somebody else, asleep for me?[48]

If St Ursula really had lived at all she might be alive in heaven now, and if she was, Rose might be there too. If St Ursula had had a vision, not merely a dream,[49] of an angel bearing a message, perhaps Ruskin would also. He discussed the matter rationally in *Fors* 71:

> You will say, perhaps, — It is not a proper intellectual state to approach such a question in, to wish anything about it. No, assuredly not, — and I have told you so myself, many a time. But it is an entirely proper state to fit you for being approached by the Spirits that you wish for, if there are such. And if there are not, it can do you no harm (XXVIII, 736).

He also looked at the question of his own mental balance deliberately. At the end of October Ruskin had spent a week in Verona and inadvertently walked through the streets in his dressing-gown. He later told the story in *Fors* to show how 'my head certainly does not serve me as it did once'.[50] To Joan Severn, who had been worried by something he had written, he predicted that as he went on she would 'not be so much alarmed for the effect of what I may say on the public, as for the effect of what I may imagine on my own mind. However . . . I'm not losing my head yet . . .'[51]

A few days after writing this letter Ruskin began looking back through the diary he had kept at Broadlands the year before. Ruskin was thinking of the 'teaching' he had received there, when a medium had seen Rose trying to speak to him.[52] On 21 December he began praying for a new sign from Rose.[53] Three days later, on Christmas Eve, the first messages came. Anxious 'lest any inaccuracy of my memory should cast doubt on any part of this story in my own mind, or others',[54] Ruskin tried to keep record of these days in his diary and in letters to Joan Severn. Of these unpublished letters Van Akin Burd has recently given account.[55] By stitching the two together one can form an idea of what happened, but the order of events and the significance of several remains unclear. Much depends on Ruskin's identification of the two plants in St Ursula's bedroom in Carpaccio's painting of the *Dream* as dianthus and vervain. From Venice he had written to the Keeper of the Kew Herbarium requesting a specimen of dried vervain. Unsolicited, but evidently suggested by conversation, was a Christmas gift of a pot of dianthus from Lady Castletown, an Irish acquaintance staying in Venice. It came with a note: ' "from St. Ursula out of her bedroom window, with love" '.[56] When the two plants arrived within a short time of each other, Ruskin read them as having been sent 'with St. Ursula's and somebody else's love, the one spoken, the other known . . .'[57] Also on Christmas Eve, it seems, arrived a letter from Mrs La Touche to Joan Severn, sent on to Ruskin by Joan. He received it 'as a direct command from St. Ursula' that he should forgive Rose's mother for having separated them.[58] Another gift, this time of some shells of a type Ruskin had been drawing on an occasion when Rose's father had refused to let him see her, told him that he must also forgive Mr La Touche.[59] These arrived, it seems, on Christmas morning, as did a study of another detail from the *Dream*, a metal pitcher, which Ruskin had commissioned from Bunney.[60] Later Ruskin was to go to Rawdon Brown's. He felt impelled to make a detour by way of St Mark's, then that Ursula and Rose wished him to pray in the Church. In the afternoon Ruskin visited the home of Piero Mazzini, the gondolier who worked the ferry from the Riva degli Schiavoni and who accompanied Ruskin when in Venice.[61] Mazzini had eleven children, of whom one young married daughter had recently had a child. To Ruskin her 'simple Venetian beauty' was exactly that of the Madonna. Passing San Giorgio degli Schiavoni on the way back to the centre, he went in and found an example of vervain in flower in Carpaccio's *Baptism of the Sultan*. In letters to Joan, Ruskin described this first phase of the 'Christmas Story' as one of 'happy effortless obedience'. Next came a period in which 'The virtue required was throughout Defiance and Resistance.' There was an encounter with a gondolier, 'a horrid monster with inflamed eyes, as red as coals'.[62] Twice that evening Ruskin got lost in the fog on the lagoon. On the morning of the 26th came 'Illustration of the meaning of the temptations of St. Anthony'. Afterwards Ruskin called this 'The Red man's day'.[63]

Throughout Christmas week and the first days of January the teachings continued. On the 27th Ruskin showed Toni, Rawdon Brown's servant, his copy of the vervain in the *Dream*. Toni told him that on the feast of Christ the Redeemer the church of that name on the Giudecca was hung with vervain wreaths. This brought 'useful thoughts' on 'the power of the Father in Heaven and of the Son in and on all the earth . . .'[64] Other messages came as Ruskin lay awake at night, or through random openings of his mother's Bible.[65] The dreamlike fortnight was followed by ten days of 'finding precious things', discoveries in the Correr Museum and State Archives, 'prosperous' work[66] on the Ducal Palace. Towards the end of January came 'A terrific fit of depression . . . all coming after extreme excitement and overwork', illness and bad dreams, and by the 25th, *'dim eclipse of all Christmas light'*.[67] Even intense moonlight on the Salute was 'in my present tone of mind, ghastly like corpse light'.[68]

For the rest of his time in Venice Ruskin's state of mind alternated between depression and self-confidence. He had frequent struggles with 'piggish disbelief and with devil's trials', 'slips and failures in duty' and 'faithless thoughts'.[69] He hoped 'to be helped out of it, for it's too strong for me, without help'. But more instructions than signs of affection came from St Ursula and Rose, who had 'taken up with each other directly   and between them, I lead rather a hard life of it — they *will* . . . scold if ever I grumble at anything'.[70] It now seemed to Ruskin that 'in the Christmas teaching, it was nearly all St Ursula and very little of Rosie'. He began to ask himself about Rose, 'I do wonder why she leaves me so long without sign.' Sometimes he blamed his own dependence on 'selfish affection or hope',[71] sometimes he rebelled: 'Its all very fine, these pretty saints thinking one's to get on with nothing but sermons and no kisses. — but one rather tires of it sometimes . . .'[72] St Ursula and Rose failed Ruskin in one way, friends failed him in others. Both in England and in Venice there were 'nasty wants of sympathy in the best people, and of understanding in the wisest'.[73]

Loneliness intensified at the thought of his father, when he heard of the death of Joseph Couttet, his old Alpine guide and remembered early holidays in Venice.[74]

Ruskin saw it as his duty to overcome illness and sadness by force of will,[75] and had some success. He was 'greatly pleased' with his new lodgings on the Zattere, even amused by the steamer that tied up in front.[76] Away from the fashionable hotel district, he could use the quay in front of the Calcina for chopping firewood, a habitual form of exercise at Brantwood.[77] Ruskin often seemed in better health than many of his friends.[78] He kept social engagements, and made new friends among young Venetians.[79] Several Guild employees were already in Venice; another, Charles Fairfax Murray, came up to join him in April. In May more intimate friends, the Talbots, arrived from England, and perhaps supplied some of the domestic affection he had been missing.[80] Near the end of his stay Ruskin took measure of himself:

> Everything going well (but so slowly!), except my own mind, which is in a quite discomfited and disgraced state considering what it was at Christmas, except only in taking shame to itself for all failure, and resigning itself to what of distress it has to bear, and to what pleasure it can take; my clear duty being now to be as happy as I can, so redeeming what I can of the past which has been so lost or miserable — happy for the sake of others always, without wanting, for pride's sake, that they should know how hard it costs to be happy. Not but that I've more capacity in that kind still than thousands, or than I ever hoped to have, lately.[81]

One thing kept Ruskin in Venice so long: 'I stay only for the hardest work — if I had an hour to spare I should be off instantly — the place is a mere horror to me — dreadful as the ruins of one's dearest home.'[82] It was his work that was 'going well (but so slowly!)'. Slowest of all was his copying from Carpaccio. *The Dream of St Ursula* dragged on until March. Ruskin had intended to draw *The Death of St Ursula* next. The saint 'asleep — that other way' on her bier should have been the twin to the saint motionless in her bed.[83] But when the Academy authorities took the picture down Ruskin was disappointed; she seemed older and less beautiful.[84] So after 'shaking myself together for new start', Ruskin transferred to the Correr Museum to copy the large dog in the corner of *Two Venetian Ladies and their Pets*.[85] This painting, otherwise known as *The Courtesans*, was of two fine but unsaintly ladies trying to amuse themselves with various dogs and parrots on a balcony. Ruskin attributed a satirical purpose to Carpaccio in painting this subject (XXIV, 365), but there may have been an element of not letting St Ursula 'have it all her own way' in his interest (see p. 153).

Ruskin was now less exclusively occupied with her, more able to give

attention to the 'work . . . [he] came to Venice to do'.[86] From January
to May he wrote furiously. In so doing he did not carry out his 'intended'
plan, but went beyond it. He put off, in effect gave up, the idea of
revising *The Stones of Venice* radically (see p. 151). Instead he put his
new material and new thoughts into a new history of Venice. This, *St
Mark's Rest*, he determined to 'work at like a Saracen, and let nobody
else get more rest than St. Mark gives them'.[87] Three chapters were
published by the end of April. The *Guide to the Principal Pictures in
the Academy of Fine Arts at Venice*, another new project, was already
in print in March. The *Guide* was perhaps the natural outcome of
having spent so much time in the Academy that winter. Yet the more
Ruskin did, the more he found to do. Apart from his own Venice work,
being available laid him open to involvement in the work of others,
particularly that of a young Venetian antiquarian, Alvise Zorzi (see
pp. 183-7). Every month, of course, there was *Fors Clavigera* to write.
In March Ruskin was contemplating spending the whole summer in
Venice,[88] but in the end decided to go home in early May.[89] Just as he
was packing up new discoveries in St Mark's 'brought necessity of
staying . . . another fortnight'.[90] Ruskin continued finding things right
up to the last moment,[91] but by now could no longer put off leaving,
for he had arranged to meet George Allen and his son in the Alps on the
way back to England.[92] He left satisfied that 'much is done' but also
dissatisfied: 'I came to Venice meaning to do nothing but finished
work! and the lot of scrawls and rags I've done!! worse than ever.'[93]
Ruskin spoke of returning to Venice in the autumn,[94] but then decided
that it was not necessary, for St Ursula's sake at least: 'little Bear is
going to come here to spend the winter with me . . .'[95] There can be
little doubt that he had gone through a period of madness in Venice at
the end of 1876. At Brantwood in February 1878 Ruskin suffered a
second and far worse attack. Others were to follow before he came
back, in 1888, for a few unhappy days.

This long winter of 1876-77 was Ruskin's last working visit to
Venice. It produced no monumental work such as *The Stones of Venice*
had been. *St. Mark's Rest*, the *Guide to . . . the Academy* and the eight
letters of *Fors Clavigera* written there are 'scrawls and rags' compared
to the old book. They are confused and confusing, structureless,
scrappy, full of statements of intention never carried out. There is
obscurity, sentimentality, over-simplification, furious abuse. Yet
through the confusion and intemperance there is consistency of
thought. The writings of the winter of 1876-77 are concerned with the
'religion of Venice'.[96] This does not mean Catholicism, although aspects
of Catholicism figure largely. They are the traditional rather than the
doctrinal ones: saints, relics, ceremony, symbolism, hierarchy. But
there is also the Protestant emphasis on the Bible as guide which is

constant in all Ruskin's work. And no less important is Ruskin's use of aspects of Venetian culture belonging more properly to secular experience: laws, trade regulations, lay confraternities, governmental hierarchy, civic order, military conduct, modes of entertainment. But in Ruskin's Venice of the late 1870s the 'Venice of St. Mark's Rest' (XXIV, 234), the political and social are never without religious implications, the temporal is perfected only in the spiritual (XXVIII, 739). Political authority is an image of divine authority, the law of the state a version of Gospel law, the capacity to be amused a condition of innocence. *The Stones of Venice* had re-created an ideal Venice. The writings of 1876-77 perform the same function, but at one remove. In the late forties and fifties he had created his ideal out of what remained of the masonry of the city. Ruskin had described the Venetians as he imagined them to have been. Now he is held by Venice's image of herself, and of The City, by Venetians' concept of themselves, and of Man. Ruskin's later ideal of Venice has little to do with the 'actual' city, or with what 'really happened' in Venetian history. It has everything to do with the images and ideals Venetians proposed to themselves, realized or not.

In 1876-77 Ruskin's experience of Venice is divided, the material separate from the immaterial. Towards the end of Christmas week Ruskin wrote in his diary that he 'had never seen Venice look so dead before, or been so dead in it'.[97] Yet at the same time Venice was providing him with a language of vision.[98] To Norton he wrote of both the dead and the living Venice:

> Time was, every hour in Venice was joy to me. Now, I work as I should on a portrait of my mother, dead. I am pleased with myself when I succeed; interested in the questions of the meaning of such and such a bend of lip, such and such a winding vein, pulseless. You will be interested in the history of her life, which I can thus write. So am I; and 'happy' — in that way in my work. But it is a different happiness from having my mother to read Walter Scott to me.
>
> There is also now quite an enormous separation between you and me in a very serious part of our minds. Every day brings me more proof of the presence and power of real Gods, with good men; and the religion of Venice is virtually now my own — mine at least (or rather at greatest) including hers, but fully accepting it, as that also of John Bunyan, and of my mother . . .[99]

Here Ruskin seems to suggest that his work regards the dead city only. In fact the religion of Venice, the reading of the tradition through which spiritual power speaks, is his main concern.

If *Fors Clavigera* was composed of commentary on 'what is passing at the time' and illustration of 'things that are for ever true' (XXVII, 250), the eight numbers written between September 1876 and May

1877 are of the second kind. Relatively little is said of contemporary events. Ruskin collects eternal truths from his usual sources: Plato, Dante, the Bible. But Venetian material dominates. Ruskin could rightly claim, as he did in a note to Letter 71, that 'my Sheffield friends must not think I am neglecting them, because I am at work here in Venice, instead of among them. They will know in a little while the use of my work here' (XXVIII, 747). He did not 'want to write about Venice, but about Sheffield' (see p. 154), yet in writing about Venice he was writing for Sheffield.

In the body of this letter for November 1876 Ruskin set out 'some of the long-promised opinions of Carpaccio on practical subjects' (XXVIII, 732). They were not things 'opined' so much as 'known', prophecies, messages, 'truths necessary to human life', by their nature irrefutable. Carpaccio's 'book' consisted of only eighteen to twenty pictures. They represented the lives of three saints, Jerome, George and Ursula. At different times and in various ways Ruskin was drawn to all of them, but St Ursula is principal here. The reasons for this may have been personal, but what was most intimate to Ruskin was also of most universal significance. To concern oneself with St Ursula is to cut all remaining links with modern philosophy. She is the only one of the three saints of whom history contains not 'the slightest material trace' (XXVIII, 733). This makes her the diametric opposite of John Stuart Mill's 'utility embodied in a material object' (XXVIII, 734). Even to find amusement in St Ursula's story, as Carpaccio did, is to break with scepticism: 'if he did not actually believe that the princess and angel ever were, at least he heartily wished there had been such persons, and could be. Now this is the first step to real faith' (XXVIII, 735). For Ruskin now the question of 'real faith' is the main one. St Ursula had a secular role too. She was a princess, and held her place in the 'Feudal Ranks', which Ruskin describes (XXVIII, 736-40). But 'temporal offices are only perfected, in the Feudal System, by their relative spiritual offices' (XXVIII, 739), and the main point of the legend, given here as compiled by James Reddie Anderson, is neither economic nor social nor political. The story has 'practical bearings' which

> if you will note that the chief work of the Princess is to convert the savage minds of the 'English', or people of Over-sea, from the worship of their god 'Malcometto,' to the 'rule of St. John the Baptist,' — you may guess to be in some close connection with the proposed 'practice' of St. George's Company . . .' (XXVIII, 740).

The matter of religion had hardly arisen when Ruskin had written of St Ursula in Fors before, in 1872 (XXVII, 342-7). Then she had been used as a model of happy human and social conduct to be set against disagreeable behaviour observed in a railway carriage. The two descriptions of *The Dream of St Ursula* differ accordingly. In 1872 Ruskin had stressed the girl's domestic virtues, expressed in the furniture and objects in her room, her clothes and the angel's, the way her hair is combed. Four years later he does not describe the saint at all.[100] Then he saw a girl dreaming (XXVII, 344). Now Carpaccio 'wishes to tell you that it was no dream, — but a vision; — that a real angel came, and was seen by Ursula's soul, when her mortal eyes were closed' (XXVIII, 744). The angel's message is read closely. He wears 'subdued purple and grey', carries the martyr's palm, the fillet borne by the Greek angels of victory, the shroud with which the Etruscans veiled their tombs. He is colourless, calm, sorrowful, the 'Angel of Death'. Many of the details Ruskin describes in 1876 he had not seen in 1872, for the picture had been too high and in darkness. But he is also now much more inclined to pore over symbols of another world than the furniture of this. All hopes of union with Rose have had to be transferred to heaven. The tenets of Carpaccio's religion, not of his morality, therefore take first place, and images of earthly happiness are replaced by promises of another life:

> For this is the first lesson which Carpaccio wrote in his Venetian words for the creatures of this restless world, — that Death is better than *their* life; and that not bride-groom rejoices over bride as they rejoice who marry not, nor are given in marriage, but are as the angels of God, in Heaven (XXVIII, 746).

Constantly discovering new symbolism in paintings, Ruskin also creates it out of the circumstances of his life in Venice. In *Fors* 72 Ruskin describes the view from his hotel room early one stormy morning (XXVIII, 756). Thunderclouds pile up, making it hard to distinguish the dome of the Salute from the roof of a ruined abbey beside it. Restless gulls over the Grand Canal signal that outside the lagoon the wind is already wild. The scene stands for nineteenth-century England. Ruskin, perhaps alone, discerns the threat. He would like to draw, in peace, two little shells found on the islands, but cannot:

> For this green tide that eddies by my threshold is full of floating corpses, and I must leave my dinner to bury them, since I cannot save; and put my cockle-shell in cap, and take my staff in hand, to seek an unencumbered shore. This green sea-tide! — yes, and if you knew it, your black and sulphurous tides also ... (XXVIII, 757-8).

Ruskin's stormy sunrise is his unhappy equivalent to St Ursula's visionary dawn and the 'eternal Morning' of her martyrdom (XXVIII, 745, 746). St Ursula had laid down two conditions for agreeing to marry the English king's son: his people must become Christian, and she must be allowed to go on a pilgrimage. Ruskin's setting out with cockle-shell and staff for 'an unencumbered shore' is his counterpart to her travelling, 'rejoicing, over the sea, hopeful to see . . . holy graves . . .' (XXVIII, 766). His story and hers, Carpaccio's 'Myth of Venice' (XXVIII, 761), the Book of Revelations and Dante's *Inferno*, all bear the same teaching: that the world is divided into men 'who mind earthly things', and those 'who mind heavenly things'. Happiness is a Christian state: 'if you seek first the Kingdom of God and His Justice . . . after your numbered days of happy loyalty, you shall go to rejoice in His Fatherland, and with His people' (XXVIII, 761-2, 767).

Such were the 'practical opinions' of Carpaccio. Ruskin now promised that in its seventh year *Fors* would 'take a directly practical character, giving account of, and directing, the actual operations of St. George's Company' (XXIX, 13). This resulted in some strange recommendations. In Letter 73 the Yorkshire operatives are ordered to draw boundaries around the Sheffield district, carry out a census of its population, its needs and income, establish a commissariat to collect and distribute food, and to 'elect a duke of Sheffield . . . Elect a doge, if, for the present, to act only as purveyor-general: — honest doge he must be, with an active and kind duchess' (XXIX, 21). Ruskin's political advice had religious connotations. In the 'Feudal Ranks' the duke or doge was the temporal equivalent of the spiritual office of bishop (XXVIII, 739). Each was a link in parallel chains of authority both ending in the King of Kings, a concept 'lost to Protestant minds'. By using the Venetian name for 'duke' Ruskin underlines the ancient, foreign, Catholic notion of authority he is proposing.

The city also takes on a transcendental aspect. Plato's ideal city had been given to readers of *Fors* at the beginning of 1874. Ruskin's excerpt ends:

'I understand; you speak of that city of which we are the founders, and which exists in idea only, for I do not think there is such an one anywhere on earth?'

'In heaven,' I replied, 'there is laid up a pattern of such a city; and he who desires may behold this, and, beholding, govern himself accordingly. But whether there really is, or ever will be, such an one, is of no importance to him, for he will act accordingly to the laws of that city and of no other?'

'True,' he said (XXVIII, 24).

Of all real cities Venice was for Ruskin the one that most nearly conformed to that pattern. He hoped to make Sheffield do so. Having drawn on the Venetian constitution in Letter 73, he turns to the Republic's statute book in Letter 74. The 'business for this month' of February 1877 was to be 'the regulation of our Sheffield vegetable market' (XXIX, 33). For this Ruskin quotes from a series of laws passed between 1516 and 1725 laying down strict standards for the quality of fruit sold in the markets of the city, and from regulations excluding middle-men from the melon trade. From these documents *Fors* readers may 'judge of the methods taken by the Duke and the statesmen of Venice for the ordering of her merchandize, and the aid of her poor' (XXIX, 43). Venice had 'other merchandize' too, and Ruskin had once been more concerned with that: 'pure gold, and ductile crystal, and inlaid marble, — various as the flowers in mountain turf. But her first care was the food of the poor; she knew that her first duty was to see that they had each day their daily bread.' Now that his own priorities have changed, so have those attributed to the Venetian state. The laws of Venice echo the Lord's prayer, just as her 'monarchical' constitution is a microcosmic version of divine authority. The two stand and fall together. Now that Venice has no doge and is 'Free', she has 'all the glorious liberties of British trade', the 'Devil's laws' in the form of taxes on the food and drink of the poor, and Ruskin, 'having been here through the entire autumn, . . . [has] not once been able to taste wall-fruit from the Rialto market, which was not *both* unripe and rotten . . .' (XXIX, 41, 43-4).

Here law merges into 'myth', as Ruskin pursues the symbolic significance of the matter of bad fruit. Last time he had been in Venice Ruskin had told of a boy selling rotten figs and had hinted at 'what this fruit "that could not be eaten, it was so evil," sold cheap before the palace of the Dukes of Venice, meant, to anyone who could read signs . . .' (XXVII, 336). He now explains that the meaning of the fruit depends on the meaning of the palace:

> the perfect type of such a building as should be made the seat of a civic govern-ment exercising all needful powers. How soon you may wish to build such an one at Sheffield depends on the perfection of the government you can develop there, and the dignity of state which you desire it should assume. For the men who took counsel in that palace 'considered the poor,' and heard the requests of the poorest citizens, in a manner of which you have had as yet no idea given you by any government visible in Europe (XXIX, 33).

Within the building the nobles conduct themselves in the manner praised by the psalmist; outside the builder has taken for his corner-stones figures from the Bible. Adam and Eve at one end, Noah at the other, they are images of disobedience to known command. Ruskin transmits Venice's warning to herself to England. It is made stronger by the fact that Venice did disobey her own ancient laws, and hence her own Lords fell, 'as a fig-tree casteth her untimely figs; and the sentence is spoken against them, "No man eat of the fruit of thee hereafter" ' (XXIX, 37).

The boy with his cheap figs is only possible as a consequence of that fall.

Ruskin had long been 'one who could read signs'. Of one source of signs he was no longer in control. St Ursula had become detached from Carpaccio's picture and assumed an independent life as 'Little Bear'. Without her counsel nothing was to be done in St George's Guild (XXVIII, 770). Ruskin deliberately left the three pages written for *Fors* at sunrise on Christmas Day unaltered. He attributed peculiar authority to this entry; it was 'to be of considerable importance to our future work' (XXIX, 30n.). The vervain, dianthus and pitcher he had just received are symbolic of service of the household Gods, service of the Father of the Gods, and of Christ's first and last miracles. They are meant not only for Ruskin but for his 'Sheffield friends': 'by specialty of sign sent to you in Venice, by the Saint whose mission it was to convert the savage people of "England over-sea"' (XXIX, 32). Throughout the 'business' of regulating the Sheffield vegetable market St Ursula issues instructions to Ruskin and his Companions. She intervenes with stories about dogs illustrating right relations between man and animal, or with readings from the New Testament: 'Little Bear *will* have us hear a little reading still' (XXIX, 36, 37). She closes the letter with some obscure 'little myths' meant for guidance on the Eastern Question (XXIX, 45-6). Some readers found all this incomprehensible. At the beginning of Letter 75 Ruskin conceded that

> all great myths are conditions of slow manifestation to human imperfect intelligence . . . whatever spiritual powers are in true personality appointed to go to and fro in the earth . . . can only be revealed, in their reality, by the gradual confirmation in the matured soul of what at first were only its instinctive desires, and figurative perceptions (XXIX, 54).

But St Ursula did not continue to reveal herself 'in true personality', and there were no more messages to pass on. Meanwhile Ruskin continued to use Venetian institutions and Venetian symbols as ideal types. He offers the Mariegola of the School of St Theodore as a model of law, the school itself as a model institution (XXIX, 62-6). Both were appropriate for St George's Company. The saint whom, with St Mark, Venice had chosen for her standard-bearer, waged holy war against material evil. The school or confraternity defended its members against the same, and was religious but not clerical. But Ruskin finds it hard to concentrate on that war. He breaks off exposition and describes the buds on the dianthus, St Ursula's flower. The rising sun fills the opening petals with light, which break as if the Adriatic breakers had all been changed into crimson leaves at the feet of Venice Aphrodite. And my dear old Chamouni guide, Joseph Couttet, is dead ... And thinking of him, and of others now in that other world, this story of St. Theodore, which is only of Life in this, seems partly comfortless (XXIX, 67).

The flower had been of general significance as symbol of the service of God. Perhaps because of the failure of revelation, it here becomes a private symbol of a person lost, and of physical love. This may explain Ruskin's reticence in explaining why '*Fors* has become much more distinctly Christian in its tone', a matter he speaks of in Letter 76 (XXIX, 86). Of the first of the 'vital causes' he says only that 'since *Fors* began, "such things have befallen me" personally, which have taught me much, but of which I need not at present speak'. Perhaps he could not speak of 'such things' at a time when they were threatened by his own loneliness and by the scepticism of others. The second 'vital cause', which he goes into at length, tells us not how he recovered his faith but how his religious convictions developed in relation to his knowledge of art (XXIX, 87-91).

By now Ruskin's 'days here in Venice ... [were] surcharged with every kind of anger and indignation' (XXIX, 118). Both *Fors* 77 and 78, the last numbers to be written before leaving for home, are angry documents. The aspect of authority most present is sternness, judgement, not caring for the poor. ' "Fear God. Honour the King" ' Ruskin proposed as the golden legend of St George's schooling (XXIX, 97). It was to be embroidered on every child's dress. God is unequivocally 'the only Despot' (XXIX, 111). Ruskin wishes for a return of the institutions of confession and inquisition (XXIX, 113-15). The Venice of these letters is different from that of the autumn and Christmas period. Modern Venice comes to the fore and ancient Venice recedes, the 'real' lays waste the ideal. She is once more seen as a city of sin, disorder, destruction, as Babylon, not Jerusalem, Bedlamite, not visionary, a warning, not a pattern. On one of the capitals of the Ducal Palace 'Solomon's head has been broken off by recent republican movements in Venice; and his teaching superseded by that of the public press' (XXIX, 116). The Venetian carnival is ' "turning the grace of God into fury" ' (XXIX, 120). A witches' sabbath is to be staged in St Mark's Square, 'certainly, next to the square around the Baptistery of Florence, the most sacred earth in Italy'. In a private letter of the time Ruskin wrote: 'I see the Judgment of God on this city more than His mercy.'[101] Ruskin turns his anger not only against Venice but also against Sheffield, despairing of both cities and of his attempts to marry the two. Under the Ducal Palace sculpture of the Father in creation and the Archangel Michael purging evil a photographer has stuck his advertisement. Photography enables Ruskin to send a picture of the capital to Sheffield, but

> by whose help do you think it is that you have no real ones at Sheffield, to see instead? Why haven't you a Ducal Palace of your own, without need to have the beauties of one far away explained to you? . . . are you never the least ashamed that what little good there may be in . . . [your own good artefacts] is borrowed from Greece or Venice; and that if you got all your best brains in Sheffield, and best hands, to work, with that sole object, you couldn't carve such another capital as this which the photographer has stuck his bill upon? (XXIX, 126-7).

Venice and Sheffield were to be linked in their ideal states once more before Ruskin left for England. On 20 May Ruskin

> found in St. Mark's the Duke and his people, and had a glorious hour, in the quiet gallery, with the service going on. I alone up there, and the message by the words of the old mosaicist given me; and found, returning home, that the Sheffield men had accepted my laws; and wrote to them in return that they should stand rentless.[102]

Of this mosaic of people, clergy, and doge 'serene in mind' Ruskin was to commission several copies for the Guild Museum.[103] It was perhaps as important to him as an earlier 'find', an inscription from the church of San Giacomo del Rialto. On a St George's cross were cut words Ruskin translates as

> 'Be thy Cross, oh Christ, the true safety of this place.' (In case of mercantile panics, you see.)
>   On the band beneath it —
>   'Around this temple, let the merchant's law be just — his weights true, and his agreements guileless.'[104]

The mosaic symbolized a perfect relationship between authority and people, harmony between church and state. The inscription expressed the regulation of commerce by Christian principles. Together they proved that men had once at least aspired to behave in accordance with God's law. Human conduct, whether political or economic, was not necessarily determined by 'natural laws' inconsistent with Christian teaching. The newspapers might speak of St George's Company as an experiment. On the contrary,

> the very gist and essence of everything St. George orders is that it shall *not* be

new, and not an 'experiment'; but the re-declaration and re-doing of things known and practised successfully since Adam's time.

Throughout the winter of 1876-77 Venice was a continual source of things 'known and practised successfully since Adam's time'. A highly organized state with sophisticated laws and institutions, Venice had surrounded herself with legends and prophecies. Civic and religious ideals were expressed simultaneously. There was much that could be transferred directly to the Company of St George, itself a mythical creation but strictly regulated by rules and commandments.

Companions of St George and regular readers of *Fors Clavigera* might be expected to puzzle out the meanings with which Ruskin invested Venetian laws, inscriptions, sculptures and paintings, or the titles of his own books. The tourists who bought his two part *Guide to the Principal Pictures in the Academy of Fine Arts at Venice* at the entrance to the Galleries could not.[105] It is literally a guide. Ruskin writes as if he in person were conducting a visitor around. His manner is intolerant, impatient and characteristically didactic. Commenting on the fee for admission, Ruskin adds that if he were Prefect of Venice, travellers would have to pay 'a good deal more' to get into the city at all, 'that I might be sure you cared to come' (XXIV, 150). Marching his reader from room to room, Ruskin pushes him past certain pictures, orders him to linger before others. The visit is hurried, highly selective and allows no freedom of choice.

In this the *Guide* reflects the specific worries and hopes of 1876-77. It is not representative of his interest in Venetian painting as a whole. It gives little time and less praise to Titian and Tintoretto.[106] Only one Titian, *The Assumption*, is discussed at any length. First Ruskin commends it:

as a piece of oil painting, and what artists call 'composition' with entire grasp and knowledge of the action of the human body, the perspectives of the human face, . . . the picture is deservedly held unsurpassable (XXIV, 153).

Told to 'Enjoy of it what you can', the admirer is cut short by a denunciation of the painter for not believing either in his own representation of the assumption or that it ever took place at all. Titian painted it for amusement, but not being 'innocent', is not even capable of true amusement: 'On the contrary, a strange gloom has been cast over him, he knows not why'.[107] Closing roughly with 'And that is all I care for your noticing in the Assumption, just now', Ruskin goes on to Tintoretto. Here there is no contempt, but consideration is cut off even more sharply:

Nothing comes near Tintoret for colossal painter's power, as such. But you need not think to get any good of these pictures; it would take you twenty years' work to understand the fineness of them as painting; and for the rest, there is little good in them to be got (XXIV, 154).

This is hardly an adequate reason for turning away. In *Modern Painters* Ruskin had not been inhibited from trying to illustrate Tintoretto's power as a painter. Elsewhere, in the Epilogue to the Travellers' *Stones*, Ruskin refers to the iconographical problems with which works of the greater Venetians present the 'ordinary traveller' (XI, 235). Again the explanation does not hold, for the same applies to Carpaccio and Bellini.

The main point is not in fact a logical one. It is that there is simply no time: 'of the wrong and truth, the error and the glory of these pictures, I have no time to speak now; nor you to hear' (XXIV, 154). Ruskin's chosen audience would not have long in the Venetian Academy. In his imagination, if not in terms of actual days, their guide was equally rushed. Ruskin had not renounced admiration for Tintoretto or even Titian.[108] He spoke of giving 'further illustration of the complete works of Tintoret' in the projected (but unrealized) new edition of *The Stones of Venice* (XXIV, 205). In future years Ruskin was to spend large sums on employing a young artist, Angelo Alessandri, to copy Tintoretto's works for the Guild Museum. But his own time was to be given to what he felt was immediately 'needful work' (XXIV, 204).

Led to a room containing an 'entirely sincere and noble' Cima da Conegliano, the visitor is told to 'Grudge no time on *it*; but look at nothing else here.' Titian's *Presentation of the Virgin* may be 'interesting to artists', but is 'To me, simply the most stupid and uninteresting picture ever painted by him' (XXIV, 157-8). Veronese's *Annunciation* is another 'artist's picture'. Of all late Renaissance painters, Veronese is the one Ruskin chose to make an example of in the *Guide*. In an appendix he gives, with commentary, the text of Veronese's interrogation by the inquisitors (XXIV, 187-90). The exercise of the painter's faculty independent of theological considerations is investigated and censured, and Ruskin approves. Yet Ruskin's position is not simply that religion is all-important and painting as such not at all. Workmanship in detail is consistently praised. One thing is pointed out to the general spectator in the Veronese *Annunciation*: a little rose-bush in a glass vase for which a good opera-glass is needed (XXIV, 158-9). There were sentimental reasons for Ruskin's liking this, but scale also enters into it. The reader is to examine Mantegna's 'microscopically minute' brush-strokes with 'a magnifying glass of considerable power' (XXIV, 156). For though 'wholly without sentiment', Mantegna is full of 'little pretty things' (XXIV, 157).

In his ideal painters Ruskin finds both sentiment and prettiness. The preferred period of the *Guide* is the 'Carpaccian epoch' (1480-1520) (XXIV, 155). Its representatives are Carpaccio and Gentile Bellini. Ruskin says nothing of the artists, and little of their paintings. He concentrates wholly on their image of Venice. What they give is

> the perfectly true representation of what the Architecture of Venice was in her glorious time; trim, dainty, — red and white like the blossom of a carnation, — touched with gold like a peacock's plumes, and frescoed, even to its chimney-pots, with fairest arabesque, — its inhabitants, and it together, one harmony of work and life, — all of a piece, you see them . . . with everybody looking out of their windows (XXIV, 163).

Everything is graceful, minute, somewhat playful. It is a miniature city, ordered by decoration. There is nothing of the passionate, defiant heroism of the Venetian ideal of *The Stones of Venice* or *Modern Painters*. As if to underline the difference Ruskin insists on eliminating a small ambiguity in his description of St Mark's in *The Stones of Venice*. There he had likened the white marble foliage on top of the church 'to the tossed spray of sea waves' (see X, 83). Bellini shows us that these waves 'were not, at all events, meant to be like sea foam white in anger, but like light spray in morning sunshine. They were all overlaid with gold' (XXIV, 163). Quick now to deny hedonistic versions of beauty, Ruskin differentiates between this gilding and the cheap fake of English prosperity. Venice rose under the eyes of the builders of the Old Testament: 'these, in their myriads stood by, to watch, to guide; — it might have been, had Venice willed, to bless' (XXIV, 164). The gold and bright colour was not that of 'vicious luxury'. Nor is order imposed by the machinery of government; it is natural, domestic, blissful. The reader is asked to enter the picture of 'old St. Mark's Place, before it was enlarged', with its

> trim, dainty, happily inhabited houses, mostly in white marble and gold, with disks of porphyry; — and look at the procession coming towards you underneath them — what a bed of moving flowers it is! Not Birnam wood coming, gloomy and terrible, but a very bloom and garland of good and knightly manhood — its Doge walking in the midst of it — simple, valiant, actual, beneficent, magnificent king (XXIV, 164-5).

The nobles of Venice had been known by Ruskin's predecessors for their political cunning, the severity of their rule. Ruskin depicts them as the flower of chivalry, their head as 'simple'. This is the 'vision of living Venice' with which Ruskin wishes the reader to end his first visit to the

Academy. Of all painters, however, it is Carpaccio who unites spiritual and temporal virtues most perfectly. The readers is not to judge Carpaccio so much as judge himself by Carpaccio. By him 'You may measure yourself, outside and in, – your religion, your taste, your knowledge of art, your knowledge of men and things . . .' (XXIV, 159). In Carpaccio all passion, all painter's faculty is subordinate to intellectual purpose. Religious enthusiasm is restrained by 'essentially Venetian, – prosaic, matter of fact . . . common sense'.[109]

But Ruskin postpones discussing his paintings. Part II of the *Guide* opens with remarks on Carpaccio's failure to paint nature well. Ruskin had discovered the same deficiency in other Venetian painters in *Modern Painters* I (III, 170-2). It is characteristic of Ruskin that he explores new values but the old ones remain, though they may move down the list of priorities. Affection for the picturesque also persists. To show the visitor an example of Carpaccio's architectural ideal, Ruskin sends him to the 'desolate little courtyard of the School of St. John the Evangelist' to look at a 'Giocondine' ruin.[110] Returning to the Academy, he must stay in his gondola and imagine how it was before recent 'improvements'. Exercising his 'charity of imagination', the reader is to remove the hated iron bridge built by an English engineer in the 1850s and replace the paving stones in the courtyard by grass (XXIV, 172). Ruskin seems to lose all sense of hurry here. He meanders inconclusively through the history of the Scuola della Carità, the building reconstructed to house the Academy collection and school.

Finally we come to the one picture analysed with any degree of completeness in the whole *Guide*, Carpaccio's *Return of the Ambassadors*. Like the Bellini, it represents the ideal nation-city:

> Here is the great King of ideal England, under an octagonal temple of audience; all the scene being meant to show the conditions of a state in perfect power and prosperity. A state, therefore, that is at once old and young; that has had a history for centuries past, and will have one for centuries to come.
>
> Ideal, founded mainly on the Venice of his own day; mingled a little with thoughts of great Rome, and of great antagonist Genoa; but, in all spirit and hope, the Venice of 1480-1550 is here living before you (XXIV, 176).

Garden and city 'mingle inseparably' here, where everything is clean and pure, every creature, befittingly dressed, keeps his rightful place. The King takes political counsel in the pavilion, the monkey sits on the ground outside, and

> Crowds on the bridges and quays, but untumultous, close set as beds of flowers, richly decorative in their mass, and a beautiful mosaic of men, and of black, red, blue, and golden bonnets. Ruins, indeed, among the prosperity; but glorious

ones; – not shells of abandoned speculation, but remnants of mighty state long ago, now restored to nature's peace ... what was left of them spared for memory's sake (XXIV, 177).

There is no conflict here, no unsatisfied desire, no decay, no movement. It is only the setting for the action, but even the action is suspended. Carpaccio shows the moment of hiatus between the landing of the ambassadors and the moment when the king will give them his attention and hear St Ursula's answer to the marriage proposal (XXIV, 178). It is a subject very near to Ruskin himself. He had lived in such a hiatus himself for many years, waiting for Rose's answer.[111] Yet Ruskin reads the situation as a joke, imagining the prince's impatience, the ambassador's pompous words as he says that they must wait for the king's attention before giving the news:

A piece of play, very nearly, the whole picture; a painter living in the midst of a prosperous city, happy in his own power, entirely believing in God, and in the saints, and in eternal life; and, at intervals, bending his whole soul to the expression of most deep and holy tragedy, – such a man needs must have his times of play ... (XXIV, 179).

Of Carpaccio's 'deep and holy tragedy' Ruskin tells us nothing in the *Guide*. This, the only picture of the series in which St Ursula does not appear, is the only one described. He intends to 'take up St. Ursula's pilgrimage, undisturbed' in another Part of the *Guide*. Like many of Ruskin's intentions, this was never carried out. Perhaps this was not the time nor the place to speak of the things that concerned him most. It is as with the unfinished Titian *Deposition* of which Ruskin says, near the end: 'The picture which he left unfinished might most fittingly be called the Shadow of Death. It is full of the profoundest metaphysical interest to me; but cannot be analysed here' (XXIV, 182).

Like the Academy *Guide*, *St Mark's Rest* was a hurried book, improvised, and never really finished. It seems to have grown out of the difficulty of revising *The Stones of Venice*. Ruskin had arrived expecting to find it an easy task.[112] But by mid-November he was feeling oppressed by the old book, 'weak in the detail of her history; and warped by my sectarian prejudices'.[113] He spoke of it as an incomplete work he was obliged to finish only because it was begun. To Carlyle he wrote wearily of his progress, mentioning for the first time a new project:

nothing got into form, and new claims on me – it seems, from my old work. For, coming here only to put myself into some temper of fancy, in recasting the Stones of Venice, I have got a new clue, utterly unseen by me when I wrote it –

which will give — and ought to give me, many hours of added toil; but I believe I shall now leave the book a sound piece of work, and connect it with a short history of Venice for the schools of St George . . .[114]

The 'new clue' probably had something to do with the religion of Venice. In December he was asking one of his Oxford pupils for information about the Christianity of the first Venetians.[115] He had already written something for the short history,[116] but by the end of January had changed his mind about his intended audience.

The title Ruskin first proposed was: 'St Mark's Rest The History of Venice Written for the Guidance of English Travellers While they visit her Ruins.'[117] It was to be a 'Catholic history'.[118] The recasting of the Protestant *Stones* could therefore be postponed. Instead there would be 'a little one for travellers, extracts only, not to supersede the big edition — but a sop in the pan meanwhile'.[119] Of the two travellers' books, priority was to be given to *St Mark's Rest*: 'The English come up from Rome after Easter and I want to be ready for them.'[120] Ruskin managed to get Part I, the first three chapters, out on St Mark's Day, 25 April. In the Preface he warned that publication would proceed 'as I can get my chapters done'.[121] Four followed in October, but Part III, consisting of one chapter only, had to wait until July 1879. The material which later became chapters IX, X and XI first appeared as supplements and appendices at irregular intervals between December 1877 and May 1884. Only one of the three was by Ruskin himself. They differ from the chapters proper in being studies in coherent series of works of art rather than excursions round apparently miscellaneous monuments and documents. James Reddie Anderson's account of Carpaccio's St George paintings and Alexander Wedderburn's description of mosaics in St Mark's are systematic, somewhat dull, sensibly limited in scope. Though this is what Ruskin wanted of his pupils, his own readings of signs and symbols is informed, as theirs were not, by an idiosyncratic vision of Venice as a whole. None of these last three chapters was written specifically for the project that emerged, by fits and starts, out of the experience of the winter of 1876-77.[122] Essays in iconography might appropriately be added, but the main body of *St Mark's Rest* is, in conception and style, something rather different. It is a guide-cum-history for strangers visiting an ideal city.

St Mark's Rest was distributed as a guide. On sale at the Academy door, it was also available from Bunney, now appointed agent for the sale of Ruskin's books in Venice.[123] This history of Venice was to be read 'while you are here within her walls' (XXIV, 255). As Catherine Williams has remarked, the instructions given the reader are intimate and 'fussy'.[124] 'Go first into the Piazzetta, and stand anywhere in the shade, where you can well see its granite pillars,' are Ruskin's first words

(XXIV, 207). The traveller is later commanded to take his gondola over to the steps of San Giorgio Maggiore to read of the siege of Tyre, the taking of the pillars, and then sent into the church, 'down the steps on your right hand', to look at the tomb inscription of the Doge who took them (XXIV, 208, 216). Chapter IV consists of a precise itinerary around a series of relief sculptures. Ruskin had always insisted on closeness to the object. But in *St Mark's Rest* he had a special motive for taking such a firm hold on his traveller-reader. Ruskin is imposing the conditions under which he is permitted to see Venice. Unable to make sure his tourists care by charging a fee to enter the city as he had suggested in the Academy *Guide*, Ruskin selects by means of his subtitle. At some point between February and April 1877 he discarded 'The History of Venice Written for the Guidance of English Travellers While they visit her Ruins' and substituted 'The History of Venice, Written for the Help of the Few Travellers Who Still Care for Her Monuments.' His first choice had been conventionally nostalgic, and placed the burden of loss upon the city. His second is uningratiating, and places responsibility upon the travelling public. It is not so much Venice that is ruined (she is, but that is not Ruskin's main preoccupation here), but a mode of travel. There was a time, Ruskin implies, when to care was the norm. He was not thinking only of his own childhood.

The 'traveller of the modern school' had come to Ruskin's notice on the way down to Venice in August 1876 (XXIX, 575-7). In the Alps he had been horrified by a group of people in conversation failing to notice the 'dramatically exciting mountain scene' before them. Modern travellers came to Geneva 'merely to buy jewellery and live in a fashionable hotel'. It is not a minor matter; 'it means the blood of all nations degraded into atheists and usurers . . . ' These tourists pervert the Swiss, and pervert themselves. They become travellers to 'that eternal ice' of the Inferno, instead of 'Christians, and travellers to the Celestial mountains above the crystal sea'. For, as Ruskin recalls from *Modern Painters* II, the sight of beauty consists in the concurrence of physical sight and 'the acknowledgement of Spiritual Power' (XXIX, 577). If the Alps were the celestial mountains, Venice was the celestial city. There too was 'Spiritual Power' to be acknowledged. In one of the first Venetian numbers of *Fors Clavigera* Ruskin had attacked the rationalists' scorn of 'all relics and old bones' (XXVIII, 766). He intended to make use of his Geneva notes 'concerning the unrejoicing manner of travel adopted by the sagacious modern tourist, and his objects of contemplation, for due comparison with St. Ursula's'. He was thinking of St Ursula's pilgrimage. Ruskin made much of the amusement with which she, her eleven hundred maidens, Prince, Pope and cardinals set out 'rejoicing, over the sea, hopeful to see . . . holy graves'. St Ursula is the ideal

Christian tourist. Her joy in her 'objects of contemplation' is dependent on her interest in the difference between good and bad. When Ruskin's Sheffield friends 'know faithful and good men from miscreants', they too will be

> amused by knowing the histories of the good ones – and very greatly entertained by visiting their tombs, and seeing their statues. You will even feel yourselves pleased, some day, in walking considerable distances, with that and other objects, and so truly seeing foreign countries, and the shrines of the holy men who are alive in them, as well as the shrines of the dead (XXIX, 23-4).

St Mark's Rest is such a pilgrim's guide to Venice, to the tombs of her good men, the images of her saints, her 'relics and old bones'. St George occupies the best part of three chapters.[125] The School of St Theodore lists the saint's body first in the inventory of its property. Ruskin quotes the passage at length, challenging his traveller to be scornful:

> Oh reader, who hast ceased to count the Dead bones of men for thy treasure, hast thou then thy treasure of the living Dead laid up in the hands of the Living God, where the worm doth not corrupt, nor the conquered King of Terror any more break through and steal? (XXIV, 231.)

The first monument of the city is a shrine. St Mark's was built on the spot where the evangelist's body, brought from Alexandria to Venice, became unbearably heavy, miraculously indicating the place where he was to rest. This aspect of the church gives this book its title. *The Stones of Venice* had ignored it. Now Ruskin was 'struck, almost into silence, by wonder at my own pert little Protestant mind, which never thought for a moment of asking what the church had been built for!' (XXIV, 277). Ruskin did not here 'speak as a Roman Catholic'; he was 'a mere wandering Arab ... seeking but my cup of cold water in the desert ... or an Indian, – with faint hope of ever seeing the ghost of Laughing Water' (XXIV, 277-8). Saints may or may not reveal themselves 'in true personality' (XXIX, 54). But the soul's 'instinctive desires and figurative perceptions' are not to be despised. Revelation is to be desired, and faith reverenced and envied, though difficult to attain. Even now

> the old leaven is yet so strong in me that I am very shy of being caught by any of my country people kneeling near St. Mark's grave.
> 'Because – you know – it's all nonsense: it isn't St. Mark's – and never was,' say my intellectual English knot of shocked friends.
> I suppose one must allow much to modern English zeal for genuineness in all

commercial articles. Be it so. Whether God ever gave the Venetians what they thought He had given, does not matter to us; He gave them at least joy and peace in their imagined treasure, more than we have in our real ones (XXIV, 278).

Ruskin imagines the sceptic's objections in terms similar to those in which he foresaw his friends' doubts about his having received messages from the insubstantial St Ursula on Christmas Day.[126] He has no more mercy on them than he has on himself. In *Stones* he had

fancied actually that the main function of St. Mark's was no more than of our St. George's at Windsor, to be the private chapel of the king and his knights . . .

'Chiesa DUCALE.' It never entered my heart once to think that there was a greater Duke than her Doge, for Venice; and that she built, for her two Dukes, each their palace, side by side. The palace of the living, and of the, — Dead, — was he then — the other Duke?

'VIVA SAN MARCO.'

You wretched little cast-iron gas-pipe of a Cockney that you are, who insist that your soul's your own . . . as if anybody else would ever care to have it! is there yet life enough in the molecules, and plasm, and general mess of the making of you, to feel for an instant what that cry once meant, upon the lips of men? (XXIV, 279-80).

Sectarian protestants, intellectuals and cockneys would not have been enlightened as to such meanings by the standard guidebook of the time. One night in Assisi in 1874 Ruskin had laid awake 'planning attack on Mr. Murray's guides'.[127] Arriving in Venice in the autumn of 1876 he had again been

so disgusted with reading the new edition of Murray's guide that I feel as if I must forswear the whole London world, and come and live in an old boat or a chalet — or anywhere where I shouldn't see the hateful English.[128]

St Mark's Rest alludes frequently, and always with contempt, to Murray's *Handbook for Travellers in Northern Italy*,[129] the Reverend Smedley's *Sketches from Venetian History* (XXIV, 209, 297), and, more generically, 'your modern English explainers', 'any modern guidebook', or 'other illumined writings of the nineteenth century' (XXIV, 225n., 295, 297). They would tell the story of the recovery of the body of St Mark 'with proudly polished, or loudly impudent, incredulity' (XXIV, 294-5). They put the crusades down to commercial appetite, as Ruskin himself had once done (XXIV, 209; cf. IX, 24). At the bookshop in Venice Ruskin will find novels, but not the lives of the saints (XXIV, 347). He must quote from the Bible continuously, for there is a 'remote possibility you may have thought its carriage unnecessarily expensive' (XXIV, 227). But he can be sure that his travellers are well armed with Murray and the like. Such books supply amusing anecdotes about Venetian superstition, attribute mercenary motives of their own time and country to twelfth-century Venice, and pander to the material preoccupations of their readers. The *Handbook* gave particulars of the number of bricks in the railway bridge, the state of Venetian commerce, where to buy glass ornaments and where to stay. For Ruskin's 'hateful English' did not come to Venice to live in old boats, or go to the Alps to stay in chalets. Like his Geneva tourists in the luxury hotels, they came to

> the Grand Hotel, — or the Swiss pension — or the duplicate Danieli with the drawbridge, — or wherever else among the palaces of resuscitated Venice you abide, congratulatory modern ambassador to the Venetian Senate (XXIV, 232-3).

For Ruskin, of course, Venice could not be 'resuscitated' along contemporary commercial lines. Like her 'other Duke', she might yet be alive, if one could read the signs. But they are not to be found in Murray's city, which begins where Ruskin's ends. Ruskin marks the frontier by pointing to a fading Giorgione fresco:

> therein is seen the end of my Venice, — the Venice I have to tell you of. Yours, of the Grand Hotels and the Peninsular steamers, you may write the history of, for yourself.
> Therein, — as it fades away — ends the Venice of St. Mark's Rest (XXIV, 234).

Eccentric as a cicerone, Ruskin could not be otherwise as a historian. The 'Venice of St. Mark's Rest' not only comes to an end in 1600; she has no political, military, economic or even ecclesiastical history. Ruskin has nothing to tell us of the structure, development or actions of the Venetian state, or any other institution. He gives vast generalizations about the periods of Venetian history, but shows no further interest in chronology. What he does tell us, about the acts of a few doges, about the building of churches, the raising of pillars, the meanings of sculptures or mosaics, is all evidence of intentions, imagination, beliefs and virtues aspired to, not of the actual course of events. Ruskin knew he was not providing his readers with what they might be expecting from a history of Venice. After six chapters he asks:

> Are you impatient with me? and do you wish me, ceasing this preamble, to begin — 'In the year this, happened that,' and set you down a page of dates and Doges to be learned off by rote? (XXIV, 268).

Behind his challenge lies a conviction that 'practical history' is of little significance, that 'ideal history' is all-important. This belief had taken a long time to mature. Since the 1850s Ruskin had been expressing a series of preferences as regards the writing of history. He had favoured visual evidence over written evidence, was more interested in 'nations' than in their governments, in 'national feeling' than in events.[130] Dissatisfied with 'common history' Ruskin suggested that the production of a 'True historical ideal ... is a task which the closing nineteenth century may propose to itself' (V, 126). Yet the nature of the ideal remained vague. During the 1860s he continued to express scepticism about the relevance of governments to nations, emphasized the need for sympathy rather than knowledge, and for the history of households rather than the history of wars (XVII, 245; XVIII, 126; XVII, 379-80). Still Ruskin made no positive proposals of a general nature, and made no real attempt to put his preferences into practice. He may have been prevented from doing so by religious doubts and consequent uncertainty about the nature of man's past. In a letter to Froude of 1864 Ruskin wrote:

> there is no law of history any more than of a kaleidoscope. With certain bits of glass — shaken so, and so — you will get pretty figures, but what figures, heaven only knows. Add definite attractions and repulsions to the angles of the tube — your figures will have such and such modifications. But the history of the world will be forever new (XXXVI, 465).

During the next decade Ruskin was to rediscover a determining force in history. In 1869 he returned with greater energy to the attack on 'modern historical inquiry' and 'the merely historical investigator', who labours over 'veracity of externals' while incapable of understanding 'veracity of vision' (XIX, 309-10). This comes in *The Queen of the Air*, Ruskin's study of the Greek Athena myth. Myth and legend were to play an important part in the elaboration of a general view of history. In 'The Tortoise of Aegina', an undelivered lecture of 1870, he wrote:

> Remember, in all your historical investigations, there are two entirely distinct branches of them. One is this history of the Acts of men; the other, the history of their Thoughts. In general, it matters to the future very little, comparatively, what men did; but it matters everything to know why they did it. For the event to them, and to us, depends always not on the deed merely, but the intent of it; so that even the truth of the deed itself is often of little importance, compared with the results of it (XX, 381-2).

It does not matter whether the William Tell story is true; what matters is that it was believed (XX, 382). In saying this Ruskin was making a case not for the history of ideas but for the history of ideals. One was not to study all thought or intention, only that which is good. In the tenth lecture of *The Eagle's Nest* series of 1872 Ruskin advised his Oxford students that self-interest, being only a destructive force, was to be no part of their historical studies (XXII, 265-7). Its material effects could be seen all too clearly in modern England, but man's inner nature is essentially good:

> in the reading of all history, your first purpose must be to seek what is to be praised; and disdain all the rest: and in doing so, remember always that the most important part of the history of man is that of his imagination. What he actually does, is always in great part accidental; it is at best a partial fulfilment of his purpose; and what we call history is often . . . merely a record of the external accidents which befall men getting together in large crowds . . . It is therefore a true historian's work diligently to separate the deed from the imagination; and when these become inconsistent, to remember that the imagination, if precious at all, is indeed the most precious.[131]

In St George's schools children were to learn the histories of five cities, but only 'what has been beautifully and bravely done; and . . . the lives of the heroes and heroines' (XXVII, 157). *St Mark's Rest* had been first conceived for these children, but they were not a special case. Shortly before leaving for Venice in 1876 Ruskin had set out, in *Fors* 67, sixteen aphorisms for the Companions of St George. In one he asserted that 'Intellectual education consists in giving the creature the faculties of admiration, hope and love' (XXVIII, 656). One of the means to this was by 'the sight and history of noble persons'. In his last aphorism he elaborated:

> Since all noble persons hitherto existent in the world have trusted in the government of it by a supreme Spirit, and in that trust, or faith, have performed all their great actions, the history of these persons will finally mean the history of their faith; and the sum of intellectual education will be the separation of what is inhuman, in such faiths, and therefore perishing, from what is human, and, for human creatures, eternally true.

Ruskin's belief in the 'eternally true' underlies all the writings of 1876-77. It explains why 'truths necessary to human life' (XXVIII, 732) can be transferred directly from Plato, or Dante, the Bible or Carpaccio, to the nineteenth century. It makes it possible for Sheffielders to build a Ducal Palace, or go on pilgrimages, or adopt the trade laws of Venice.

It also makes possible the writing of a history such as *St Mark's Rest*. Ruskin selects from the past of Venice what is to be praised, discards what is 'perishing'. The history of Venice after 1600 is a 'diary of expiring delirium' best ignored (XXIV, 255). To the period 1520-1600, a time of 'luxurious use, and display, of the powers attained by the labour and meditation of former times', Ruskin makes little reference. A whole volume of *The Stones of Venice* had been devoted to those periods. *St Mark's Rest* deals only with her virtuous time, now extended to include the fifteenth century, and arranged in three epochs (XXIV, 254). The first, 421-1100, is the time of 'growth and mental formation':

> At the close of this epoch Venice had fully learned Christianity from the Greeks, chivalry from the Normans, and the laws of human life and toil from the ocean. Prudently and nobly proud, she stood, a helpful and wise princess, highest in council and mightiest in deed, among the knightly powers of the world.

The second, 1100-1301, is 'that of her great deeds in war, and of the establishment of her reign in justice and truth'. The third, 1301-1520, is 'that of religious meditation . . . marked by the establishment of schools of kindly civil order, and by its endeavours to express, in word and picture, the thoughts which until then had wrought in silence'. Of Venice's 'great deeds in war' Ruskin gives one illustration, deliberately omitting any account of fighting or killing (XXIV, 213-14). Of the administrative side of establishing her reign or her schools of kindly civil order we are told nothing.

Ruskin's material is the Venetian imagination. Many of his protagonists are figures in sculptures and mosaics: the saints, prophets, trades and virtues of Venice. The 'most precious "historical picture" ' in the world is a mosaic in St Mark's of Venetians' concept of themselves: 'the Priests, the Clergy, the Doge, and the people of Venice . . . are an abstract, at least, or epitome of those personages, as they were, and felt themselves to be, in those days' (XXIV, 295-6). The 'real' Venetians of whom Ruskin speaks are also types. Domenico Michiel leading the crusade is religious zeal in combat, his relations with his allies exemplify loyalty. Defeating the Saracens he personifies wisdom and might; the charter he draws up for the regulation of the Venetian subjects in Palestinian cities is a model of good government (XXIV, 208-13). Ruskin's Venetians do not react to the pressure of circumstance, they behave in accordance with patterns of belief. When they put out the eyes of deposed doges they were 'deliberately' applying the city's 'practical law against leaders whom she had found spiritually blind: "These, at least, shall guide no more" ' (XXIV, 269). The choosing of Doge Selvo proceeds according to the type of divine election, his mode of acceptance is emblematic of modesty and bounty, his battles enact the principles of chivalry (XXIV, 271-4). Not all the articles of Venetian faith are religious. But the climax of the book is a celebration of the religion of Venice. Doge Selvo married a Greek girl, during whose reign work was done in St Mark's which 'first interpreted to her people's hearts, and made legible to their eyes, the law of Christianity in its eternal harmony with the laws of the Jew and of the Greek' (XXIV, 275-6). The centre of *The Stones of Venice* had been a secular building. The Ducal Palace confessed human imperfection (X, 359). St Mark's expresses the union of faiths in 'eternal harmony'.

Ruskin realized that his version of Venetian history would be thought ingenuous. He recognized that the way we view relations between religion and state depends on the 'assumptions of theory in which we may approach this matter' (XXIV, 258). One might see Venetian idealism as 'a cloak for their commercial appetite as modern church-going is for modern swindling'. Or one might see it as 'an exquisite dream of mortal childhood . . . a beautifully deceived heroism of vain hope'. This is the pessimistic view of 'modern enlightenment', born of personal sorrow. Ruskin offers a third approach:

the only modest, and therefore the only rational theory, is, that we are all and always, in these as in former ages, deceived by our own guilty passions, blinded by our own obstinate wills, and misled by the insolence and fancy of our ungoverned thoughts; but that there is verily a Divinity in nature which has shaped the rough hewn deeds of our weak human effort, and revealed itself in rays of broken, but of eternal light, to the souls which have desired to see the day of the Son of Man (XXIV, 259).

St Mark's Rest tries to show 'a Divinity in nature' shaping the 'histories of the religion and policy of Venice' (XXIV, 258). Those histories were for Ruskin 'only intense abstracts of the same course of thought and events in every nation of Europe'. In 1880 Ruskin began a projected series of histories of European towns collectively entitled 'Our Fathers Have Told Us'. In the *Bible of Amiens*, the only one completed, Ruskin affirms with clearer conviction, the principle explored in *St Mark's Rest*. Historians may look to politics, to financial self-interest, or the progress of science for an explanation of history, but all the while

the two ignored powers – the Providence of Heaven, and the virtue of men – have ruled, and rule, the world, not invisibly; and they are the only powers of which history has ever to tell any profitable truth. Under all sorrow, there is the force of virtue; over all ruin, the restoring charity of God. To these alone we have to look; in these alone we may understand the past, and predict the future destiny of the ages (XXXIII, 38).

The Bible of Amiens was begun partly in response to 'the request of a young English governess, that I would write some pieces of history

which her pupils could gather some good out of ...' (XXXIII, 21).
Ruskin saw history as a matter of education, not of research. This
separated him from his oldest friend in Venice, Rawdon Brown. Brown
had spent his life transcribing and editing State papers.[132] He was
curious, cautious but sure. He saw his work as the gathering of quantities
of minute facts in preparation for an undramatic but accurate portrait.
Ruskin had come to distrust literal fact as much as he did systems. He
did not assemble details into generalizations. He would be excited by
the discovery of a single document or an inscription, and make a principle of a single piece of evidence. Ruskin did not have the patience or
the inclination to collect and collate on a large scale. Yet he respected
the 'long & faithful work' of those who did.[133] And now, as in *The
Stones* time, he needed to draw on their knowledge. The centralized
and highly bureaucratic nature of the Venetian republic meant that the
state archives were vast, filling twenty-nine rooms in the ex-convent of
the Frari. Brown and Lorenzi again acted as guides.

Ruskin and Brown met sometimes during the winter of 1876-77,
but they did not live near each other. Brown was now quite old, and
though Ruskin enjoyed rowing, 'the up and down canal breaks the
forearms in a way impossible to me'.[134] Therefore information passed
largely by letter.[135] The correspondence shows Ruskin repeatedly
asking for a particular book, or for advice on what to read on a particular subject. Sometimes he asks for information directly, dates, help
with translation or interpreting a symbol. Occasionally messages were
passed through Brown to Lorenzi, who also found material for Ruskin
and helped with deciphering inscriptions. They contributed much,
though indirectly, to the mid-winter numbers of *Fors*, the Academy
Guide, and especially *St Mark's Rest*. Though ultimately 'careless of
afterwards remediable mistakes' (XXIV, 204), Ruskin submitted drafts
of chapters to Brown that he might save him from 'ludicrous and
regrettable errors'.[136] But the differences between them were too great
for smooth adjustment. Brown's period was the Renaissance, and there
were irate comments on Ruskin's treatment of his seventeenth-century
'high-heeled friends'.[137] Ruskin was used to Brown's bad temper,[138] but
was still 'a little mortified' when his 'confidence in your probable
correctness of historic instinct' was not reciprocated when it came to
architectural matters.[139] Ruskin also thought that 'Papas ought to be
more interested in their son's books' than Brown seemed to be in *Fors
Clavigera*.[140] In fact Brown's scoring and margin comments in his copy
of *Fors* shows that he did not so much ignore as strongly disapprove of
the pamphlet. By some abuse of Germans in Letter 39, for example, he
had written in large capitals: 'TRASH'. Ruskin tried to pacify Brown
without yielding on questions important to him. One letter begins 'My
DEAR Papa — Will you just evermore be good enough, — and youll be

ever so much more *comfortable* to understand that *"whenever* you think *Im* wrong — *you're* wrong!"' It ends with the half-serious warning, 'Some day you'll kill *me*, with always scolding . . .'[141]

Just before publication proofs of *St Mark's Rest* went not only to Brown and Lorenzi but also to Giovanni Veludo, Librarian of the Marciana at that time.[142] It had probably been Brown who had introduced Ruskin to Veludo. Most of his contacts with Venetians had been acquired and maintained through Brown in the past. By now Ruskin had some independent contacts as well, for he was beginning to be recognized in Venice. Nicolò Barozzi, the man who had pressed Ruskin to have *The Stones of Venice* translated in 1869, was one of a large number of scholars who had done much to stimulate a patriotic and scientific interest in Venetian matters throughout the nineteenth century. This they had done in spite of the Austrians; now, with encouragement from Rome, historical studies flourished. Although Venice still had no university, there were many and active cultural institutions, such as the Ateneo Veneto, the Academy, the Istituto Veneto and the young and vigorous Deputazione per la Storia Patria, each of which had its own periodical publication. Now Ruskin found that in his absence he had been honoured by two of these. The Deputazione per la Storia Patria, of which Barozzi was a founder member, had elected both Brown and Ruskin honorary members.[143] In 1873 Giovanni Battista Cecchini, then Secretary, had succeeded in getting Ruskin made an honorary member of the Academy.[144] This, and another coincidence, meant that Ruskin was given a warm welcome when he went there to copy *The Dream of St Ursula*:

> they're — what do you think — going to take my dear little princess down for me, and give her to me all to myself where I can look at her all day long. It really happens very Fors-y that the very person whom I found facing the frescoes by Cimabue at Assisi should be now inspector of the Academy at Venice, and that the Historical Society of Venice had just made me a member last month, so I can get anything done that I want almost.[145]

Ruskin sympathized with the Academy's financial problems, offered to pay for repairs to another painting in the same series, and donated a number of his works to the Academy library.[146] Relations were not entirely formal. The man he had met in Assisi in 1874, Guglielmo Botti, seems to have won Ruskin's friendship as well as his respect.[147] Ruskin had other friends among the Armenian fathers of the island of San Lazzaro, and they too were learned men.[148]

Yet Ruskin remained on the fringes of Venetian scholarly circles. More than with contemporaries and established figures, he formed lasting relationships among the younger generation of artists and writers to whom he could be adviser, protector, Master. Ever since the *Stones* period Ruskin had employed local artists to take casts and measurements and make copies.[149] But Raffaele Carloforti, Alvise Zorzi and Angelo Alessandri were more than employees. The same is true of Giacomo Boni, with whom Ruskin came into contact a few years later. All had substantial interests in common with Ruskin and maintained independent correspondence with him when he was not in Venice.[150] Their backgrounds and interests overlap. Three were Venetian by birth, Carloforti was living in the city at this time. All four of them studied at the Academy. Carloforti and Zorzi were already friends in 1876, Alessandri and Boni became close subsequently.[151] Carloforti and Alessandri were painters, Zorzi and Boni were of a more archaeological turn of mind. But all were conscious of a specifically Venetian inheritance, and members of informal circles meeting to discuss artistic and historical questions.[152] Except for Carloforti they all attained positions of some importance in the cultural professions.[153] But in the late 1870s and early 80s they were barely out of their student days, none of them rich enough to pursue their interests freely. To a varying extent they all received financial, moral and intellectual support from Ruskin, and formed affectionate ties with him. Arriving in Venice in September 1876 Ruskin had been met at the station by his Venetian 'Papa', Rawdon Brown. Leaving the city in May 1877 he was seen on to his train by two 'sons', Carloforti and Zorzi, and took with him a third, Angelo Alessandri.[154]

Ruskin's Venetian disciples had much in common with each other, not least their admiration for Ruskin. Yet apart from the occasional message to be passed from one to the other, Ruskin kept his relationship with each separate. They met Ruskin at different times, and their functions were individual. Raffaele Carloforti had probably met Ruskin in Assisi in 1874.[155] By March 1876 Ruskin was 'maintaining [him] in art study at Venice' on a monthly allowance of £7 10s which he continued to receive for a year at least (XXVIII, 583, 633, 729, 769 and XXIX, 50). He was to do architectural and sculpture studies for the Guild, with which he was still associated in 1899.[156] Otherwise we know little of him. Of Alessandri, whom Ruskin probably met in the Academy in February 1877, and who was to become one of the steadiest and most valued of the Guild colour copyists, we know a great deal more. But his relationship with Ruskin did not become steady until 1879, and is best told by their correspondence. The only Venetian closely, almost exclusively, associated with the visit of 1876-77 is Count Alvise Piero Zorzi. Born in 1846, Zorzi had gone to the Academy school as a boy and as a young man continued to frequent the institution.[157] There he met, in 1873, a Mrs Margaret West, 'a very cultured lady and a clever painter'. She advised him to read Ruskin and to send him some of his work on early Venetian sculpture. Zorzi was planning a book on 'Artistic Venice' which was to include

topography, changes in names and their spelling, studies of façades and interiors of buildings which had been destroyed, notes on objects carried away from the city, notices of ubiquitous rebuilding, and much else referring to the monumental heritage of Venice, especially of Venice unknown.

Ruskin might have sympathized with the underlying intention, but laboriously detailed accounts, especially in Italian, tended to weary him. He did not reply. It was a more concentrated work that was to bring Zorzi Ruskin's admiration. Zorzi seems to have begun working on a critique of the restoration of St Mark's in 1875.[158] It was a detailed and comprehensive attack on work that had been in progress since 1818.[159] The Austrians had begun by selling jewels from the church treasury in order to pay for repair of the roof, but that had only been the start of a long-term project. In 1856 the Emperor Franz Josef had set up a perpetual fund to pay for the work. Since 1853 it had been in the hands of Giovanni Battista Meduna.[160] Meduna seems to have followed a crude version of Viollet-le-Duc's criterion of making all the parts of a building conform to the principles of its 'original epoch'. He had tried to make St Mark's look 'as new'. On the north and south façades the very varied, horizontally zigzagged marbles were replaced by regular, vertically-veined new marble. On the outside of the building capitals and reliefs were replaced by copies. Inside a fifteenth-century altar was removed because out of place in a 'Byzantine' building, while the old stone mosaics were replaced by glass ones in a new design. Much of the work was contracted out to private firms. Some were suspected of deliberate vandalism intended to create more work for the company.[161] Although Zorzi was not the first to criticize the innovations,[162] they had, by and large, been much admired. Viollet-le-Duc himself had written in praise of the thoroughness with which Italy was restoring her monuments, citing St Mark's as an example.[163] In November 1876 the *Gazzetta di Venezia* commended Salviati and Company, the British-owned glassworks firm responsible for the new mosaics, for their services to art and the nation.[164] Shortly afterwards comes a report of a move to prevent the Italian parliament from halving the money available for restoration in Venice and Milan.[165] The *Gazzetta* took up the cause with a front page article in bold type:

Now that the south side has been restored, everyone can see that the main façade is untidy, for it is loose and threatens to collapse; the floor is impassable and the Zeno Chapel in great disorder . . .[166]

Such a time of excitement probably favoured debate. Certain developments suggest that a shift towards more cautious restoration policies had already begun. Soon after Unification the Italian government had appointed provincial committees to catalogue monuments and works of art and advise on measures to be taken.[167] During the later seventies changes were taking place in these 'Commissioni Consultive dei Monumenti ed Oggetti d'Arte e di Antichità.' In some cases they were replaced by 'Commissioni Conservatrici dei Monumenti ed Oggetti d'Arte e di Antichità.'[168] The Venetian commission, dissolved in March 1876, was reconstituted in November with at least one admirer of Ruskin, Nicolò Barozzi, among its members.[169] On a less official level the Circolo Artistico Veneziano discussed a motion that protest should be made to the Minister about continuing desecration of Venetian architecture.[170] Zorzi was to find a ready welcome from some sections of the population. He tells of reading his paper on St Mark's to a 'number of artists, colleagues, fellow-citizens, fellow countrymen and foreigners', among them Carloforti.[171] The group acclaimed the essay and recommended publication. It was in getting it printed that Zorzi met with difficulties. The problems, however, were due to his criticisms of individuals rather than to his ideas. Rinaldo Fulin, Barozzi's colleague on the Deputazione di Storia Patria, was prepared to publish the paper in the *Archivio Veneto* if Zorzi would omit his 'virulent attacks' on the engineers. Ruskin's friend, Countess Bermani, also tried to persuade him to spare the feelings of Meduna. Zorzi's richer relatives refused to help. Tecchio, a parliamentary deputy and editor of the newspaper the *Adriatico*, offered uncensored but inevitably piecemeal publication.

It was here that someone from outside could help. Carloforti told Ruskin about Zorzi and on 7 December there was an enthusiastic meeting. Zorzi, who knew no English, read long extracts from his essay. In 'very English Italian' Ruskin declared fellowship. He proposed to finance the publication and write a prefatory letter. It was one of the rare occasions on which Ruskin felt less isolated from the world immediately around him. 'I am yours! I am yours! I am at last a Venetian!', he exclaimed.[172] A month later we find him studying Venetian dialect.[173] Collaboration with Zorzi on *Osservazioni intorno ai restauri interni ed esterni della basilica di San Marco* brought Ruskin certain pleasures.[174] There were reverential visits to Zorzi's mother, a member of one of the oldest of Venetian noble families, calls on Zorzi's delicate young Polish fiancée, Eugenia Szczepanowska, evenings with Zorzi himself on the Zattere. They talked of politics and religion. Ruskin told Zorzi of revelations 'with such conviction that I was amazed'. But when they went together to the Academy it was only Carloforti's jokes that prevented them from quarrelling about Renaissance painting. Ruskin chose to make a pupil of Eugenia, not Zorzi, who had 'no patience'.[175]

Nor could they agree easily on the wording of Ruskin's prefatory letter. Zorzi saw the battle in practical, administrative terms. Ruskin enjoyed the young man's fury, but envisaged a holier war. He did not care for local political struggles:

> You have been thinking, my dear friend, too much of the Prefecture of Venice — and not enough of the Soul of Europe. It is neither your part nor mine becomingly to play the part of police officers detecting petty theft. We are antiquaries and artists, defending a monument of Christianity.
>
> You shall forgive me — but I *must*, for your sake as for my own, insist on the word 'Religion' being introduced in page 12 . . . (XXXVII, 220).

The writing, translating and revising of the letter took from February until Easter.[176] It cost Zorzi some frustration and Ruskin considerable worry and effort. Eventually, in June, the book was published. On the 30th a letter pledging support appeared in the *Gazetta di Venezia*. Most of its 61 signatories were artists, architects or academics. The roles played by individuals, groups and governments in the controversy that followed are not yet clear. It caused much excitement in William Morris's Society for the Protection of Ancient Buildings in 1879 (XXIV, lxi, lxii). Some Venetians felt themselves unjustly accused, or that the English intervention was belated and tactless.[177] For by then restoration had been stopped and the matter being investigated. Arguments continued to flare up during the 1880s. Boni, helped by Alessandri, probably played an important part in bringing change.[178] With such public argument Ruskin could and would have little to do. As he wrote to one St Mark's campaigner, 'I don't believe we can save it by any protests.'[179] Instead he gave his efforts to having pupils and employees make visual and written records, and, unwillingly, to appealing for funds to finance them.[180]

In the meantime Ruskin had had his first total mental breakdown. Less than a year afterwards, in January 1879, he heard of an impending visit from Venice. He reacted with something approaching panic. In the course of this letter Ruskin's handwriting, at first calm, slides quickly out of control:

> Dear Count Zorzi
>
>   I have your letter sent me by Miss Yule, and was glad to hear of you, through her, but greatly alarmed by hearing you, like poor Carloforti, were thinking of coming to see me in England. You would NOT see me if you did. There are literally, thousands of people who want to see me, and whom I could help, if *I* were a thousand men in good health — instead of one man, old and ill.
>
>   I have not 'abandoned' *you* — but my brains have abandoned *me*. Have you not been told, or don't you believe that I was raving mad for two months? —

held down in my bed some times by three men? — Do you suppose I can after such warning — allow myself to be excited or grieved, when I *cannot* help. The only chance you or any other of my friends have of seeing more of me is by remembering that it is *I* who want help, now — and that the only help they can give me is by sparing me the pain of writing sad letters like this, and by staying quiet till I call for them.

Ever affectionately Yrs.

J Ruskin[181]

For nine years Ruskin was to avoid direct contact with Venice. He was yet to call for some of his Venetian friends, and to help them to continue what he had left unfinished. But for Ruskin himself Venetian work was virtually at an end.

III.5 1888

On 18 February 1881 Ruskin wrote to Rawdon Brown:

My dearest Papa
  Your lovely steady hand is a miracle! mine shakes all over the place unless I try hard to keep it steady. I've been thinking of little else than Venice and you for the last year — for I felt that both were like to be moved out of their place — Venice, violently — you, tenderly: — but that both would soon be lost to *me*.[1]

Two days later Ruskin's second attack of madness began. It may have been brought on in part by the death of 'Papa Carlyle' two weeks earlier. His Venetian father figure died in August 1883. But Ruskin's fears were in one sense justified, for he and Brown never met again. Ruskin suffered further attacks of madness in 1881 and 1882. In the autumn of 1882 he travelled in Italy but did not go to Venice. Ruskin did, however, call Alessandri from Venice to Pisa to join him and W.G. Collingwood, his secretary and assistant. He also brought to Tuscany another young Venetian, a man he had never met. Giacomo Boni must have written to Ruskin in 1881 enclosing a drawing, saying something of his position with the firm of architects restoring the Ducal Palace and of his strong Ruskinian views on the matter of restoration. Ruskin had responded in 'eager recognition',[2] but with a note of warning:

so far as in me lies, I will not fail you: most thankful shall I be to have your drawings and your help, at your own price . . . only of course, so far as you can retain your position and influence at Venice, — no other man can be so nobly useful, and you most [sic] not at present be [sic] yourself the mischief of acknowledge [sic] connection with me — only if any mischange [sic] should give you leisure or freedom, here am I ready to give you all kinds of work — you and Alessandri together. You will be my most honoured helpers — and most trusted, and I hope my life may be spaced [sic] long enough to be of material service to you both.[3]

Now, in Pisa in October 1882, Ruskin had need of assistance, not just with water colour studies of architectural detail, which were entrusted to Alessandri, but with measuring the inclination of the Duomo and Baptistry. The ideal man for the job was clearly Boni, with his official position, architectural training and marvellous head for heights, something for which Ruskin had also been noted.[4] This was not all they had in common. Boni also spoke excellent English, could

> draw like Lippi, & ... has read Carlyle, & me, & Pope! And he's *so* nice, altogether & it's a great thing for *him*, for he has scarcely ever been ten miles from Venice in his life — and he sees Pisa — Lucca, & Florence now for the first time.[5]

The Italian journey of 1882 gave Ruskin new energy and hope. On his return to England he took up the Slade Professorship once more. From Oxford and Brantwood Ruskin watched over and guided the young men who, he hoped, would continue his work. In Venice Anderson and Wedderburn collected information, Alessandri and Carloforti copied paintings and sculptures. Boni sent information about inscriptions, sculptures, the lion of St Mark, but remained independent.[6] He gave lectures on Ruskin, fought restoration, studied techniques for conservation, invented schemes as eccentric as Ruskin's had been.[7] Ruskin worried about his health, and told him repeatedly that if his opponents became too violent he was to leave Venice and come to him.[8] But he admired the young man all the more for the passion with which he expressed views similar to his own. Once Boni wrote of the meanness of Italian education, citing the example of

> a professor of philosophy who has earned a good reputation because he read a paper of his ten years ago — of which nobody understood a word, — he told me malicious things about our preventing so many respectable *commendatori* to make all the monuments, new, perfect, and white, — then he said that his ideal was 'una pollastra lessa' at dinner, and as to men, and women especially, he did not believe any one of them. — I had to turn around and rush away because a [*sic*] felt a knot in the throat and a great envy of smashing his face. —[9]

The year of their most intense correspondence was 1884. In 1885 came Ruskin's worst delirious illness. After that he could no longer carry such wide responsibilities, and he supervised his pupils and employees less closely, though they continued to exchange letters.

Ruskin made one more visit to Venice. The journey of 1882 had done him so much good that in 1888 his cousin and friends thought another might be of benefit. In July 1888 he set off with Arthur Severn, only to exchange him in Rouen for another companion, Detmar

Blow, a young architectural student. In Venice Alessandri and Boni were waiting for him. They were to have a 'happy hour' together.[10] But Ruskin had been nursing hopes of something more than memories. For the past two years he had been meeting and corresponding with a young art student, Kathleen Olander. This had been a matter of anxiety both to her parents and to the Severns, but not to Kathleen herself. A letter from Milan made clear to her what she had not understood, that Ruskin wanted her to be his wife.[11] Her reply, saying that she could not, reached Ruskin in Bassano on 4 October.[12] A week later Ruskin travelled to Venice, but after a few days had to get away from 'the elements of imagination which haunt me here'.[13] Ruskin's last 'Diary for Continental Journey'[14] ends with three entries:

September 28th. Friday. Among the kindest people in the world —
September 30th. Sunday — but I don't know what is going to become of me.
October 10th. VENICE. And less still here . . .[15]

Notes

Preface and Acknowledgements

1 Unpubl. letter from John James Ruskin to Georgiana Burne-Jones of 10 September 1863 in the Fitzwilliam Museum, Cambridge.
2 Examples of which are easily accessible in Robert Hewison's catalogue of the *Ruskin and Venice* exhibition at the J.B. Speed Art Museum, Louisville, Kentucky in 1978.

I.1 The English View of Venice before Ruskin

1 Andrew M. Canepa, 'From Degenerate Scoundrel to Noble Savage: The Italian Stereotype in 18th Century British Travel Literature', *English Miscellany*, No. 22 (1971), p. 107.
2 George B. Parks, *The English Traveler to Italy: The Middle Ages (to 1525)* (Rome, 1954), p. 581.
3 Corpus Christi Cambridge MS. 407, but taken from Parks, ibid., pp. 580-1.
4 In Samuel Purchas, *Hakluytus Posthumus or Purchas His Pilgrimes* (Glasgow, 1905), VII, 542; quoted by Parks, ibid., pp. 581-2, with modern spelling.
5 Anon., *The Pylgrymage of Sir Richarde Guylforde to the Holy Land, A.D. 1506*, Camden Society Reprint No. 51 (1851), pp. 8-9; quoted by Parks, ibid., p. 583, as given here.
6 J.R. Hale, *England and the Italian Renaissance: The Growth of Interest in its History and Art* (1954), pp. 11, 28.
7 See William Bouwsma, 'Venice and the Political Education of Europe', in, *Renaissance Venice*, ed. J.R. Hale (1973), p. 460.
8 Hale, *England and the Italian Renaissance*, p. 29.
9 Hale says that in general 'Taste . . . was vulgar, admiring a work in terms of its materials . . . and . . . ingenuity', ibid., p. 27.
10 Ibid., p. 23.
11 George B. Parks, 'The Decline and Fall of the English Renaissance Admiration of Italy', *Huntington Library Quarterly*, 31, No. 4 (August 1968), 342.
12 Bouwsma, op. cit., p. 451.

13   On the necessity of actually visiting Italy at this time see Ruth Kelso, *The Doctrine of the English Gentleman in the Sixteenth Century*, University of Illinois Studies in Language and Literature, 14, Nos. 1-2 (Urbana, 1929), 145.

14   E.H. Sugden, *A Topographical Dictionary to the Works of Shakespeare and His Fellow Dramatists*, Publications of the University of Manchester, No. 168 (Manchester, 1925), pp. 543-6.

15   *The Works of Ben Jonson*, eds. C.H. Herford, P. and E. Simpson (Oxford, 1925-52), II, 53.

16   *The Whole Works of Roger Ascham*, ed. Rev. Dr J.H. Giles (1864-65), III, 163.

17   Sugden, op. cit., p. 546.

18   *The Arden Edition of the Works of William Shakespeare: Othello*, ed. M.R. Ridley (1958), III. iii. 206-8.

19   Ibid., III. iii. 357.

20   Canepa, art. cit., pp. 121-2.

21   Bouwsma, op. cit., p. 461.

22   An English translation of Gasparo Contarini, *The Commonwealth and Gouvernment of Venice*, came out in 1959; Paolo Sarpi made his first London appearance in Italian, *Istoria del Concilio Tridentino* (1619), and then in translation, *The History of the Quarrels of Pope Paul V with the State of Venice* in 1626 and *The History of the Inquisition* in 1639; Paolo Paruta's, *Politick Discources* appeared in 1657 and *The History of Venice* in 1658.

23   Bouwsma, op. cit., p. 454.

24   Zera Fink, 'Venice and English Political Thought in the Seventeenth Century', *Modern Philology*, 38, No. 2 (November 1940), 155-72.

25   Giuliano Procacci, *History of the Italian People*, trans. Anthony Paul (1973), p. 200.

26   James Howell, *S.P.Q.V. A Survay of the Signorie of Venice, of Her Admired Policy, and Method of Government Etc., with a Cohortation to All Christian Princes to Resent Her Dangerous Condition at Present* (1651).

27   See Myron Gilmore, 'Myth and Reality in Venetian Political Theory', in Hale, *Renaissance Venice*, pp. 431-44.

28   *The Ready and Easy Way to Establish a Free Commonwealth and the Excellence Thereof, Compared with the Inconveniences and Dangers of Readmitting Kingship in this Nation* (1660), rpt. in *The Complete Works, Prose and Poetical, of John Milton*, (1875), p. 448.

29   Howell, op. cit., Preface.

30   Ibid., p. 199.

31   Bem.MS.L.4.

32   Howell, op. cit., p. 35.

33   Loc. cit.

34   Howell, op. cit., p. 40.

35   Loc. cit.

36   Jean Gailhard, *The Present State of the Republick of Venice, as to the*

Government, Laws, Forces, Riches, Manners, Customes, Revenue, and Territory of That Common-wealth With a Relation of the Present War in Candia (1669).

37 See (p. 25) John Moore, and most of those who followed him.

38 Gailhard, op. cit., pp. 153-8.

39 Ibid., p. 169.

40 Ibid., p. 13.

41 Parks, 'The Decline and Fall of the English Renaissance Admiration of Italy', p. 353. Parks cites the appearance in 1677 of *The History of the Government of Venice*, a translation of Amelot de Houssaye's account of the city; it included a chapter on 'the Principal Causes of the Decadence of the Republic'.

42 Jean Gailhard, *The Present State of the Princes and Republics of Italy with Observations on Them*, (1668), p. 106.

43 Gilbert Burnet, *Some Letters Containing an Account of What Seemed Most Remarkable in Switzerland, Italy Etc.* (1686; rpt. 1972), p. 133.

44 Ibid., p. 129. On the misery and 'dispeopling' of Italy and France, see pp. 4 and 42, on the danger of the lagoon drying up, p. 129.

45 Ibid., p. 151.

46 Ibid., pp. 150-1.

47 Ibid., p. 159.

48 Venetian military dependence on foreigners had, of course, been reflected eighty years before in *Othello*.

49 Burnet, op. cit., p. 147.

50 Ibid., pp. 143, 149-50.

51 Ibid., p. 130; on paintings and Palladian churches, p. 132.

52 Ibid., pp. 129-30. For Ruskin's reaction see *Letters from Venice*, pp. 31-2, and for Hester Thrale's see below.

53 Joseph Addison, *Remarks on Several Parts of Italy, Etc. in the Years 1701, 1702, 1703* (1705), rpt. in *The Miscellaneous Works of Joseph Addison*, ed. A.C. Guthkelch (1914), II, 52-4. Addison denies that the sea is shrinking away.

54 Ibid., II, 57.

55 Ibid., II, 59, 61-2.

56 Ibid., II, 54.

57 Paul R. Baker, *The Fortunate Pilgrims: Americans in Italy 1800-1860* (Cambridge, Mass., 1964), p. 12.

58 Arturo Graf, *L'anglomania e l'influsso inglese in Italia nel secolo XVIII* (Turin, 1911), pp. 244-82.

59 *The Yale Edition of Horace Walpole's Correspondence*, ed. W.S. Lewis (New Haven, Conn., 1937-date), XVIII, 63.

60 Ibid., XX, 46-7.

61 *The Correspondence of Thomas Gray*, eds. Paget Toynbee and Leonard Whibley (Oxford, 1935), I, 182.

62 *The Travel Diaries of William Beckford of Fonthill*, ed. Guy Chapman

(Cambridge, 1928), I, 95.

63   Given in Robert Halsband, *The Life of Lady Mary Wortley Montagu* (Oxford, 1956), p. 185.

64   IX, xxiv; Ruskin was reading her letters in the summer of 1849.

65   *Boswell on the Grand Tour: Italy, Corsica, and France 1765-66*, eds. Frank Brady and Frederick A. Pottle (1955), p. 11; see also p. 109.

66   *The Dunciad*, Bk. IV, lines 299-310.

67   *Travel Diaries of William Beckford*, I, 93-4.

68   *Boswell on the Grand Tour*, p. 11.

69   *Memoirs of My Life*, ed. George A. Bonnard (1966), p. 135.

70   *The Letters of Edward Gibbon*, ed. J.E. Norton (1956), I, 193.

71   Samuel Sharp, *Letters from Italy Describing the Customs and Manners of That Country in the Years 1765 and 1766* (1766), p. 11.

72   Ibid., pp. 11-12.

73   Ibid., p. 17. Shelley shows what could be done with the same image by one of another disposition. 'The gondolas themselves are things of a most romantic & picturesque appearance; I can only compare them to moths of which a coffin might have been the crysallis'; *The Letters of Percy Bysshe Shelley*, ed. Frederick L. Jones (Oxford, 1964), II, 42. Ruskin also uses the coffin image in 'Velasquez the Novice'; see I, 539.

74   Sharp, op. cit., p. 31.

75   Ibid., pp. 29-30.

76   Herbert Barrows, 'Convention and Novelty in the Romantic Generation's Experience of Italy', *Bulletin of the New York Public Library*, 67 (June 1963), 372.

77   Lawrence Sterne, *A Sentimental Journey through France and Italy* (1768; rpt. 1967), p. 52.

78   Michael Lloyd, 'Hawthorne, Ruskin and the Hostile Tradition', *English Miscellany*, No. 6 (1955), pp. 109-33. Lloyd's article deals with the 'hostile tradition' as a nineteenth-century phenomenon only.

79   J. Voisine, 'Voyageurs anglais à Venise au XVIIIe siecle', in *Venezia nelle letterature moderne; Atti del Primo Congresso dell'Associazone Internazionale di Letteratura Comparata*, ed. Carlo Pellegrini (Venice, 1961), p. 62.

80   See Graf, op. cit., pp. xi, 48.

81   Guiseppe Baretti, *An Account of the Manners and Customs of Italy; With Observations on the Mistakes of Some Travellers with Regard to That Country* (1768), II, 143-54.

82   Baretti used Mrs Thrale's second marriage to insult her in his *Strictures on Signora Piozzi's Publication of Doctor Johnson's Letters* (1788), rpt. *Prefazioni e Polemiche*, ed. Luigi Piccioni (Bari, 1911), pp. 329, 331.

83   It was another of the books John James Ruskin drew his son's attention to in the autumn of 1851. He copied out extracts, asking his son whether Mrs Piozzi's observations were still accurate, in his letters of 14-15, 17-18 November 1851; unpubl. letters, Bem. MS. L. 4. Ruskin replied enthusiastically,

but corrected her on some points; see *Letters from Venice*, pp. 69-75.

84 Hester Thrale (afterwards Piozzi), *Observations and Reflections Made in the Course of a Journey through France, Italy and Germany* (1789), II, 151.

85 Ibid., II, 163.

86 See Marino Berengo, *La Società veneta alla fine del settecento: ricerche storiche*, (Florence, 1955), p. 1n.

87 Thrale, op. cit., II, pp. 180-1.

88 Ibid., II, 173. This was one of the extracts sent to Ruskin by his father.

89 Ibid., II, 152.

90 Loc. cit.

91 Ibid., II, 151, 157, 175.

92 See A.J. Finberg's *Life of J.M.W. Turner, R.A.* (Oxford, 1939: 2nd edn 1961) pp. 36-40.

93 *Travel Diaries of William Beckford*, I, 86.

94 Ibid., I, 85.

95 Ibid., I, 95.

96 Ibid., I, 102-3. For one of Ruskin's many Venetian sunsets, see *Letters from Venice*, p. 71.

97 *Travel Diaries of William Beckford*, I, 78-9.

98 Ibid., I, 85.

99 Ibid., I, 80.

100 Ibid., I, 81.

101 Ibid., I, 82, 100, 83.

102 Ibid., I, 98.

103 Ibid., I, 85-90. I am grateful to Robert Hewison for drawing my attention to Ruskin's note on these passages in his unpublished diary entry of 1850, Bodl. MS. Eng. Misc. C.217, fo. 60.

104 *Travel Diaries of William Beckford*, I, 107.

105 Roderick Marshall, *Italy in English Literature 1755-1815: Origins of the Romantic Interest in Italy*, Columbia University Studies in English and Comparative Literature, No. 116 (New York, 1934), p. 167n. See also Voisine, art. cit., p. 71 and F.C. Roe, 'Venise et la littérature anglaise', also in *Venezia nelle letterature moderne*, ed. Pellegrini, p. 56.

106 The whole 1783 edition was burnt at Fonthill in 1801, except for four or five copies (one of which Samuel Rogers took). *Italy: With Sketches of Spain and Portugal* (1834) in part based on *Dreams*, must have been what Ruskin saw — unless Rogers lent him his stolen volume.

107 John Moore, *A View of Society and Manners in Italy: With Anecdotes Relating to Some Eminent Characters* (1781). This went into five editions by the end of the decade.

108 Ibid., I, 144.

109 Voisine, art. cit., I, 144.

110 Moore, op. cit., I, 59.

111   Ibid., 1, 57-8.

112   Ibid., I, 59.

113   Ibid., I, 70.

114   Ibid., I, 157.

115   Thrale, op. cit., II, 162.

116   Moore, op. cit., I, 179.

117   Ibid., I, 237.

118   Joseph Forsyth, *Remarks on Antiquities, Arts, and Letters during an Excursion in Italy in the Years 1802 and 1803* (1813), p. 362.

119   Voisine, art. cit., p. 71.

120   Lady Sydney Owenson Morgan, *Italy* (1821), II, 473-6. William Stewart Rose, translator of *Orlando Furioso*, lived a year in Venice, married a Venetian, and expressed similar views; see *Letters from the North of Italy Addressed to Henry Hallam Esq.* (1819), II, 68.

121   Morgan, *Italy*, I, 17.

122   See C.P. Brand, *Italy and the English Romantics* (Cambridge, 1957). Beatrice Corrigan's *Italian Poets and English Critics, 1755-1859: A Collection of Critical Essays* (Chicago and London, 1969) has a useful introductory essay on the rediscovery of Dante, Petrarch and Boccaccio, mentioning Ruskin's contribution to the understanding of Dante (pp. 23-4). On the mid-century exiles, see H.W. Rudman, *Italian Nationalism and English Letters: Figures of the Risorgimento and Victorian Men of Letters* (1940).

123   *The Letters of Percy Bysshe Shelley*, ed. Jones, II, 43.

124   *Julian and Maddalo*, lines 450-7.

125   *The Letters of Percy Bysshe Shelley*, ed. Roger Ingpen (1909), II, 649.

126   *Lines Written Among the Euganean Hills*, lines 106-10. Ruskin used a slightly longer passage including these lines to head a chapter of 'Velasquez the Novice', I, 543; the editors note that he 'compresses, and rearranges' the lines.

127   *Lines Written Among the Euganean Hills*, lines 129-33.

128   Barrows, op. cit., 372, 374.

129   *The Poetical Works of Lord Byron*, ed. E.H. Coleridge (1905), p. 465.

130   Ibid., p. 464.

131   *Childe Harold*, IV, Stanzas 19, 25.

132   Ibid., Stanza 1.

133   Ibid., Stanzas 13, 14, 17. Ruskin uses the same two comparisons in the opening of *The Stones of Venice*, IX, 17. Byron influenced Ruskin's view of Venice enormously, as we shall see.

134   *Childe Harold*, IV, Stanzas 15, 25.

135   Ibid., Stanzas 3, 18.

136   Robert Gleckner, *Byron and the Ruins of Paradise* (Baltimore, 1967), p. 310.

137   *Childe Harold*, IV, Stanza 29.

138   *Byron's Letters and Journals*, ed. Leslie Marchand (1973-date), V, 129.

139   *Memoirs, Journals and Correspondence*, ed. Lord John Russell (1853), III, 24.

140   Morgan, *Italy*, II, 450.

141   Samuel Rogers, *Italy: A Poem* was first published anonymously in 1822 but, it was the 1830 edition, illustrated with engravings from Turner, Stothard and others, that was enormously successful. Within two years 7,000 copies had been sold, one of them to Henry Telford as a birthday present for the son of his partner, John James Ruskin (XXXV, 79). Here Ruskin calls Rogers, justifiably, 'a mere dilettante' in comparison to Byron.

142   *Landscape Annual* for 1831, p. 1.

143   *The Complete Works of William Hazlitt*, ed. P.P. Howe (1930-34), X, 267.

144   Morgan, *Italy*, II, 452.

145   Rogers, *Italy: A Poem* (1830 edn), p. 48.

146   *Heath's Picturesque Annual* for 1832, pp. 162-5. Ritchie was a journalist, editor and hack novelist.

147   Examples of love stories are 'The Bridge of Sighs' and 'The Intrigues of Venice' in the *Forget-Me-Not* for 1826. Some mystery tales with varying degrees of Gothic horror are 'Il Fascino', 'A Tale of Venice' and 'Ippolito' in *Friendship's Offering* for 1828, 1831 and 1834 respectively, and 'The Gondola' in the *Keepsake* for 1831.

148   Rogers, op. cit., p. 57. Rogers tells several stories from Venetian history, including that of the abduction of the brides by pirates in 954, and the old favourites of the two Foscari and Marin Faliero. The Foscari story appears again in 'The Palace of the Foscari' in the *Landscape Annual* for 1830. Lord Morpeth uses ceremonial in his poem 'The Nuptials of the Doge of Venice with the Adriatic Sea' in the *Keepsake* for 1830.

149   *Landscape Annual* for 1830, p. 221 and for 1831, pp. 32, 67, 77. Roscoe edited the *Landscape Annual* from 1830 to 1836, when the Ruskins' friend, W.H. Harrison, took over.

150   *The Gem* for 1829, p. 217.

151   *The Complete Works of William Hazlitt*, X, 267-8.

152   *Landscape Annual* for 1830, p. 187 and for 1831, pp. 102-3; see also *Heath's Picturesque Annual* for 1832, pp. 175-6. Forsyth's comments are in *Remarks*, pp. 362-3.

153   Joseph Woods, *Letters of an Architect from France, Italy, and Greece* (1828), I, 255-6. In *The Seven Lamps* Ruskin used Wood's comments to show that his own view of the Palace was not 'altogether trite or accepted' (VIII, 206).

154   *Heath's Picturesque Annual* for 1832, p. 178.

155   Morgan, *Italy*, II, 456.

156   Ibid., II, 461.

157   *Finden's Illustrations of the Works of Byron* (1833), I, 'The Piazzetta'.

158   See Ingrid Daemmrich's 'The Ruins Motif as Artistic Device in French Literature (Part I)', *The Journal of Aesthetic and Art Criticism*, 30, No. 4 (summer, 1972), 449-57.

159   *Diary, Reminiscences, and Correspondence of Henry Crabb Robinson*, ed. Thomas Sadler (1869), II, 197.

160 Morgan, *Italy*, II 452.
161 C.B. von Miltitz in a description of the Bridge of Sighs, p. 27.
162 *Diary . . . Henry Crabb Robinson*, II, 85.

I.2   1835

1   The best account of their backgrounds is Helen Gill Viljoen's *Ruskin's Scottish Heritage: A Prelude* (Urbana, 1956).
2   For these journeys and Ruskin's geological interests see Robert Hewison, *John Ruskin: The Argument of the Eye* (1976), pp. 13-20.
3   The diary survives in transcript, and is Bem.MS.T.48.
4   It is the song of the flower girls in 'Velasquez the Novice', I, 541.
5   Hewison, for example, op. cit., pp. 16-17.
6   I, xxix, letter to James Hogg of 13 February 1834.
7   'Etna' appears in II, 278; the one about Vesuvius is unpublished and appears in Bem.MS.T.28.
8   *Family Letters*, I, 220, letter to John James Ruskin of 21 February.
9   We know that Ruskin knew the 1830 volume from the letter to W.H. Harrison of 30 January 1841 (see I, 445 and n.), that John James bought the volume for 1834 (*Family Letters*, I, 286n.), and from 1835 to 1844 Ruskin himself contributed something to every volume. This was by no means the only annual Ruskin was familiar with. He contributed to the *Spiritual Times* of 1830, the *Amaranth* of 1839, and both *Heath's Book of Beauty* and the *Keepsake* volumes of 1845 and 1846, and John James Ruskin had bought the volumes for 1834 (*Family Letters*, I, 286). Ruskin certainly knew the *Continental Annual and Romantic Cabinet* for 1832 (see II, 430), *Heath's Picturesque Annual* for 1835 (III, 221), and the *Landscape Annual*, of which he recommended a friend to buy any old volumes he might find (I, 428, letter to Edward Clayton of 3 December 1840).
10 XXXV, 91. This number also contained another of 'St. Mark's, and the Doge's Palace at Venice'.
11 See above, n. 9, and XXXV, 140.
12 I, 445, letter to W.H. Harrison of 30 January 1841.
13 This and the following purchases are recorded in John James Ruskin's account books and are given in *Family Letters*, I, 286n. and 301n.
14 For Forsyth and Rose see above, pp. 26 and 196, n.120.
15 *Family Letters*, I, 303, letter from Margaret to John James Ruskin of 21 February 1835.
16 Ibid., I, 297, letter to John James Ruskin of 18 February 1835.
17 Loc. cit.
18 This verse letter, largely unpublished, survives in transcript, Bem.MS.T.28.
19 Loc. cit.
20 *Diaries*, I, 4, 13 June 1835. 'Cyan.' refers to the 'cyanometer', an instrument

Ruskin used to measure the blueness of the sky.

21 Ibid., I, 20-3, 11-14 July 1835.

22 Ibid., I, 25, 15 July 1835.

23 Ibid., I, 26.

24 Ruskin himself satirized it in 'The Ascent of the St. Bernard: A Dramatic Sketch', I, 519.

25 *Diaries*, I, 4, 9 June 1835.

26 Ibid., I, 70, 23 September.

27 XXXV, 182, where the drawing is reproduced.

28 Four lines are given in Robert Hewison, *Ruskin and Venice* (1978), p. 9, otherwise unpubl., Bem.MS.T.28.

29 I, 453, letter to Clayton of 16 May 1841.

30 Samuel Rogers provides the names of the hero and heroine, Marcolini and Bianca (see *Italy: A Poem* (1830 edn), pp. 68, 85), Shakespeare that of the second protagonist, Orsino. In character Bianca is an attempt at a Portia type; she is witty and sets her aspiring lovers an appearance and reality test. The dwelling on the island mad-house (II, 508) probably comes from *Julian and Maddalo*, the idea that Venetians cannot survive away from their own city (II, 480) from *The Two Foscari* (I.1).

31 I, 547-51. This character, Peter Hayward, resembles Samuel Sharp in many respects. For Sharp see above, p. 21.

32 The city rises from the 'altar' of ocean as in *Lines Written Among the Euganean Hills*.

33 For an analysis of Turner's changing approach to Venice, his cautious progress from detailed architectural studies to poetic assembly, see Hardy S. George, 'Turner in Venice', unpubl. Ph.D thesis, University of London, 1970.

I.3   1841

1 In *Praeterita* (XXXV, 134) Ruskin was to give a more sentimental picture of his own and his father's reactions to the return to London.

2 Ruskin had been writing for Loudon's *Magazine of Natural History* since 1834. *The Poetry of Architecture*, his study of cottages and villas, largely picturesque, in relation to their natural settings and national character, first appeared in parts in the *Architectural Magazine* between November 1837 and December 1838.

3 *Diaries*, I, 158, 28 February 1841. In the rest of this section all letters and diary entries dated September to December are of 1840, and all dated January to June are of 1841, unless otherwise stated.

4 *Diaries*, I, 186, 12 May.

5 Ibid., I, 86, 88-9, 11 and 15 October.

6 Ibid., I, 94, 22 October.

7 Ibid., I, 107, 108, 110, 113, 8, 9, 15 and 25 November.

8 *Diaries*, 1, 120, 136, 137, 143, 146, 159, 6 December, 6, 17, 27 January and 1 March.

9 Jean Charles Léonard Simonde du Sismondi's history had been first published in sixteen volumes in 1803-18, but Ruskin was probably using the three-volume edition of 1838. His copy, now at Bembridge, has extensive scoring and notes in the first two volumes.

10 *Diaries*, I, 122, 9 December.

11 Ibid., I, 130, 30 December.

12 Ibid., I, 161, 3 March.

13 Ibid., I, 173, 16 April.

14 Ibid., I, 127, 18 December; see also 166, 17 March.

15 Ibid., I, 176, 20 April.

16 Ibid., I, 183.

17 Ibid., I, 184, 7 May.

18 Ibid., I, 184, 8 May.

19 Ibid., I, 185, 9 May.

20 Ibid., I, 185-6, 12 May.

21 I, 447, letter of 16 May.

22 *Diaries*, I, 184, 7 May.

23 Ibid., I, 184-5, 8 May.

24 The diary is unpublished and exists in transcript at Bembridge, MS.T.49. This is from her entry for 7 May, fo.222.

25 Ibid., fo.232, 17 May.

26 Ibid., fo.226, 12 May.

27 *Diaries*, I, 186, 12 May.

28 Bem.MS.T.49, fo.222, 7 May.

29 Mary Richardson went on 7 May, Ruskin on 13 May (*Diaries*, I, 187).

30 *Diaries*, I, 188, 15 May.

31 Bem.MS.T.49, fos.219, 224, 6 and 10 May.

32 *Diaries*, I, 185, 12 May.

33 Ibid., I, 187, 14 May.

34 Ibid., I, 187-8, 15 and 16 May.

35 Ibid., I, 189, 16 May.

36 I, 453, letter to Clayton of 16 May.

37 *Diaries*, I, 185, 9 May.

38 Venetian trade was on the increase during the 1830s and 1840s, partly because the city had been made a free port; see Tullio Bagiotti, *Venezia da modello a problema* (Venice, 1972), p. 216. The lagoon and the Grand Canal were, however, silting up. The San Nicolò entry to the lagoon had been closed to ships for many years, and now the Malamocco entry was becoming difficult. Protective jetties were being built to correct this. One was completed in 1838, another in 1857. Frederick C. Lane gives an account in *Venice: A Maritime Republic* (1973), pp. 453-4.

39 Bem.MS.T.49, fos.218-19, 6 May.

40   I, 434-5, letter of 12 February.
41   The title was abbreviated in subsequent volumes.
42   II, 227-8. The poem is of 1844.

II.1   1845

1   *Diaries*, I, 212. Comments on the previous year's journey are scattered through pp. 212-19, 10 September-24 October.
2   Ibid., I, 220, 20 November.
3   Ibid., I, 247. Woodburn was apparently regarded as an authority, for he was sent to Venice by the British government in 1851 to value a collection of paintings up for sale; this emerges from John James Ruskin's unpublished letter to his son of 23 March 1852, Bem.MS.L.4.
4   Unpubl., n.d., Bodl.MS.Eng.Lett.C.32, fos.136-7.
5   Unpubl. letter to the Rev. W.L. Brown, Bodl.MS.Eng.Lett.C.32, fo.161.
6   III, 668-9, letter of 12 October 1844 to Liddell.
7   I, 493-4, letter to the Rev. Edward Clayton of 17 June 1843.
8   *Diaries*, I, 249.
9   For Ruskin's critical mediaevalist reading during the 1840s see Nicholas Shrimpton's unpublished doctoral thesis, 'Economic, Social and Literary Influences upon the Development of Ruskin's Ideas to *Unto This Last* (1860)', pp. 150-82, Bodl.MS.D.Phil.C.2063 (1976).
10   *Diaries*, I, 265.
11   Ibid., I, 311.
12   *Ruskin in Italy*, pp. 35-6, 43, letters of 23 and 27 April 1845. All letters in this section are of 1845 and are from Ruskin to his father unless otherwise stated.
13   Ibid., p. 52, letter of 5 May.
14   Ibid., p. 128, letter of 25 June.
15   Ibid., p. 130, postscript of 26 June.
16   Ibid., p. 95, letter of 2 June.
17   Ibid., p. 140, letter of 9 July.
18   Ibid., p. 57, letter of 10 May.
19   Ibid., p. 142n., letter of 26 June from John James Ruskin to his son.
20   Ibid., pp. 142-3, letter of 10 July.
21   Ibid., p. 244, letter of 23 July from John James Ruskin to his son.
22   Ibid., p. 168, letter of 6 August.
23   Unpubl. letter of 17 August 1845 from John James Ruskin to his son, Bem. MS.L.3.
24   *Ruskin in Italy*, p. 194, letter of 6 September.
25   Ibid., p. 196, letter of 7 September.
26   Ibid., p. 197, letter of 7 September.
27   Ibid., p. 221, letter of 10 October.
28   Ibid., p. 183, letter of 23 August.

29   Ibid., p. 198, letter of 10 September.
30   Ibid., p. 199, postscript of 11 September.
31   Ibid., p. 198, letter of 10 September.
32   Ibid., p. 199, postscript of 11 September.
33   Ibid., pp. 201, letter of 11 September.
34   Ibid., p. 209, letter of 23 September.
35   Ibid., p. 218, letter of 1 October.
36   Ibid., pp. 201-2, letter of 14 September. Later Ruskin found that what he had thought was scraped marble was in fact painted stucco — the old marbles had been taken away, it seems; p. 224, letter of 14 October.
37   Ibid., p. 209, letter of 23 September.
38   Ibid., p. 198, letter of 10 September.
39   Ibid., pp. 199-200, letter of 11 September.
40   Ibid., p. 201, letter of 14 September.
41   For these projects and the policies of successive administrations on town planning during the nineteenth century see Giandomenico Romanelli, *Venezia Ottocento*: Materiali per una storia architettonica e urbanistica della città nel secolo XIX (Rome, 1978).
42   *Ruskin in Italy*, pp. 198, 202, 224, letters of 10, 14 September and 14 October.
43   Ibid., pp. 198-9, letter of 10 September.
44   *Diaries*, I, 185, 9 May.
45   *Ruskin in Italy*, p. 201, letter of 14 September.
46   Ibid., pp. 199, 209, 222, postscript of 11 September, letters of 23 September and 11 October.
47   Ibid., p. 205, letter of 16 September.
48   See Ruskin's letter to Prout of 21 February 1844, in III, 664.
49   *Ruskin in Italy*, p. 219, letter of 4 October.
50   Ibid., p. 202, letter of 14 September.
51   Ibid., p. 219, letter of 4 October.
52   Ibid., p. 210.
53   Ibid., pp. 211-12.
54   In the 1883 Epilogue to *Modern Painters* II (IV, 354).
55   *Ruskin in Italy*, p. 212, letter of 24 September.
56   Ibid., pp. 144-5, letter of 11 July.
57   Ibid., p. 185, letter of 24 August.
58   Ibid., p. 212, letter of 24 September.
59   Ibid., p. 145, letter of 11 July.
60   Ibid., p. 185, letter of 24 August.
61   Ibid., p. 212, letter of 24 September.
62   Ibid., p. 217, letter of 30 September.
63   IV, 394, letter of 21 September (surely misdated).
64   *Ruskin in Italy*, p. 223, letter of 11 October.
65   Ibid., p. 214, letter of 26 September.

66   Loc. cit. For an account of the friendship see M.J.H. Liversidge, 'John Ruskin and William Boxall: An Unpublished Correspondence', *Apollo*, 85, No. 59, N.S. (January 1967), pp. 39-44.

67   *Ruskin in Italy*, p. 214, letter of 26 September.

68   Ibid., pp. 215-16, both letters of 28 September. Anna Jameson's *Sacred and Legendary Art* appeared in book form in 1850.

69   *Ruskin in Italy*, pp. 216, 230, letters of 30 September and 23 October.

70   Ibid., p. 219, letter of 4 October.

71   Ibid., p. 224, letter of 13 October.

72   See the description of the 1833-43 manuscript, IV, 361-2 and Robert Hewison, *John Ruskin: The Argument of the Eye* (1976), p. 66.

II.2   1846

1   Unpubl. letter of 10-13 September, Bem.MS.L.3.

2   *Ruskin in Italy*, p. 229, letter of 23 October.

3   *Diaries*, I, 321-2, 4 January 1846.

4   *Ruskin in Italy*, pp. 186-7, letter to Margaret Ruskin of 24 August 1845.

5   Ibid., p. 187n.

6   Ibid., p. 187.

7   John James Ruskin's travel diary for 1846 is with that for 1833 in Bem.MS. 33.A.

8   Unpubl. letter from John James Ruskin to his son of 15-16 September 1851, Bem.MS.L.4.

9   Bem.MS.33.A., entries for 18 and 19 May 1846.

10   This part of the letter to W.H. Harrison of 25 May 1846 is unpublished, and is Bodl.MS.Eng.Lett.C.32, fo.243.

11   Unpubl. letter from John James Ruskin to W.H. Harrison of 20 June 1846, Bodl.MS.Eng.Lett.C.32, fo.244.

12   Unpubl. letter from John James Ruskin to W.H. Harrison of 28 July 1846, Bodl.MS.Eng.Lett.C.32, fo.248.

13   Unpubl. letter from John James Ruskin to W.H. Harrison of 14 July 1846, Bodl.MS.Eng.Lett.C.32, fo.247.

14   *Diaries*, I, 337-8, 17 May 1846.

15   Ibid., I, 337, 16 May 1846.

204 Ruskin and Venice

16   Ibid., I, 338-41, 17-29 May 1846. For several days no entries appear, but he also made notes elsewhere. He refers to the 'smallest notebook', 'Yellow paper note book' and 'sheets' of series of capitals (*Diaries*, I, 341, 29 May and 1 June 1846). Ruskin had probably begun using the system he was to use in 1849-50, or something approaching it (see Robert Hewison, *Ruskin and Venice* (1978), pp. 54-5). He is also comparing his findings with those of Robert Willis, *Remarks on the Architecture of the Middle Ages, Especially of Italy* (Cambridge, 1835), to which he refers on 27 May (*Diaries*, I, 339).

17   Bodl.MS.Eng.Lett.C.32, fo.243, letter of 25 May 1846, partly published in VIII, xxiii.

18   XXXVI, 63-5, letter of 30 August 1846.

19   XXXVI, 61, letter to Dr John Brown of 27 June 1846. Brown had written to Ruskin about *Modern Painters*, and thus became his friend.

20   Loc. cit.

21   III, 213-14. In speaking 'Of Truth of Water' Ruskin does castigate Canaletto for failing to record the Venice of fishing-boats and fruit markets, the Venice Ruskin had drawn with Harding in 1845. The scene Ruskin describes in some respects is a reversion to that earlier, picturesque city, but modified by the intrusion of contrast between past and present. The seamen are 'the last of the old Venetian race, who yet keep the right Giorgione colour on their brows and bosoms, in strange contrast with the sallow sensual degradation of the creatures that live in the cafés of the Piazza . . .' (III, 515-16).

22   VIII, xxvii, letter to W.H. Harrison of 18 September 1847.

23   Unpubl. letter to the Rev. W.L. Brown of July 1847, Bodl.MS.Eng.Lett.C.32, fos.264-5.

24   Loc. cit. The heterogeneous nature of Ruskin's reading at this time would appear from the list of books bought given in his letter to his father of 29 July, given in VIII, xxvi.

25   See Mary Lutyens, *The Ruskins and the Grays* (1972), p. 222, letter to Effie of 24 June 1849.

26   For accounts of the revolution see G.M. Trevelyan, *Manin and the Venetian Revolution of 1848* (1923) and Paul Ginsborg, *Daniele Manin and the Venetian Revolution of 1848* (Cambridge, 1979).

27   *Trevelyan Letters*, p. 7, letter of 24 June 1848.

28   Ibid., p. 9, letter from Effie of 15 July 1848; *Diaries*, II, 367, 16 July 1848. Ruskin also had a bad cough, and there was considerable friction between Effie and old Mrs Ruskin, Ruskin taking his mother's part; see Lutyens, *The Ruskins and the Grays*, pp. 126-8.

29   Lutyens, *The Ruskins and the Grays*, p. 128.

30   VIII, xxix, letter from John James Ruskin to W.H. Harrison of 12 August 1848.

31   Unpubl. part of letter to W.H. Harrison of 24 October 1848, Bodl.MS.Eng. Lett.C.32, fo.318.

32   See Denis Mack Smith, *Victor Emanuel, Cavour and the Risorgimento*

(1971), pp. 16-18.

33 Unpubl. letter to John James Ruskin of 25 August 1848, Bodl.MS.Eng.Lett. C.32, fo.313.

34 VIII, xxxii-xxxiii, letter to W.H. Harrison of 24 October 1849.

35 Unpubl. letter of 7 November 1848, Bodl.MS.Eng.Lett.C.32, fo.322.

II.3   1849-50

1 Mary Lutyens, *The Ruskins and the Grays* (1972), p. 186, letter to Effie of 27 April 1849.

2 Ibid., p. 190, letter from John James Ruskin to Mr Gray of 29 April 1849.

3 Ibid., p. 184, mistakenly dated 25 April 1849. The Brescia rebellion had been crushed in March.

4 XXXVI, 100-1, letter to George Richmond of 20 May 1849.

5 Lutyens, *The Ruskins and the Grays*, p. 199, letter to Effie of 3 May 1849.

6 Ibid., pp. 201, 231-6, letters to Effie and Mr Gray of 10 May and 5 July 1849.

7 Ibid., p. 216, letter of 14 June. In the rest of this section all letters dated from June to December are of 1849, and all dated January to May are of 1850, unless otherwise stated.

8 Ibid., p. 221, letter of 24 June.

9 Ibid., p. 222, same letter.

10 G.M. Trevelyan, *Manin and the Venetian Revolution of 1848* (1923), p. 236. The Austrians lost 7,000 men through disease, a few hundred in battle.

11 Unpubl. letter from John James Ruskin to his son, n.d., Bem.MS.L.3.

12 Ibid.

13 *The Times*, 1 September 1849.

14 Lutyens, *The Ruskins and the Grays*, pp. 248-50.

15 XXXVI, 104, letter to the Rev. W.L. Brown, Ruskin's Christ Church tutor, of 11 December.

16 *Effie in Venice*, p. 39.

17 Unpubl. letter from John James Ruskin to W.H. Harrison of 4 August, Bodl. MS.Eng.Lett.C.33, fo.11.

18 Unpubl. letter from John James Ruskin to his son of 27 November, Bem. MS.L.3.

19 Lutyens, *The Ruskins and the Grays*, p. 255, letter from John James Ruskin to his son of 25 September.

20 Letter from Effie to Pauline Trevelyan of 27 October, *Trevelyan Letters*, p. 19.

21 As Effie told George Gray in January. This is one of the passages in Mary Lutyen's transcript (Bem.MS.T.46, fo.142) of Effie's letters in the Pierpont Morgan Library but omitted from the published edition.

22 *Effie in Venice*, p. 84, letter of 10 December.

23 *Trevelyan Letters*, p. 20, letter from Effie of 27 October.

24   *Effie in Venice*, p. 70, letter of 15 November.

25   Ibid., p. 69, same letter.

26   Ibid., pp. 125-6, letter of 27 January.

27   Tullio Bagiotti, *Venezia da modello a problema* (Venice, 1972), pp. 219-20. Venetian status as a free port, suspended in 1848, was not restored until 1851.

28   *Effie in Venice*, p. 82, letter of 3 December.

29   Ibid., p. 71, letter of 19 November.

30   Ibid., p. 78, letter of 27 November.

31   Ibid., p. 79, letter of 3 December.

32   Ibid., pp. 81-2, same letter.

33   Ibid., p. 91, letter of 22 December.

34   Ibid., p. 106, letter of 6 January.

35   Trevelyan, op. cit., p. 61.

36   *Effie in Venice*, p. 91, letter of 22 December.

37   Ibid., p. 129, letter of 27 January.

38   Ibid., pp. 92, 151, letters of 22 December and 3 March.

39   *Trevelyan Letters*, pp. 23-4, letter from Effie of January.

40   *Effie in Venice*, p. 86, letter of 10 December and Ruskin 's letter to Brown of 8 January quoted below.

41   Of the Tintorettos in the Scuola di San Rocco Effie said 'we only looked at two because they are so very large and they take so much mind out of you looking and entering into them thoroughly that it is extremely fatiguing . . .' and parrots Ruskin in similar fashion on the capitals of the Ducal Palace in two unpublished passages in Mary Lutyen's transcript, Bem.MS.T.46. fos.87 and 92, letters of 19 and 24 November. In the published part of the first letter she says 'when I want you to get a fuller description . . . than I have time to give you I will refer to the particular page in Murray . . .' (*Effie in Venice*, p. 73).

42   *Effie in Venice*, p. 99, letter of 22 December.

43   As in getting the brother of her gondolier out of conscription, ibid., p. 125, letter of 27 January.

44   Ibid., p. 89, postscript of 18 December.

45   Ibid., p. 92, letter of 22 December.

46   *Trevelyan Letters*, p. 23, letter from Effie of January.

47   *Effie in Venice*, p. 54.

48   Unpubl. passage from letter of 4 November in Mary Lutyen's transcript, Bem.MS.T.46, fo.69.

49   *Effie in Venice*, p. 80, letter of 3 December.

50   Unpubl. letter from John James Ruskin to his son of 27 November, Bem.MS. L.3.

51   *Effie in Venice*, p. 77, letter of 27 November.

52   Ibid., p. 123, letter of 18 January.

53   Ibid., pp. 127, 189, letters of 27 January and 22 December.

54 Ibid., p. 111, n.d.

55 Ibid., p. 126, letter of 27 January.

56 Ibid., p. 134, letter of 3 February and unpubl. passage in letter of 22 December given in Mary Lutyen's transcript, Bem.MS.T.40, fo.120.

57 *Effie in Venice*, p. 144, letter of 18 February.

58 Ibid., pp. 116, 149, letters of 18 January and 24 February.

59 From a passage copied by Effie in her letter of 24 February, ibid., p. 146.

60 Loc. cit.

61 XXXVI, 104, letter to the Rev. W.L. Brown of 11 December.

62 Unpubl. letters from John James Ruskin to his son of 29 October, 28-29 December, 14 and 3 December respectively, Bem.MS.L.3.

63 *Four Years at the Court of Henry VIII* (1854).

64 *Letters from Venice*, p. 165, letter of 6 February 1852.

65 IX, xxviii, letter to Charles Eliot Norton of May 1859.

66 Unpubl. passage from one of Ruskin's notebook diaries of 1849-50, Bodl.MS. Eng.Misc.C.216, fo.13v.

67 In his *Ruskin and Venice* (1978), pp. 54-5; see pp. 56-60 for examples of pages from Ruskin's notebooks, which are at Bembridge.

68 Unpubl. letter to W.H. Harrison of 12 December, Bodl.MS.Eng.Lett.C.33, fo.20.

69 Unpubl. letter of 15-16 February, Bem.MS.L.3.

70 Copied by Effie in her letter of 24 February, *Effie in Venice*, pp. 145-6.

71 *Letters from Venice*, p. 86, letter of 7 December.

72 X, xxvii, letter to John James Ruskin of 11 October 1851.

73 *Effie in Venice*, p. 84, letter of 10 December.

74 *Trevelyan Letters*, p. 27, letter of 27 January.

75 Unpubl. letter of 14 December, Bem.MS.L.3.

76 IX, xxix, letter of 23 December.

77 IX, xxix-xxx.

78 *Diaries*, II, 455, 30 December.

79 Unpubl. Bodl.MS.Eng.Lett.C.33, fos.31-5. It is curious that Cook and Wedderburn should not have included this most interesting letter, especially since there is so little covering this winter, so I have quoted from it at length.

80 Effie was probably reflecting her husband's views when she wrote in her letter of 10 December that the power of the priests 'only lasts during the mass, and the Romish Church is so shaken to its very root' (unpubl. passage in Bem. MS.T.46, fos.107-8).

81 *Trevelyan Letters*, p. 30, letter from Effie to Pauline Trevelyan of 1 April.

82 For example, Joan Evans, *John Ruskin* (1954), p. 165; John D. Rosenberg, *The Darkening Glass: A Portrait of Ruskin's Genius* (1963), p. 80.

83 *Ruskin in Italy*, p. 200, letter of 11 September.

84 As does Richard Ellman, in 'Overtures to *Salome*', *Golden Codgers: Biographical Speculations* (New York, 1973), pp. 39-59.

85 *Ruskin in Italy*, p. 200, letter of 11 September.

86 Rosenberg, op. cit., p. 80.
87 Unpubl. letters from John James Ruskin to his son of 6 November 1851 and 22 March 1852, Bem.MS.L.4.
88 XXIX, 89-90, *Fors Clavigera* 76.
89 Samuel Rogers, *Italy: A Poem* (1830 edn), pp. 48-50.

II.4   1851-52

1 *Diaries*, II, 468.
2 'Do *get on* now with 2nd Vol. Stones & *3rd M. Painters*' he wrote to him in a letter of 15-16 September 1851 (Bem.MS.L.4). The emphases indicate that this was not the first urging, and suggest which of the two books he looked forward to most.
3 *Effie in Venice*, p. 176, letter to John James Ruskin of August 1851.
4 *Trevelyan Letters*, p. 30, letter from Effie of 1 April 1850.
5 *Letters from Venice*, p. 1, letter to John James Ruskin of 2 September 1851. In the rest of this section all letters dated September to December are of 1851 and all dated January to June are of 1852 unless otherwise stated. Also all letters from Ruskin are to John James Ruskin unless otherwise stated.
6 *Effie in Venice*, pp. 173-4.
7 In his letter of 17 November 1849, Bem.MS.L.3.
8 Unpubl. letter of 27 November 1849, Bem.MS.L.3.
9 Loc. cit. Margaret Ruskin was 'never right near water', according to a letter of John James Ruskin to his son of 8 July 1848, also Bem.MS.L.3.
10 Letter of 27 November, Bem.MS.L.3.
11 This is indicated by John James Ruskin's letter of 16-17 December 1849 (Bem.MS.L.3) in which he wrote: 'you surely utterly mistake my letter mentioning Byron & Gibbon — I could not liken you to either except in . . . living abroad in place of at home . . .'
12 *Letters from Venice*, p. 20, letter of 24 September.
13 *Effie in Venice*, p. 208, letter of 1 November.
14 Unpubl. letters from John James Ruskin to his son of 9 September and 10 October, Bem.MS.L.4 and *Effie in Venice*, p. 216, letter of 25 November.
15 *Effie in Venice*, pp. 217-18, letter of 25 November.
16 *Letters from Venice*, pp. 39-40, letter of 15 October.
17 *Effie in Venice*, p. 327n.
18 Ibid., p. 333, letter of 4 July.
19 *Letters from Venice*, p. 27, letter of 1 October.
20 *Effie in Venice*, p. 204, letter of 27 October.
21 *Letters from Venice*, p. 182, letter of 16 February.
22 Ibid., p. 66, letter of 22 November, by which time their season was over.
23 *Effie in Venice*, p. 205, letter of 27 October. For Viscount Fielding's efforts to convert the Ruskins see pp. 337-8, letter of 10 July.

24 They had met Cheyney in the summer of 1850 (see ibid., pp. 169-70). In an unpublished letter of 30 May 1870, Bodl.MS.Eng.Lett.D.1, fo.195, Ruskin told Brown to give his love to Cheyney and 'I am always terribly afraid of him — & yet very fond of him though he may not believe it.' Cheyney was of great help to the Ruskins in the robbery affair, for which see below, pp. 94-5.
25 *Effie in Venice*, p. 194, letter of 28 September.
26 See *Letters from Venice*, p. 106, letter of 27 December, for example.
27 *Effie in Venice*, pp. 198, 200, 228, 264, letters of 10, 14 October, 7 December and 8 February.
28 Ibid., p. 245, letter of 10 January.
29 Ibid., pp. 285, 275, letters of 7 March and 24 February.
30 Ibid., p. 334, letter of 4 July.
31 Ibid., p. 230, letter of 14 December.
32 Ibid., pp. 266-7, letter of 8 February.
33 Ibid., pp. 263-4, the same letter.
34 Loc. cit.
35 Loc. cit.
36 *Letters from Venice*, p. 110, letter of 28 December.
37 Ibid., pp. 31-2, letter of 5 October.
38 Ibid., p. 60, letter of 16 November.
39 Loc. cit.
40 XI, xxvii, letter of 23 June.
41 *Letters from Venice*, p. 161, letter of 2 February.
42 Ibid., pp. 100, 182, letters of 22 December and 16 February.
43 Ibid., p. 10, letter of 14 September.
44 Ibid., pp. 27-9, letter of 3 October.
45 Ibid., pp. 154-5, letter of 27 January.
46 Ibid., p. 130, letter of 9 January.
47 Ibid., p. 138, letter of 16 January.
48 Ibid., p. 166, letter of 7 February.
49 *Effie in Venice*, p. 266, letter of 8 February.
50 *Letters from Venice*, p. 187, letter of 20 February.
51 Ibid., p. 111, letter of 28 December.
52 Unpubl. letter from John James Ruskin of 11 February, Bem.MS.L.4.
53 *Letters from Venice*, pp. 170-1, letter of 8 February.
54 Unpubl. letters from John James Ruskin of 21, 23, 30-31 December and 3, 11 January, Bem.MS.L.4.
55 *Letters from Venice*, p. 156, letter of 28 January.
56 Ibid., p. 57, letter of 12 November.
57 Ibid., p. 128, letter of 8 January.
58 Ibid., p. 281, letter of 17 May.
59 Ibid., p. 248, letter of 11 April.
60 Unpubl. letter from John James Ruskin of 27-28 February, Bem.MS.L.4.
61 Ibid., letter of 18 December.

62 Unpubl. letters from John James Ruskin between 9 September and 28 January, Bem.MS.L.4.

63 Ibid., letter of 18 December, in which he expressed fears of 'another Salisbury'.

64 Ibid., letter of 11 February.

65 Ibid., letter of 29 August, in which he told his son 'Your Expenditure is £1670 in place of £1170. p annum . . .'

66 Ibid., letter of 9 September.

67 Ibid., letter of 16-17 April: 'I have Strong opinions about Italy & especially Venice I am convinced Italy ennervates Venice relaxes, you cannot be so amphibious without disease Your flesh gets fishified — your Throat like a Turtles . . .'

68 Ibid., letter of 15-16 September.

69 Ibid., letter of 29 August, 9 and 11 September.

70 Ibid., letter of 25 November.

71 XXXVI, 115, letter of 24 May 1851.

72 *Letters from Venice*, p. 244, letter of 9 April.

73 Unpubl. letter of 16-17 April, Bem.MS.L.4.

74 Ibid., letter of 11 December. The plates were of fragments, rather than the views the public wanted.

75 Ibid., same letter.

76 Ibid., letter of 20 March.

77 The first two, not published at the time, are given in XII, 593-603; the third was adapted for Appendix 7 to *Stones* III, XI, 258-63.

78 Unpubl. letters of 16-17, 19, 20, 22, 23 and 25 March, Bem.MS.L.4.

79 Ibid., letter of 19 March.

80 Ibid., letter of 20 March.

81 XXXVI, 114-15, letter to Henry Acland of 24 May 1851.

82 Unpubl. letter from John James Ruskin of 23 March, Bem.MS.L.4.

83 Ibid., letter of 6-7 January.

84 Ibid., letter of 11 February.

85 Ibid., letter of 13 February.

86 Ibid., letter of 9 December; see X, 81. Robert Hewison drew attention to John James Ruskin's role in editing his son's draft of this chapter in his lecture 'Notes on the Construction of *The Stones of Venice*' given at the Ruskin Conference at Leicester in September 1977.

87 Letter of 13 February, Bem.MS.L.4. This material is given in XI, 289-307.

88 Loc. cit.

89 *Letters from Venice*, pp. 184-5, letter of 18 February.

90 Ibid., p. 188, letter of 21 February.

91 *Ezekiel*, 21, 31.

92 Canto IV, Stanza 1.

93 Samuel Rogers, *Italy: A Poem* (1830 edn), p. 47.

94 See Appendix I, X, 441-3. For Shelley's description see p. 194, n.73.

95   *Childe Harold*, Canto IV, Stanza xviii.
96   *Letters from Venice*, p. 207, letter of 2 March.
97   Unpubl. letter of 13 March, Bem.MS.L.4.
98   XXXVI, 115, letter to Henry Acland of 24 May 1851.
99   *Letters from Venice*, pp. 246-7, letter of 11 April.
100 Unpubl. letter of 1 September, Bem.MS.L.4.
101 Unpubl. letter of 5-6 December, Bem.MS.L.4.
102 In the Brenta villas of 'The Vestibule', 'Torcello' and 'Murano' respectively.
103 X, 92. John Unrau gives a detailed discussion of Ruskin's treatment of the
     'laws of St. Mark's architectural chivalry' in 'A Study of Ruskin's
     Architectural Writings', Bodl.MS.D.Phil.C.596-7 (1969), pp. 80-113.
104 X, 170; see *Ezekiel*, 27, 11.
105 XXXVI, 125, 129, letters to John James Ruskin of 9 January and 7 February.
106 Unrau, op. cit., p. 156.
107 *Letters from Venice*, p. 261, letter of 26 April.
108 X, 365. Could Ruskin have meant 'eight feet above the ground' here? Even
     allowing for the raising of the level of the square eight feet above eye level
     seems exaggerated.
109 *Trevelyan Letters*, p. 34, letter of 1 March 1851.
110 Ibid., p. 37, letter of 22 September 1851.
111 Ibid., p. 58, letter of 6 September 1853.
112 *Letters from Venice*, p. 22, letter of 26 September.
113 Ibid., p. 141, letter of 18 January 1852.

III.1   1869

1   XXXVI, 566, letter to Constance Hilliard, niece of Lady Trevelyan.
2   IX, xxvii-xxix, letter of May 1857.
3   *Diaries*, II, 437, 8 September 1849.
4   *Trevelyan Letters*, p. 89, letter of 24 September 1854.
5   XXXVI, 288, letter to John James Ruskin of 4 August 1858.
6   XXXVI, 440, letter of 7 April 1863.
7   XXXVI, 408, letter of 10 May 1862.
8   *The Winnington Letters; John Ruskin's Correspondence with Margaret Alexis
    Bell and the Children at Winnington Hall*, ed. Van Akin Burd (1969), p. 226,
    letter to the children of Winnington Hall perhaps of 19 February.
9   XXXVI, 338, letter of 18 June 1860.
10 XXXVI, 440, letter of 7 April 1863.
11 *Monumenti per servire alla storia del palazzo ducale di Venezia ovvero serie di
    atti pubblici dal 1253 al 1797 che variamente lo riguardono tratti dai veneti
    archivii* (Venice 1868) is dedicated to Ruskin.
12 *Trevelyan Letters*, p. 253.
13 Ibid., p. 254, letter of perhaps 21 March 1863. Rose was going back to

Ireland. Her London house was in Grosvenor Street.

14   XXXVI, 509, letter of 11 June 1866.

15   Without mentioning Rose's name Ruskin told Brown, in an unpublished letter of 26 August 1875, of the death of a girl 'of whom I have before now enough pained you by telling' (B. L. Add.MS.36, 304).

16   *The Winnington Letters*, p. 596, letter of 19 November 1866. Lily was one of the girls at Winnington School where Ruskin went often during the late 1850s and 1860s.

17   XXXVI, 550, letter to Margaret Ruskin of 25 May 1868.

18   XXXVI, 559, letter to Mrs C.E. Norton, n.d. but of 1868.

19   XXXVI, 563, letter to George Richmond of 11 March 1869.

20   XXXVI, 564, letter to Norton of 27 April 1869.

21   See XXXVI, 565, letter to Constance Hilliard of 9 May 1869.

22   XXXVI, 566, letter to Joan Agnew of 12 May 1869.

23   It would seem from the *Diaries* that he was in Venice from 9-13 May, 15-19 June and 28 July-3 August. He does not appear to have been there on 2 July, as would be suggested by the letter to Margaret Ruskin in XXXVI, 573, so this letter may be wrongly dated.

24   XXXVI, 566, letter to Constance Hilliard of 9 May 1869.

25   XXXVI, 567, letter to Joan Agnew of 12 May 1869.

26   *Diaries*, II, 668, 13 May 1869.

27   Ibid., II, 674, 1 and 2 August 1869.

28   XXXVI, 573, letter to Margaret Ruskin given as of 2 July 1869.

29   XXXVI, 574, letter of 11 July 1869.

30   XXXVI, 575, letter to Margaret Ruskin of 16 July.

31   Unpubl. letter to Margaret Ruskin of 13 May 1869, Bodl.MS.Eng.Lett.C.37, fo.30.

32   Unpubl. letter to Margaret Ruskin of 13 August 1869, Bodl.MS.Eng.Lett. C.37, fo.145.

33   Alvise Piero Zorzi, 'Ruskin in Venice', *Cornhill Magazine*, No. 122, N.S. (August 1909), p. 256.

34   XXXVI, 585, letter to Norton of 18 August 1869.

35   XXXVI, 577, letter to Norton of 9 August 1869.

36   See XXXVI, 568-9, 571, letters to Norton of 13, 14 and 21 June 1869.

37   *Diaries*, II, 669.

38   XXXVI, 589, letter of 4 September 1869. William Cowper-Temple, later Lord Mount-Temple, was secretary to Palmerston. Ruskin had met him in 1852 and became a close friend of him and his wife.

III.2   1870

1   XXXVII, 4, letter of 25 January. All letters and diary entries cited in this section are of 1870.

2 *Diaries*, II, 693.

3 Unpubl. letter of 4 May, Bodl.MS.Eng.Lett.D.1, fo.197.

4 Unpubl. letter of 30 May, Bodl.MS.Eng.Lett.D.1, fo.195.

5 Unpubl. letter, n.d., Bodl.MS.Eng.Lett.D.1, fo.198.

6 *Diaries*, II, 697, 26 May and 10 June; Ruskin sent one of his drawings to Norton with his letter of 12 June, XXXVII, 6.

7 XX, li, letter to Margaret Ruskin of 13 June.

8 XXXVII, 11, letter to Norton of 12 July.

9 XXII, 79-80. The lecture was delivered in June 1871, published the following year.

10 An unpublished letter from Ruskin to Monsignor Giuseppe Valentinelli (librarian of the Marciana from 1846 to 1874) of 19 November 1871 thanks Valentinelli for giving permission for Caldara to copy this herbal. The letter is in the Marciana in Venice, MS.Marc.It.X, 468 (=12167), no. 701.

11 Catherine Williams, 'Ruskin's Late Works, c.1870-1890, with Particular Reference to the Collection Made for the Guild of St. George', unpubl. Ph.D. thesis, London University, 1967, p. 163.

III.3   1872

1 *The Professor: Arthur Severn's Memoir of John Ruskin*, ed. James S. Dearden (1967), p. 61. See also Dearden's 'The Ruskin Circle in Italy in 1872', *The Connoisseur*, 179, No. 722 (April 1972), 240-5.

2 *Diaries*, II, 727, 25-28 June 1872.

3 Ruskin seems to imply this in writing to Joan: 'I believe Arfie has a true regard for me — and mean to trust it, and make the most I can of it. We should have been happier, on the whole, had we come abroad, as we originally intended, by ourselves . . .' (unpubl. letter, n.d., Bem.MS.L.37).

4 In Ruskin's letter to Joan of 19 July he refers to 'quarreling with everybody — not Bogie . . .' (unpubl. letter, Bem.MS.L.37).

5 See Dearden, *The Professor*, pp. 53, 60.

6 *Diaries*, II, 727, 5 July.

7 According to the letter of 19 July already cited.

8 Rawdon Brown pasted the articles from the Venetian papers into his copy of volume II of *Fors Clavigera*, now in the Marciana. They appeared in *Il Tempo* for 13 July, *Il Rinnovamento* of 14 July, *La Stampa* of 17 July. On 21 July *Il Rinnovamento* printed a letter from an Antonio Quercia della Rovere in support of Ruskin, which Rawdon Brown also cut out and pasted into *Fors*.

III.4   1876-77

1   XXXVII, 136, letter to Susan Beever, Ruskin's neighbour at Coniston, of 25 August 1874.

2   XXXVII, 183, letter to Charles Eliot Norton of 30 October 1875.

3   As in 1861 (see XXXVI, 356), letter to Norton of 25 February.

4   XXXVII, 185, letter to Norton of 14 November 1875.

5   IX, 13 and XXXVII, 198, letter to HRH Prince Leopold of 10 May 1876. The Prince had attended Ruskin's lectures at Oxford and become his friend and supporter. He had met Brown on a visit to Venice (see XXXVI, lxix).

6   A few months later Ruskin told Joan Severn that he would 'never more think of influencing Oxford life; the fact, though I said nothing at the time, that not a single tutor helped me in the push I made to give the men rational motion in that Hinksey work, entirely disgusted me'. He also found the social obligations a strain in his personal unhappiness (unpubl. letter of 29 April, Bem.MS.L.41).

7   XXXVII, 205, letter to Norton of 2 August 1876. In the rest of this section all letters and diary entries dated from August to December are of 1876, and all dated from January to July are of 1877, unless otherwise stated.

8   To Carlyle Ruskin wrote only a month after the letter to Norton that he had 'good hope now of recasting the Stones of Venice into a book such as you would have a pupil of yours write. I shall throw off at least half of the present text, and add what I now better know of the real sources of Venetian energy and what I – worse – know of the causes of Venetian ruin – with some notes on modern Italy which I do eagerly hope you will be satisfied with' (unpubl. letter of 9 September, Bodl.MS.Eng.Lett.C.41, fo.135).

9   See *The Brantwood Diary of John Ruskin Together with Selected Related Letters and Sketches of Persons Mentioned*, ed. Helen Gill Viljoen (1971), p. 16n.

10 Unpubl. letter to Joan Severn of 29 September, Bodl.MS.Eng.Lett.C.41, fo.139.

11 XXXVII, 204, letter to Norton of 2 August.

12 Unpubl. letter to Mary Aitken of 9 September, Bodl.MS.Eng.Lett.C.41, fo.134.

13 Unpubl. letter to Sara Anderson of 28 August, Bodl.MS.Eng.Lett.C.41, fo.124.

14 *Diaries*, III, 904-5, 6 and 7 September.

15 XXIV, xxxv, letter to Joan Severn of 7 September.

16 Unpubl. letter to Carlyle of 9 September, Bodl.M.S.Eng.Lett.C.41, fo.135.

17 See *Diaries*, III, 911, 915, 937, entries of 18 October, 23 November and 13 February. Of this last move Ruskin told Joan Severn 'The Grand Hotel was really *too* expensive; I was getting quite ruined, so I came away to a little inn fronting the *Giudecca* . . . where I have two rooms for six francs a day instead of one for twelve' (XXIV, xxxvi, letter of 13 February).

18 Unpubl. letter to Brown of 30 April, B.L.Add.MS.36,304, fo.149.

19 *Diaries*, III, 906, 9 September. Ruskin drew the view for Norton in his letter of 5 October (XXXVII, facing 210).

20 *Diaries*, I, 184, 7 May 1841.

21 XXIV, xxxvii, letter to Joan Severn of 16 September.

22 Unpubl. letter to George Macdonald of 8 September, Bodl.MS.Eng.Lett.C.41, fo.133.

23 XXXVII, 208, letter to George Allen of 10 September.

24 Writing to Joan Severn on 29 September, Ruskin mentions time given 'most pleasantly always, to Mr. Moore' and 'interruptions' from Brown, his servant Toni, Carloforti and 'sundry Museum and studio people — on my return to Venice after three years' (unpubl. Bodl.MS.Eng.Lett.C.41, fo.139). For Carloforti and others, see pp. 182-6.

25 Unpubl. letter to Joan Severn of 17 October, Bodl.MS.Eng.Lett.C.41, fo.140.

26 *Diaries*, III, 910, 5 October.

27 *Diaries*, II, 906-9, 9-10, 21, 22, 24 September, and 2 October.

28 Ibid., III, 908, 22 September.

29 Ibid., III, 909, 27 September.

30 See letters to George Allen and Joan Severn of 21, 22 September, unpubl. Bodl.MS.Eng.Lett.C.41, fos.136-7.

31 XXXVII, 208, letter to Susan Beever of 10 September.

32 XXXVII, 208, letter to George Allen of 10 September.

33 XXXVII, 210-11, letter of 5 October.

34 Listed in XXXVII, 238.

35 A strange choice, even though Ruskin must have been reading a much edited text, presumably the 'édition originale' (1826-38, volumes published variously in Leipzig, Paris and Brussels); see Willard Trask's introduction to Giacomo Casanova, *History of My Life* (1967).

36 *Diaries*, III, 909, 29 September.

37 Unpubl. letters to Joan Severn of 17, 23 and 24 October, Bem.MS.L.41.

38 *Diaries*, III, 911-12, 19-21 and 29 October.

39 Unpubl. letter to George Allen of 24 October, Bodl.MS.Eng.Lett.C.41, fo.143.

40 Letter to Mrs Fanny Talbot, the St George's Guild helper, of 20 October, in *Dearest Mama Talbot. A Selection of Letters Written by John Ruskin to Mrs Fanny Talbot*, ed. Margaret Spence (1966), p. 57.

41 Unpubl. letters of 5 October and 15 November, Bem.MS.L.41 and Bodl.MS. Eng.Lett.C.41, fo.161.

42 Unpubl. letter of 15 November, Bodl.MS.Eng.Lett.C.41, fo.159.

43 XXXVII, 211, letter to Susan Beever of 13 November.

44 *Diaries*, III, 916.

45 *Dearest Mama Talbot*, p. 58, letter to Mrs Talbot of 2 September. See also *Diaries*, III, 907, 18 September.

46 XXXVII, 213, letter to Carlyle of 1 December.

47   XXXVII, 214, letter to Susan Beever of 2 December.

48   Unpubl. letter to Joan Severn of 19 September, Bem.MS.L.40.

49   See the summary of Van Akin Burd's lecture, 'Ruskin and Carpaccio: Studies in Vision' in *The Ruskin Newsletter*, No. 19 (autumn, 1978), pp. 8-9.

50   XXIX, 50, letter 74. To Mrs Talbot he wrote on 20 October 'I fear my head is giving way a little at last I left a book quite unaccountably to myself in a railroad carriage the other day' (*Dearest Mama Talbot*, p. 57).

51   Unpubl. letter of 9 December, Bem.MS.L.41.

52   *Diaries*, III, 919, 15 and 21 December. See also letter to Sir Richard Collins of 12 November, unpubl. Bodl.MS.Eng.Lett.C.41, fo.156. Broadlands was the home of the Cowper-Temples, friends of Ruskin and Rose.

53   *Diaries*, III, 921, 27 December.

54   Loc. cit.

55   *John Ruskin and Rose La Touche: Her Unpublished Diaries of 1861 and 1867*, ed. Van Akin Burd (Oxford, 1979), pp. 137-40.

56   Ibid., p. 137.

57   *Diaries*, III, 920, 25 December.

58   Ibid., III, 921, 27 December.

59   *John Ruskin and Rose La Touche*, p. 138.

60   *Diaries*, III, 920, 26 December.

61   For Mazzini see Ugo Ojetti, *I capricci de Conte Ottavio*, 2 vols. (Milan, 1908-9), I, 190-2.

62   *John Ruskin and Rose La Touche*, p. 139.

63   *Diaries*, III, 920, 924, 26 and 30 December.

64   Ibid., III, 923, 28 December.

65   Ibid., III, 920, 927-9, 25 December and 1-6 January.

66   *Diaries*, III, pp. 929-30, 8, 13 and 14 January.

67   Ibid., III, pp. 929-30, 8, 13 and 14 January.

68   Ibid., III, 934, 28 January; see also 1 February.

69   Ibid., III, 929, 932 and 942, 7, 22 January and 11 March.

70   *Dearest Mama Talbot*, p. 63, letter to Mrs Talbot of 8 February.

71   Ibid., pp. 64-5, letter to Mrs Talbot of 18 February.

72   Unpubl. letter to Joan Severn of 25 January, Bem.MS.L.41.

73   *Diaries*, III, 944, 26 March; see also 941, 10 March, 'my mind sore with foolishness of people making one disbelieve all piety'.

74   Unpubl. letter to Joan Severn of 25 January, Bem.MS.L.41; *Diaries*, III, 935, 952, 2 February and 13 May.

75   *Diaries*, III, 946, 10 April.

76   Unpubl. letter to Joan Severn of 17 February, Bodl.MS.Eng.Lett.C.41, fo.222.

77   Count Alvise Zorzi, 'Ruskin in Venice', *Cornhill Magazine*, No. 122, N.S. (August 1906), p. 265.

78   See *Diaries*, III, 945, 949, 30 March, 28 and 30 April.

79   For some of Ruskin's visiting see *Diaries*, III, 924, 938, 950 and 953, 29

December, 23 February, 2 and 19 May. For his Venetian pupil-friends, see pp. 182-6.

80   See *Dearest Mama Talbot*, pp. 66-8. Ruskin had again proposed that the Severns come out for a holiday (unpubl. letter to Joan Severn of 8 April, Bodl.MS.Eng.Lett.C.41, fo.260), and had had hopes of Burne-Jones joining him in the spring (XXIV, xxxviii, letter of 8 December).

81   *Diaries*, III, 950, 3 May.

82   *Dearest Mama Talbot*, p. 65, letter to Quarry Talbot of 5 March.

83   Unpubl. letter to Joan Severn of 19 September, Bem.MS.L.41.

84   Unpubl. letter to Joan Severn of 20 March, Bem.MS.L.41; see also XXIV, 366.

85   *Diaries*, III, 943-4, 21-22 March.

86   Unpubl. letter to Rawdon Brown of 21 January, B.L.Add.MS.36, 304, fo.100.

87   Unpubl. letter to H. Jowett, Ruskin's printer, of 31 Januarym Bodl.MS.Eng. Lett.C.41, fo.206.

88   *Diaries*, III, 941, 7 March.

89   Ibid., III, 947, 14 and 15 April.

90   Ibid., III, 950, 6 May.

91   Ibid., III, 953, 21 May.

92   See unpubl. letters to Allen of 9 and 12 May, Bodl.MS.Eng.Lett.C.41, fos. 276, 279.

93   *Diaries*, III, 953, 22 May; unpubl. letter to Joan Severn of 20 May, Bodl.MS. Eng.Lett.C.41, fo.283.

94   In a letter to Rawdon Brown of 30 April, unpubl. B.L.Add.MS.36,304, fo.148.

95   Unpubl. letter to Mrs Cowper-Temple of 11 September, Bodl.MS.Eng.Lett. C.41, fo.399.

96   XXXVII, 216, letter to Norton of 16 January.

97   *Diaries*, III, 924, 29 December.

98   As Ruskin told Susan Beever on Christmas Day, 'I have found there is an existing power which can, and does, speak through the tradition, to those who can read its letters.' (unpubl. letter, Bodl.MS.Eng.Lett.C.41, fo.175).

99   XXXVII, 216, letter of 16 January.

100 Except to give her age. He calls her a 'little maid of fifteen' (XXVIII, 744). This is interesting because in 1872 he had described her as 'some seventeen or eighteen years old' (XXVII, 344).

101 Unpubl. letter to Henry Willet, a *Fors Clavigera* reader, of 4 May, Bodl.MS. Eng.Lett.C.41, fo.270.

102 *Diaries*, III, 953, 21 May; see also XXIX, 148.

103 See XXX, 226 and Ruskin's description of the mosaic, XXIV, 295.

104 XXIX, 99; see also XXIV, 237, 307-8. For a discussion of its significance for Ruskin's political economy and connection with *The Merchant of Venice* see the summary of D. Blythe's lecture, 'A Stone of Ruskin's Venice', in *The*

Ruskin Newsletter, No. 19 (autumn, 1978), pp. 6-8.

105 On 7 April Ruskin wrote to Allen asking him to send thirty copies to the Academy porter, 'who has official permission to sell them. He sells for 1½ lire Italian paper, about 14 pence − giving me 1¼ lira . . .' (unpubl. Bodl. MS.Eng.Lett.C.41, fo.255). He was also to sell *Ariadne Florentina, Michael Angelo and Tintoret*, 'my other guides' and 'the New Guides', probably *Mornings in Florence, St Mark's Rest* and eventually the Travellers' Edition of *Stones* (see unpubl. letter to Allen of 13 February, Bodl.MS.Eng.Lett. C.41, fo.216.).

106 Who had been heroes of *Modern Painters* II (see above, pp. 61-2).

107 XXIV, 154. There is an implicit contrast with Carpaccio's capacity for innocent amusement here; see XXIV, 179 and XXVIII, 734-5.

108 A few months later he was to use the portrait of *The Doge Andrea Gritti*, thought then to be by Titian, as a model of perfect workmanship to be compared with Whistler's paintings.

109 XXIV, 159. Ruskin believed that religious enthusiasm was one of the things that drove Rose La Touche mad (see letter to Blanche Atkinson given in *Dearest Mama Talbot*, p. 61n.).

110 XXIV, 170. 'Giocondine' was Ruskin's new term for the style described in *Stones* as 'Early Renaissance' (XI, 20-1).

111 He was still waiting in fact. Ruskin had proposed to Rose on 2 February 1866. On 2 February 1877 he wrote in his diary: 'Eleven years, then, today, I have "waited" ' (*Diaries*, III, 934).

112 See XXXVII, 208, letter to Allen of 10 September.

113 Unpubl. letter to Sir Richard Collins of 12 November, Bodl.MS.Eng.Lett.C.41, fo.156. Collins had been tutor to Prince Leopold.

114 Unpubl. letter of 15 November, Bodl.MS.Eng.Lett.C.41, fo.159.

115 Unpubl. letter to R. Caird of 11 December, Bodl.MS.Eng.Lett.C.41, fo.166.

116 In the letter to Carlyle just quoted Ruskin said he had 'sent a little piece to be printed . . .'

117 Ruskin set out the title page in a letter to Allen of 21 January, unpubl. Bodl.MS.Eng.Lett.C.41, fo.201.

118 XXXVII, 217, letter to Susan Beever of 23 January.

119 Unpubl. letter to Allen of February, Bodl.Ms.Eng.Lett.C.41, fo.227. The 'big edition' never materialized.

120 Unpubl. letter to Allen of 21 January, Bodl.MS.Eng.Lett.C.41, fo.201-2.

121 XXIV, 204. The various parts, supplements and appendices mentioned below were not assembled into a book until 1884.

122 'The Shrine of Slaves' must have been 'intended' as the second of the 'Two separate little guides, one to the academy, the other to San Giorgio de' Schiavoni . . .' of which Ruskin speaks in the Preface to *St Mark's Rest* (XXIV, 204-5). When he received Anderson's manuscript, Ruskin replied: 'I remember our plan was that you should prepare a separate book on Carpaccio . . . I will only take such extracts as are quite needful to me,

referring the reader to the book itself' (unpubl. letter of 14 March 1877, Bodl.MS.Eng.Lett.C.41, fo.237). Wedderburn's contribution came out of some notes made for Ruskin on a visit to Venice in 1882 (XXIV, 309).

123   Ruskin instructed George Allen to send the first 500 copies of *St Mark's Rest* to Bunney, the Guild copyist, explaining that 'He is to be here what you are at Sunnysde [*sic*]' (unpubl. letter of 7 May, Bodl.MS.Eng.Lett.C.41, fo.273). Allen lived at, and published Ruskin's books from, Sunnyside, Orpington, Kent.

124   Catherine Williams, 'Ruskin's Late Works, c.1870-1890, with Particular Reference to the Collection Made for the Guild of St. George', unpubl. Ph.D. thesis, London University, 1972, p. 156.

125   Chapters IV, X and XI.

126   Ruskin wrote to Susan Beever on that day and predicted how she would react: ' "But there never was, and cannot be therefore — any St Ursula to send *real* messages." I have found that there *is* . . .' (unpubl. letter of 25 December, Bodl.MS.Eng.Lett.C.41, fo.175).

127   *Diaries*, III, 808, 31 August.

128   Unpubl. letter to Joan Severn of 22 September, Bodl.MS.Eng.Lett.C.41, fo.137.

129   XXIV, 207, 297. The 8th edition had come out in 1874.

130   See the evidence Ruskin gave to the National Gallery Commission in 1857, XIII, 545-50; see also XVI, 452.

131   XXII, 269. See also pp. 270-1 on the difference between a 'practical history of the Middle Ages' and an ideal history.

132   Paul Kaufman, 'Rawdon Brown and His Adventures in Venetian Archives', *English Miscellany*, No. 18 (1967), pp. 283-302.

133   Unpubl. letter to Brown of 25 December, B.L.Add.MS.36,304, fo.97.

134   Unpubl. letter to Brown, n.d., B.L.Add.MS.36,304, fo.94.

135   B.L.Add.MS.36, 304 contains 36 letters or notes written by Ruskin to Brown during the winter of 1876-77 (fos.93-156). Only one of these is given in Paul Kaufman's article, 'John Ruskin to Rawdon Brown: The Unpublished Correspondence of an Anglo-Venetian Friendship', *North American Review* (September-November 1925 and December-January 1925-26), pp. 112-20, 311-20.

136   Unpubl. letter to Brown of 4 March, B.L.Add.MS.36,304, fo.114; an undated letter, fo.118, shows that Ruskin did, gratefully, accept correction.

137   Unpubl. letters of 22 March, B.L.Add.MS.36,304, fos.128-30. In the first of these Ruskin, with some justification, asked Brown why he had fetched him to Venice 'if you didn't want your high-heeled friends bowled over?' Brown wrote a stiff note on the letter to the effect that he had wanted the errors in *Stones* corrected, not added to.

138   See *Letters from Venice*, p. 255, letter of 21 April 1852.

139   XXXVII, 222, letter to Brown of 8 May and unpubl. letter of 10 April, B.L.Add.MS.36,304, fo.141.

140   Unpubl. letter to Brown, n.d. but of winter 1876-77, pasted in vol. 5 of Brown's copy of *Fors Clavigera* in the Marciana.

141   Unpubl. letter to Brown, n.d., B.L.Add.MS.36,304, fo.112.

142   Unpubl. letter to Brown of 6 April, B.L.Add.MS.36,304. Veludo (1811-89), historian, archaeologist and Greek scholar, had been librarian since 1874 (Maria Luxoro, *La biblioteca di San Marco nella sua storia* (Florence, 1954), pp. 102-3).

143   Their names appear in the *Atti della Deputazione Veneta di Storia Patria* for 1876.

144   Ruskin's name first appears among the 'soci d'onore' in the *Atti della Reale Accademia di Belli Arti* for 1873. Rawdon Brown had been an honorary member since 1871. Zorzi reports that Ruskin's nomination was proposed by Cecchini, and that Cecchini had talked to Ruskin of Zorzi's work, for which, see pp. 183-6 (Zorzi, 'Ruskin in Venice', pp. 257,262).

145   XXIV, xxxvi, letter to Joan Severn of 16 September.

146   They are still in the Academy library; the first volume is inscribed by Ruskin with a Latin dedication dated 6 May 1877.

147   Ruskin described his first encounter with Botti in a letter to Joan Severn of 25 June 1874 (XXIII, xlii-xliii). He was not, as Ruskin then thought, Director of the Academy, but Professor of Restoration and since 1873 temporary Inspector of the Galleries, according to the *Atti* of the Academy for 1873. Ruskin had a 'nice visit' from Botti on 26 February and mentions him again on 30 March 1877 (*Diaries*, III, 939, 945).

148   Ruskin had become friendly with the Armenian fathers of the convent of San Lazzaro in 1870. He went to see them on 12 October 1876 and 28 April 1877 (*Diaries*, III, 910, 949). He seems to have had most contact with Padre Jacopo Issaverdens (1835-1920), whose special function it was to receive visitors. Besides the letter of 27 July 1883 published in XXXVII, 462, the archives of the convent also contain an inscribed photograph of Ruskin as an old man, and an undated letter to Issaverdens asking for advice on some coins, 'apparently of gold', offered to him by 'The attendant of the Archives'. The letter is almost certainly of 1876-77 because it was only during this winter that Ruskin worked in the *archivio di stato*.

149   In 1850 Ruskin had, through Brown, employed a certain Vason to draw and measure horseshoe arches (see Ruskin's letter to Brown of 22 April, XXXVI, 106). Since 1873 he had been paying Caldara to copy drawings in a Venetian herbal (see records of payments out of Guild funds, XXVIII, 749 and XIX, 31). In 1887 he paid a sculptor, A. Giordani, to make a cast of the Noah angle of the Ducal Palace (XXIX, 50). He may have been the man who made casts for Ruskin in 1852 (see X, 432).

150   Of letters to Carloforti only a part of one has been published (XXXVII, 739), and I have been unable to locate the correspondence. His wife and daughter emigrated to America after his death in 1901, according to distant relatives in Assisi. The Library Edition gives eleven letters from Ruskin to Zorzi, his

fiancée and her mother, taken from Zorzi's article, 'Ruskin in Venice'. The originals of seven of these are in the possession of Count Alvise Zorzi, who also has two unpublished letters. One is a note, written in French, clearly of 1877. The other, of 1879, is given below. For Alessandri's voluminous correspondence, see my article, 'John Ruskin's Correspondence with Angelo Alessandri' in *The Bulletin of the John Rylands University Library of Manchester*, 60, No. 2 (spring, 1978), pp. 404-33. In his will Boni left fifteen letters from Ruskin to himself to Eva Tea, his biographer. Dr Tea sent transcripts of these to Alexander Wedderburn in 1926 (Bem.MS.T.34). The Pierpont Morgan Library, New York, has five letters from Boni to Ruskin.

151   See Zorzi, 'Ruskin in Venice', p. 258 and Eva Tea, *Giacomo Boni nella vita del suo tempo* (Milan, 1932), I, 15-16.

152   Of his and Carloforti's associates Zorzi makes mention, 'Ruskin in Venice', pp. 257-8. Zorzi also mentions the abbot, professor Rinaldo Fulin, another of the founder members of the Deputazione per la Storia Patria. According to Eva Tea, Fulin held gatherings of artists and scholars every Friday to discuss matters of Venetian cultural interest, so Zorzi may also have attended these; Boni did, and was encouraged by Fulin to study Latin and to work in the archives (op. cit., I, 16).

153   Alessandri taught in the Academy, Zorzi was made responsible for the archaeological collections in the museum at Cividale in Friuli, and Boni became very well known as an archaeologist, principally for his excavation of the Forum at Rome.

154   See Zorzi, 'Ruskin in Venice', p. 374. Ruskin was taking Alessandri sketching in the Alps.

155   See Catherine William's entry in her catalogue of the Guild collection in 'Ruskin's Late Works'.

156   Loc. cit.

157   The following information is taken from Zorzi's article, 'Ruskin in Venice', p. 257.

158   Zorzi, 'Ruskin in Venice', p. 257. It was to appear under the title *Osservazioni intorno ai ristauri interni ed esterni ed esterni della Basilica di San Marco* (Venice, 1877).

159   The following information is taken from Ferdinando Forlati's section on 'The Work of Restoration in San Marco' in Otto Demus, *The Church of San Marco in Venice: History, Architecture, Sculpture* (Washington D.C., 1960), pp. 193-201, and from Zorzi's *Osservazioni*.

160   He was the brother of Tommaso Meduna, the engineer who in the 1840s had built the bridge linking Venice to the mainland. He had also introduced the Gothic revival to Venetian architecture.

161   Zorzi, *Osservazioni*, pp. 43-50.

162   Pietro Saccardo, Meduna's assistant, had put up some opposition to the new mosaics. He had given a lecture on the subject at the Ateneo Veneto in July 1864; Zorzi quotes at length from this paper in *Osservazioni*, pp. 141-5.

163   Zorzi reprints the article in *Osservazioni*, pp. 161-7. It first appeared under the title 'De la restauration des Anciens Edifices en Italie' in *Encyclopédie d'Architecture: Revue Mensuelle des Travaux Publiques et Particuliers*, 2nd series, I (1872).

164   *Gazzetta di Venezia*, No. 309 (21 November 1876).

165   Ibid., No. 333 (15 December 1876).

166   Ibid., No. 339 (21 December 1876).

167   Alfredo Barbacci, *Il restauro dei monumenti in Italia* (Rome, 1956), pp. 254-5.

168   The *Gazzetta di Venezia* reports such a change having taken place in the Vicenza committee, No. 249 (18 September 1876).

169   *Gazzetta di Venezia*, No. 300 (11 November 1876).

170   Ibid., No. 320 (2 December 1876).

171   Zorzi, 'Ruskin in Venice', pp. 257-8.

172   Ibid., pp. 259-62.

173   *Diaries*, III, 930, 13 January. Venetians would normally use dialect when conversing with each other; many would not know Italian.

174   Zorzi, 'Ruskin in Venice', pp. 262-5.

175   Ibid., p. 366.

176   *Diaries*, III, 936, 938, 943-4, 8, 22 February, 16 and 23 March.

177   Saccardo published a series of articles in defence of his own role and of his colleagues in the newspaper *Veneto Cattolico*, republished as *S. Marco, gl'inglesi e noi* (Venice, 1879).

178   See Eva Tea, op. cit., I, pp. 21-34. Boni's anonymously published pamphlet, *L'avvenire dei nostri monumenti: Memoria diretta alla Commissione pei Monumenti* (Venice, 1883), aroused Saccardo's colleagues to reply with another, *La Basilica di S. Marco in Venezia nel suo passato e nel suo avvenire* (Venice, 1883).

179   XXIV, 424, letter to F.W. Pullen, secretary of the Manchester Ruskin Society.

180   The 'Memorial Studies of St. Mark's, Venice' undertaken by T.M. Rooke in 1879 and 1884. Ruskin published a circular inviting subscriptions and put on an exhibition of photographs (XXIV, 412-23).

181   Unpubl. letter, by courtesy of Count Alvise Zorzi. Miss Yule would be Amy Yule, Ruskin's 'witch of Sicily' (XXXVII, 94). Ruskin had visited the Yule family in Palermo in 1874.

III.5   1888

1   Unpubl. letter, Bodl.MS.Eng.Lett.D.I, fo.204.

2   XXXVII, 374, letter of 30 August 1881.

3   This part of the letter is unpublished and is taken from Eva Tea's transcripts, Bem.MS.T.34, 30 August.

4   See *The Professor: Arthur Severn's Memoir of John Ruskin*, ed. James S.

Dearden (1961), p. 54.

5   Unpubl. letter to Joan Severn of 4 November 1882, Bodl.MS.Eng.Lett.C.45, fo.208.

6   Unpubl. letters in the Pierpont Morgan Library, 24 September and 13 December 1883.

7   An unsigned article in the *Corriere della sera* of 25 July 1925 describes Boni's various enthusiasms: 'Today it would be a crusade against drunkenness and wine; tomorrow a plan to reclaim the desert by planting broom, or to divide uncultivated land up amongst the poor; the day after it would be propaganda for introducing dancing into schools, or an improved system for fertilising the soil by fixing nitrogen from the atmosphere, . . . or for managing the waters of the Venetian lagoon. Each time I went to see him, I would hear of some new idea, which he would go to great lengths to demonstrate by means of statistics, diagrams, proofs.'

8   Unpubl. letters of 18 and 19 December 1882, Easter Day and 30 September 1883, 6 June 1884, Bem.MS.T.34. In the last of these Ruskin expresses fears of 'actual violence' or that 'these men now distinct adversaries in humiliated rage, may torment you in laborious poverty till your best strength is past'.

9   Unpubl. letter in Pierpont Morgan Library, n.d. The letter must be of July 1884 because it contains a reference to having received a Greek dictionary of which Ruskin writes in his letter of 14 July 1884 (Bem.MS.T.34).

10   XXXVII, 608, letter to Alessandri of October 1888.

11   *The Gulf of Years: Letters from John Ruskin to Kathleen Olander*, ed. Rayner Unwin (1953), pp. 77-9, letter of 25 September 1888.

12   Ibid., pp. 81-2.

13   XXXVII, 608, letter to Alessandri of October 1888.

14   *Diaries*, III, 1146.

15   Ibid., III, 1150.

Index

Academy, Venice: relations with as an
institution, 182, 220n; sale of R's
books at entrance, 172, 218n;
visits to or periods of study in:
1841, 44; 1845, 59; 1846, 64, 66;
1869, 139; 1872, 146; 1876-7,
149-50, 185. *See also* Bellini
Gentile, Bellini, Giovanni,
Carpaccio, Ruskin *Guide to . . . the
Academy*, Tintoretto, Titian
Academy Bridge, Venice (Ponte della
Carità), 170
Acland, Henry: letters to, 99, 100,
112
Addison, Joseph, 16, 18
Agnew, Joan: goes to live at Denmark
Hill, 137; marries Arthur Severn,
146; R's letters to, 130; R plans
to take to V, 138; with R in
Italy 1870, 142-3; *then see* Severn
Aitken, Mary: letter to, 214n
Alessandri, Angelo: relationship with
R, 168, 183, 188-90, 221n
Allen, George: letters to, 215n, 217n,
218n, 219n; R meets in Alps, 158
Alps 3, 41-2, 51, 136; modern tourists

in, 173, 176; R plans to dam
valleys, 139-42; R's travels and
study in: 1833, 33; 1835, 35;
1845, 54; 1849, 72-3, 74; 1851, 92;
1854, 1858, 134; seen from Venice,
29, 83, 90, 92
Anderson, James Reddie: in Venice
1876, 152; letter to, 218n; work on
Carpaccio, 160, 172
Anderson, Sara: letter to, 214n
Angelico, Fra: admiration for, 52,
64; opposed to Venetians, 137
Annuals, 29-31, 33-4, 197n, 198n
Archives, Venice (Archivio di Stato),
156, 220n,
Armstrong, Lily: letter to, 138
Arsenal, Venice: R family visit, 44;
worker kills Governor, 82
Ascham, Roger: on Venetian vice,
13-14; reaction compared to
Beckford's, 20; to Shelley's, 27
Ashmolean, R comments on holdings,
144
Assisi: R meets Botti, 182; meets
Carloforti, 183
Athens, history of to be taught, 146

224